HANDS-ON GUIDE SERIES®

Hands-On Guide to

Windows Media

Focal Press Hands-On Guide Series

The Hands-On Guide series serves as the ultimate resource in streaming and digital media-based subjects for industry professionals. The books cover solutions for enterprise, media and entertainment, and educational institutions. A compendium of everything you need to know for streaming and digital media subjects, this series is known in the industry as a must-have tool of the trade.

Books in the series cover streaming media-based technologies, applications and solutions as well as how they are applied to specific industry verticals. Because these books are not part of a vendor-based press they offer objective insight into the technology weaknesses and strengths, as well as solutions to problems you face in the real-world.

Competitive books in this category have sometimes been criticized for being either technically overwhelming or too general an overview to actually impart information. The Hands-On Guide series combats these problems by ensuring both ease-of-use and specific focus on streaming and digital media-based topics broken into separate books.

Developed in collaboration with the series editor, Dan Rayburn, these books are written by authorities in their field, those who have actually been in the trenches and done the work first-hand.

All Hands-On Guide books share the following qualities:

- Easy-to-follow practical application information
- Step-by-step instructions that readers can use in real-world situations
- Unique author tips from "in-the-trenches" experience
- Compact at 250–300 pages in length

The Hands-On Guides series is the essential reference for Streaming and Digital Media professionals!

Series Editor: Dan Rayburn (www.danrayburn.com)

Executive Vice President for StreamingMedia.com, a diversified news media company with a mission to serve and educate the streaming media industry and corporations adopting Internet based audio and video technology. Recognized as the "voice for the streaming media industry" and as one of the Internet industry's foremost authorities, speakers, teachers, and writers on Streaming and Digital Media Technologies.

Titles in the series:

- *Hands-On Guide to Windows Media*
- *Hands-On Guide to Webcasting*
- *Hands-On Guide to Video Blogging & Podcasting*
- *Hands-On Guide to Flash Communication Server*

HANDS-ON GUIDE SERIES®

Hands-On Guide to

Windows Media

JOE FOLLANSBEE

Focal Press
Taylor & Francis Group

NEW YORK AND LONDON

First published 2006

This edition published 2013
by Focal Press
70 Blanchard Road, Suite 402, Burlington, MA 01803

Simultaneously published in the UK
by Focal Press
2 Park Square, Milton Park, Abingdon, Oxon OX14 4RN

Focal Press is an imprint of the Taylor & Francis Group, an informa business

Library of Congress Cataloging-in-Publication Data

Follansbee, Joe.
  Hands-on guide to Windows Media / Joe Follansbee.
      p. cm. -- (The Focal hands-on guide series)
  Includes index.
  ISBN-13: 978-0-240-80759-1 (pbk. : alk. paper)
  ISBN-10: 0-240-80759-6 (pbk. : alk. paper) 1. Multimedia systems. 2.
Interactive multimedia. 3. Streaming technology (Telecommunications) I.
Title. II. Series.
  QA76.575.F65 2005
  006.7--dc22
                                2005027231

British Library Cataloguing-in-Publication Data
A catalogue record for this book is available from the British Library.

ISBN-13: 978-0-240-80759-1 (pbk)

Table of Contents

Chapter 1: Windows Media Quick Start

Chapter 2: Streaming Media Basics

Chapter 3: Get Ready to Capture Audio and Video

Chapter 4: Recording and Capturing Audio and Video

Chapter 5: Optimizing Your Audio and Video

Chapter 6: Encoding for Windows Media

Chapter 7: Getting Ready to Distribute Windows Media Streams

Chapter 8: Delivering Windows Media to Your Audience

Chapter 9: Get Ready to Webcast Live with Windows Media

Chapter 10: Encoding and Distributing Live Webcasts

Chapter 11: Going Beyond the Desktop

Chapter 12: Advanced Topics

Appendix: Streaming PowerPoints with Producer

Acknowledgments

Writing a book is really a team effort. It's just that the author gets all the glory. Some of the glory should go to others. My sincerest thanks go to Marc Melkonian, my technical editor, who whacked me upside the head when necessary. My friends at Online Video Service, including Tim Treanor and Matt Hickey, who provided priceless support. I would also like to thank Joanne Tracy, Angelina Ward, editor Howard Jones, Gina Marzilli, Becky Golden-Harrell, and the rest of the staff at Elsevier/Focal Press. Steve Mack first suggested I contact Focal Press about writing a book on streaming media. Dan Rayburn also offered his influential support. And I would like to express my admiration for my former colleagues at RealNetworks. They are among the few who understand Microsoft.

About the Author

Joe Follansbee is a freelance writer who got sucked into the whole Internet technology thing in 1996, when RealNetworks (the Progressive Networks) hired him out of public radio. He bailed out of the software business in 2001, although he kept his hand in with some web development and streaming media work. He went back to his first love, writing, in 2003 and published *Get Streaming! Quick Steps to Audio and Video Online* (Focal Press) in 2004. *The Hands-On Guide to Windows Media* is his second book. He's written a third book, as yet unpublished, which is a history of the 1897 three-masted schooner *Wawona*, listed on the National Register of Historic Places, and he is working on a fourth book about the tragic sinking in 1906 of a passenger vessel in Puget Sound. He also contributes to a number of magazines and newspapers in the Seattle area. He's active in local historic preservation. He lives in Seattle with his wife and two daughters.

About the Series Editor

Dan Rayburn is recognized as the "voice for the streaming media industry" and as one of the Internet industry's foremost authorities, speakers, and writers on Streaming and Digital Media Technologies for the past ten years. As a passionate leader and spokesperson in the field of streaming and digital media, Mr. Rayburn is noted for his expertise and insight pertaining to digital media business models, industry foresight, hardware and software products, delivery methods and cutting edge technology solutions globally.

He is Executive Vice President for StreamingMedia.com, a diversified news media company with a mission to serve and educate the streaming media industry and corporations adopting Internet based audio and video technology. Its website (*www.StreamingMedia.com*), print magazine, research reports and tradeshows (Streaming Media East and West) are considered the premier destinations both in person and online for professionals seeking industry news, articles, white papers, directories and tutorials.

Prior to StreamingMedia.com, he founded a streaming media services division for the Globix Corporation, a publicly traded NASDAQ company, which became one of the largest global streaming media service providers specializing in on-site event production for webcasts around the world. Prior to Globix, he co-founded one of the industry's first streaming media webcasting production companies, Live On Line, successfully acquired by Digital Island for $70 million dollars.

An established writer, Mr. Rayburn's articles on streaming media trends and technologies have been translated into four languages and are regularly published in major trade magazines and web portals around the world. He is Series Editor for a new series of Streaming Media related books for Focal Press entitled "The Dan Rayburn Hands On Guide" Series. He is co-author of the first business focused book on the industry, *The Business of Streaming & Digital Media* and his second highly anticipated book co-authored with Steve Mack, *Hands-On Guide to Webcasting* is due out in November of 2005.

Regularly consulted by the media for insight into business trends and technology, Mr. Rayburn has been featured in over one hundred print and on-line articles that have appeared in The New York Times, The Seattle Times, Crain's B2B Weekly, Broadcasting & Cable, Electronic Media, Mediapost.com, POST Magazine, ProAV Magazine, INS Asia, Internet.com, Radio Ink, EContent Magazine, Nikke Electronics and Wired.com among others. He has also appeared on many TV programs including those on CNN and CBS.

Mr. Rayburn also consults for corporations who are implementing digital media services and products in the broadcast, wireless, IPTV, security and cable industries. Over the past ten years he has helped develop, consult, and implement streaming media solutions for prestigious companies in the enterprise, entertainment and government sectors including A&E, ABC, Apple, Atlantic Records, American Express, BMG, BP, CBS, Cisco, Elektra, Excite.com, HBO, House Of Blues, ifilm, Indy 500, Intel, ITN, KPMG, Microsoft, MTV, NYTimes.com, Pepsi, Price Waterhouse Coopers, Qualcomm, RealNetworks, Sony Music, Twentieth Century Fox, United Nations, Viacom, VH1 and Warner Brothers among others.

For the past ten years, Mr. Rayburn has traveled internationally as a featured industry expert and has been sought out to keynote and speak on the current and future direction of streaming media technology, trends and business cases. A current technology advisor to many universities in the US, he has also taught Internet Broadcasting classes at New York University (NYU) and regularly lectures at numerous academic institutions. He is currently developing a series of distance learning classes with the Seattle Community Colleges, which will focus on teaching people the business and legal issues surrounding the implementation of streaming and digital media.

Mr. Rayburn holds board positions with various technology corporations in the US and Europe and works with many non-profit organizations enabling them to utilize streaming media for their projects including The Museum of the Moving Image, The International Agency for Economic Development and the X PRIZE Foundation.

Dan Rayburn's contact infromation:
917-523-4562
www.danrayburn.com

Introduction

Purpose of the Book

The *Hands-On Guide to Windows Media* is one of a series of books designed to help you use and understand one of the most important sets of technologies on the Internet: *streaming media*, specifically Microsoft's Windows Media technologies. Windows Media is Microsoft's implementation of streaming media, the process of sending audio and video predictably over a computer network in real time. It answers the question, "How do I send audio and video over the Internet without clogging up my company's network and frustrating users who depend on it?"

More and more people are demanding audio and video experiences delivered over the Internet, such as live radio or video. Many enterprises, government agencies, and other large organizations are turning to streaming media in general and Windows Media Series in particular to improve communications with internal and external audiences. The book's goal is to get you up to speed on Windows Media as quickly and painlessly as possibly, while helping you meet demands for Internet audio and video. Along the way, you'll participate in the global revolution in digital media delivery.

Scope of the Book

This book focuses on easy and effective ways to use Microsoft Windows Media technology, which is just one set of tools for sending audio and video over the Internet and corporate intranets. You'll find step-by-step instructions for using all of the basic Windows Media tools, such as the Windows Media Player, and some of the more advanced tools, including the Windows Media Server. The book will also discuss how to prepare your audio and video recordings for streaming, and how to make good choices within the Windows Media toolset, such as codecs. Finally, this book will examine some of the more advanced applications of Windows Media, such as its implementation in the world of high-definition television.

The book won't compare Windows Media with solutions developed by other vendors, such as RealNetworks or Apple Computer, although we will mention these solutions occasionally

---

to place Windows Media in context of its competitors. The book also won't discuss in detail deep-level programming within the Windows Media environment, such as plug-ins to the Windows Media Server. And the book won't offer any magic ways to make money overnight with Windows Media, although many companies are competing to provide products and services based on streaming media technology.

Who Should Read This Book

You should read this book if you do any kind of technical work with audio and video. If you've paid the least bit of attention to the debates over digital music distribution or the latest up-and-coming toys, such as portable media players, you know that the Internet is the way of the future for media distribution. Streaming media is one of the most popular media distribution methods, and you'll be forearmed with knowledge once the time comes for you to send your audio and video into the "great cloud."

If you have one of the following job titles, read this book.

- Audio Engineer
- Video Engineer
- Media Producer
- Web Designer
- Web Programmer
- Web Producer
- Teacher/Professor
    - Media Studies
    - Media Production
    - Communications
    - Computer Science

Required Skill Level

This book was written with the intermediate computer user in mind. That means you don't have to be a programming whiz or a network engineer to understand and use its concepts right away. But the book makes a few assumptions about your computer knowledge and experience:

- Minimum one year of experience with a Windows personal computer.
- Familiarity with basic Internet tools, for example, web browsers such as Microsoft Internet Explorer and Netscape Navigator, and FTP programs.
- Familiarity with basic computer terminology, for example, CPU, RAM, bandwidth, hard drive, sound card, and so on.

If you're not sure whether you fit into these assumptions, you should spend some time with a good basic computer skills book. Even if you do fit, it's a good idea to set aside some time to simply goof around with the technologies you're about to discover. Children learn by playing, so why shouldn't adults?

Whatever your learning style, by the time you're finished with *Hands-On Guide to Windows Media Series*, you'll have the knowledge to create streaming media for the Internet with Windows Media tools on your own. But the best media productions flower within a group of technicians and artists, so you should find some like-minded colleagues and build a streaming media production team, or at least make sure that other folks in your department know what you're up to. Collaboration will make everything go much more smoothly.

Why Streaming Media?

The proliferation of portable media players such as Apple Computer's iPod, Creative Labs' NOMAD Jukebox, and the Rio Cali have pretty much sealed the deal on Internet distribution of digital media. Some have even predicted the death of the compact disc, arguing that consumers will find the process of purchasing music over the Net, customizing a playlist, and loading it into a hardware device more convenient and satisfying than buying a prepackaged album of songs.

But the world of media distribution goes far beyond the work of pop artists. Nearly every form of media content, from movie trailers to training videos to pep talks by company presidents, is moving onto the Net. Today's hardware devices can't handle the sheer amount of data contained in some kinds of media, especially video. Sure, given the current pace of technology, somebody will build a handheld, portable hardware device that can store all the classic episodes of *Outer Limits*. But for the foreseeable future, putting this type of content on a server and delivering it via streaming media technology is the best option.

Streaming media is a particularly good choice for large enterprises keen to control costs while improving their audio and video communications to the public and internal audiences, such as employees. Here are some of the business benefits of streaming media:

- **Cost-effectiveness**: When you produce a video and distribute it via VHS tape or DVD, you should expect to spend about $10 a copy as a rule of thumb. Duplicating and shipping hundreds of tapes or DVDs all over the world, if you work in a global company, can cost tens of thousands of dollars. By placing the video on a streaming media server and asking people to view it by logging into a website, you've just saved your company a big chunk of money.

- **Faster time-to-market**: Days or weeks may pass before your carefully produced training video might arrive at your office in Ulaanbaatar, Outer Mongolia. By then, the information is out of date. However, if you put the video on a streaming media server immediately after it's produced, and send an e-mail to all your company offices asking your colleagues to view it, you've just saved your company a big chunk of time. And as they say, time is money.

- Uses network resources more efficiently: Some people prefer to let users download audio and video programs, arguing that multimegabyte files offer higher quality. That's true, if you're willing to inflict the World Wide Wait on people (such as bosses) who expect instant gratification. You also risk the wrath of your company's networking gurus, who will complain loudly that your video is clogging the infrastructure and making their lives miserable. Streaming media offers a much more measured and disciplined way to use networking resources, especially precious bandwidth, so that everyone stays reasonably happy.

Streaming's Great Strength: Going Live

Finally, streaming media offers something found in no other Internet-based digital media technology—live broadcasting—or in the industry's word, *webcasting*. Digital media such as music or video differs in one important way from other types of media, such as text or photographs. A single media experience changes dynamically over time. In a symphony, one note follows another in logical manner; in a movie, image replaces image in an orderly progression.

Furthermore, a user often experiences time-based media remotely as it is created. This phenomenon first appeared in the nineteenth century, when telegraph operators could hear someone sending a message in Morse code a thousand miles away. The phenomenon gained serious momentum with the invention of radio, which was almost always produced live in the early days of the industry in the 1920s and 1930s. Television took it to a new level in the 1940s and 1950s, and today, streaming media allows an individual to send live pictures of their event to a global audience almost instantaneously at very low cost. No portable media player can match the power of watching someone speak to you in real time from halfway around the planet.

The Growth of Streaming Media

The origins of streaming media go back to 1992 and the development of the *Real-Time Transport Protocol* and an audiocast of the 23rd Internet Engineering Task Force (IETF), an Internet standards body. But the streaming media industry was born in 1995, when Progressive Networks (now RealNetworks) launched RealAudio 1.0, the first commercial webcasting system. Another company, Xing Technologies, launched a streaming system based on MPEG, an open audio standard. Microsoft followed in 1996 with Netshow, later renamed Windows Media Series. Apple Computer was late to the party with QuickTime streaming in 1998. A host of other companies came up with their own systems, but most died with the Internet bust or were purchased by the leaders. RealNetworks bought Xing Technologies in 1999.

Since those early days, streaming media has exploded. What started as a novelty in the mid-1990s has now grown into a multimillion-dollar industry. The most important factor in the growth is the proliferation of high-bandwidth connections, usually via a digital subscriber line (DSL) or cable modems. A good quality streaming media experience requires lots of bandwidth. In January 2001, 7% of Americans had residential broadband service, according to a report by Arbitron, the media ratings company. Just three years later, nearly one-quarter of Americans subscribed to broadband service. Arbitron added that three-quarters of people with a broadband connection at home have watched Internet video. The growth shows no sign of stopping.

Most of the attention has focused on the consumer side of streaming, such as live radio broadcasts over the Internet, music samples, and movie trailers. In fact, marketers have identified a distinct group of people who spend a lot of time listening to online audio and watching online video. They're called *streamies*, and they have important demographic characteristics. For example, nearly half of streaming media users are between the ages of 25 and 45, and they tend to have a lot of disposable income.

People have paid less attention to the business market for streaming, which is just as important as all large organizations discover the benefits of streaming. Wainhouse Research, which tracks streaming media and similar technologies, says the market will reach nearly $1 billion by 2007.

Why Windows Media Series?

The explosive growth of streaming media in the 1990s and the shakeout in all Internet technology in the early years of this decade left four major streaming technology vendors standing: Apple Computer, RealNetworks, Macromedia (with its Flash MX technology), and Microsoft. Two companies, RealNetworks and Microsoft, dominate perhaps 90% of the space, although no one knows exactly how much each of them owns, in part because people sometimes use both vendors' technology. And when you compare each company's technology feature to feature, you see few important differences.

But if you look carefully at their marketing strategies, it's clear that RealNetworks tends toward the consumer end of the spectrum. Part of its business model relies on consumer subscriptions to its media services, and the look and feel of its flagship software, RealPlayer, definitely appeals to a younger, hipper audience. RealNetworks sells server software as well, but it's pricey.

Microsoft, on the other hand, has leveraged its ability to tie its media player and media server software to its operating systems to make strong inroads into the business market. In other words, every time an enterprise or other large organization buys dozens or hundreds of computers, or upgrades to a new version of Windows, Windows Media Series is automatically installed, making the system the default choice for that group of people.

ALERT Microsoft's strategy of bundling Windows Media Series players with its Windows operating system is controversial. The practice has raised eyebrows at the US Justice Department, and the European Union has demanded that Microsoft stop the bundling. But as a practical matter, Windows Media Player has become the default streaming media player on most new computers.

The Windows Media Choice

Microsoft's strategy has paid off. Because Windows Media Player is already installed, most people don't see the need to download and install a competing player. And in many large enterprises, information technology (IT) managers won't allow users to download players from RealNetworks or other Microsoft competitors, in part to avoid the security risks that come with downloading bits out of their control.

Furthermore, Microsoft bundles its Windows Media Series server software "free" with its enterprise server products, and all it takes is a few clicks of the mouse to install the media server. In the case of RealNetworks, organizations have to spend thousands of extra dollars to use RealNetworks' technology. To summarize, for many businesses, the shortest route from no streaming to a full-fledged system is Microsoft.

What does this mean to you? You may have chosen to learn more about Windows Media Series because you believe that it's the best product among several competitors. Or you have chosen to learn about Windows Media Series because it's the easiest and most cost-effective way to get going quickly, because all the tools are at hand and/or installed. Perhaps both reasons apply. In any case, by the time you finish this book, you'll have the knowledge to make the most out of your investment.

Career Opportunities

The peculiarities of streaming media as a distribution method have created an opportunity for forward-looking technologists to specialize. Over the years, a small, but growing cadre of people are spending most, if not all, of their time designing networks optimized for streaming, setting up live webcasts from remote locations, mapping processes for quick and efficient conversion of film and video archives to streaming, and writing business models that build on streaming media's advantages. Most of these folks have backgrounds in the major areas of networking, media production, systems design, and general business skills.

Streaming media training is still in its infancy; some individuals offer training, but as of this writing, Microsoft does not offer certifications in Windows Media specifically, although it covers some of the subject in other areas, such as Internet Information Services (IIS).

Inside the Industry

Making Money with Streaming Media

Many of you have an entrepreneurial bent, or you like to work in the freelance market, and so it's worth mentioning some of the services or skills you could offer to a prospective client after studying this book and applying your knowledge.

Live Webcasting: More and more organizations want to send a speech by a CEO or other important person over the Internet, but they don't want to invest in a full-fledged streaming media system. Once you read Chapters 9 and 10, which cover live webcasting, you'll have the knowledge to offer your services as a live Windows Media webcasting specialist.

Digital Compression: Some people specialize in the highly technical work of digital compression, which is a critical component of successful streaming media. After reading Chapters 5 and 6, which cover streaming compression, and consulting a good audio and video compression guide, such as Cliff Wootton's, *A Practical Guide to Video and Audio Compression* (Focal Press), you'll have highly desired skills in the ongoing digital media revolution.

Hosting Services: Unlike run-of-the-mill website hosting, streaming media hosting requires understanding of specialized media servers and the unique demands of streaming media delivery, particularly in relation to networking and bandwidth. If you enjoy the intricacies of protocols, packets, RAIDs, and NICS, read Chapters 7 and 8 on serving Windows Media streams, get some practical experience, and offer your services as a streaming media networking consultant.

How to Use this Book

This book is designed to get you up and going with Windows Media's streaming technology as quickly and painlessly as possible. It starts with a tutorial chapter that covers the basics and nothing more. From there, it gets into more detail on the four steps of streaming: capture, encode, distribute, and playback. In the final chapters, the book examines some of the more advanced aspects of streaming, such as streaming audio and video to mobile devices.

There are three types of sidebars used in this book: "Author Tip," "Inside the Industry," and "Alert." Each is separated from the text and gives you quick, helpful information that is easy to find.

Author Tip: Gives tips that are directly from the author's experience in the field.

Inside the Industry: Relays information about companies, behind the scenes happenings, quotes from people in the industry, a bit from a case study, statistics, market research, anything to do with the topic's industry that doesn't necessarily come from the author's experience.

Alert: Spells out important information such as technical considerations, troubleshooting, warning of potential pitfalls, and anything else that needs special attention.

Finally, an appendix gives you an in-depth look at using Microsoft Producer, a free tool for streaming PowerPoint presentations. And a glossary gives you a one-stop, all-important grounding in the terminology of streaming media in general and Windows Media in particular.

Conclusion

Streaming media is one of the fastest growing technologies for delivering digital audio and video online, and it's the technology of choice for live webcasting over the Internet. Anyone who has a technical or business connection to media, including the recording industry, television, corporate media production, or media education, should master the basics of streaming and Microsoft's Windows Media technologies. In Chapter 1, you'll learn how to get up and running within a day.

CHAPTER 1

Windows Media Quick Start

You need to get up to speed as quickly as possible on the basics of streaming media and Windows Media Series. Maybe you're on a tight deadline or you have to learn this stuff in between 63 other projects that were due yesterday. You've come to the right place!

This chapter walks you step-by-step through a number of important installations. By the time you're finished, you'll be streaming a video file. Just to make things extra fast, the instructions assume that most default settings, automatically set by the installer, work for you. However, for this chapter to make sense, the text makes a number of further assumptions:

- You have a source audio or video file in a "raw" format, that is, a file with the extension **.wav** or **.avi**.
- You are allowed to install software on your system.
- You are familiar with the basics of using an FTP client.
- You are running a computer with Windows® XP operating system, preferably Windows XP Professional.
- You have access to a computer running at least Windows Server™ 2003 Standard Edition with Windows Media® Services installed.
- You have permission to upload files to a Windows Media Server and a Microsoft Internet Information Services (IIS) web server.
- You know something about writing HTML.

Even if you're not sure about all of the above, we can still get started. By the time you finish this chapter, you'll know how to:

- Update Windows Media Player
- Use the main player features
- Prepare your media file for encoding

- Install a Windows Media Encoder 9 Series
- Encode your media file
- Publish your media file
- Troubleshoot the installation process

Update Your Media Player

Unless you've built your own system from parts or bought a "bare bones" system, there's a better than 99% chance that Windows Media Player is already installed on your hard drive. But you may not have the latest version, especially if you don't have the latest version of the Windows operating system and its service packs.

Inside the Industry

What Is a Media Player?

The term *media player* refers to a piece of software that transforms digital signals transmitted over a computer network into signals that generate pressure waves in speakers, or patterns of light and color on a computer monitor. A software media player performs the same function as Thomas Edison's original 1877 phonograph and similar devices that followed. On a phonograph, a needle followed the hills and valleys of a groove etched in wax. A diaphragm converted the needle's vibrations into sound that humans could perceive. A phonograph is just an analog version of a twenty-first century piece of high-tech. Radios and televisions do something similar, converting invisible radiation (radio and television signals) into sound waves and visible light.

Author's Tip

If you're not part of the information technology team at your company, or you haven't talked with your Internet service provider (ISP) for a while, now is a good time to make contact with your high priests of networking and tell them your plans. They will appreciate being "in the loop," especially when it comes time to streaming your audio and video files.

Using the Player Update Feature

Fortunately, updating the player is free and easy. First, start up your player. A typical location is Start → Programs → Accessories → Windows Media Player. You'll use the Player Update feature built into your version of the software. Here's the procedure, as illustrated in **Figure 1-1**.

1. Click the Help menu
2. Select Check for Player Updates

The player will now contact the Microsoft network and check whether there's a new version. If so, installation will begin. As of this writing, the latest version of Windows Media Player is 10.

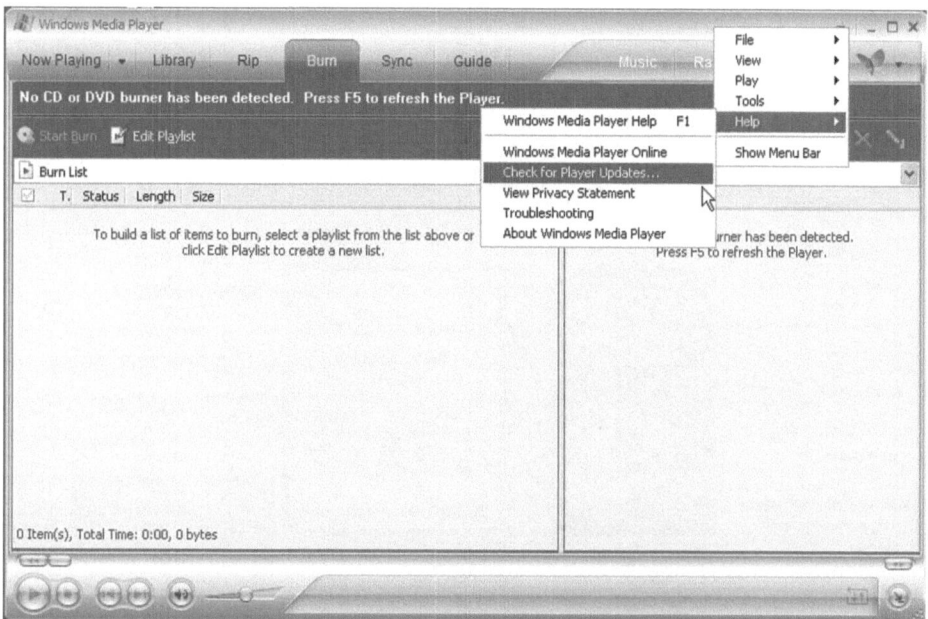

Figure 1-1
To update your player, click Help, then Check for Player Updates.

Updating via the Microsoft Website

You also can update your player via the Microsoft website. It takes only a little longer, and it gives you an opportunity to get familiar with Microsoft's Windows Media webpages.

Unfortunately, Microsoft has decided to offer its latest version of the player only to XP users. (See the QuickTip below for update information for non-XP users.) Here's the procedure for Windows XP:

1. Go to Microsoft's Windows Media page:
   http://www.microsoft.com/windowsmedia/
2. Click the "Windows Media Player 10 for XP" button, as shown in **Figure 1-2**. (By the time you read this, the webpage may have changed somewhat, but the link will still be the same.)

Author's Tip

From now on, the instructions assume you are logged on to the Internet. You're going to be downloading some large files, so if you're on a dial-up connection, be patient. If you're on a DSL/cable line or better, be happy.

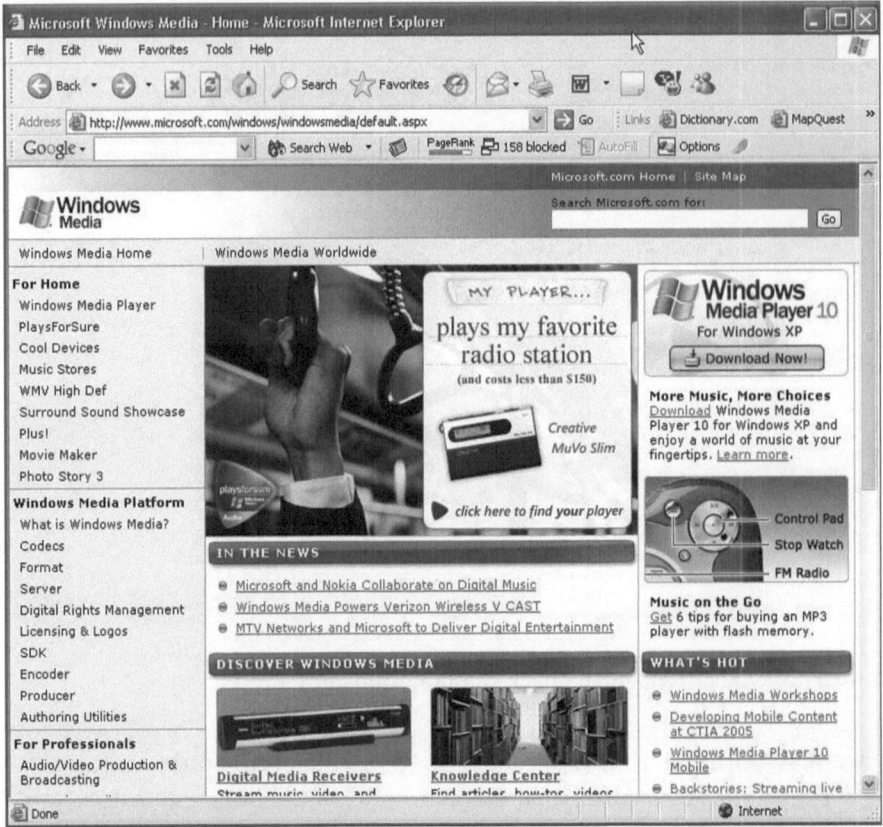

Figure 1-2
Click the "Windows Media Player 10 for XP" button on the Microsoft Window Media Player page to begin updating your player.

3. In the Windows Media Player Download Page, click the "Download" button.

4. In the File Download box, click "Save," and place the installer in a directory on your hard drive where you can find it later.

5. Click Start → Run... → Browse..., find the directory where you put the installer, select it, and click OK.

6. Accept the Supplemental End Users License Agreement.

7. In the "Welcome to Windows Media Player 10" window, click Next.

8. Review the options under "Select Your Privacy Options," though it's safe to go with the defaults, as shown in **Figure 1-3**. Click Next.

9. Review the options under "Customize the Installation Options." It's safe to use the defaults. Click Finish.

The player is now installed.

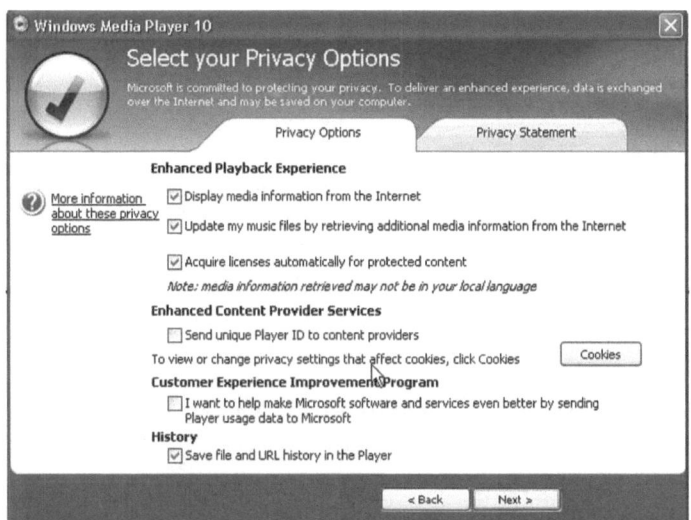

Figure 1-3
The Windows Media Player Installer offers several privacy options. You should also review the Privacy Statement.

ALERT If you have configured other applications to play certain file types, such as MP3 audio, Windows Media Player will now be the default player for those file types. If you'd prefer otherwise, uncheck the relevant boxes.

Overview of Main Player Features

The Windows Media Player offers a rich array of media management tools that go beyond simple playback of streaming media. This section covers the player's main features, as shown in **Figure 1-4**.

The main features are arranged under tabs (and one arrow) at the top of the user interface: Now Playing, Library, Rip, Burn, Sync, Guide, and three tabs for MSN Music: Music, Radio, and Movies & TV.

Now Playing

Now Playing shows you what is currently streaming. Depending on how you accessed the stream, the Now Playing panel shows more information about the stream, or, if you're listening to music or a radio station, a colorful *visualization*, an often hypnotic graphical representation of the sounds you're hearing.

Author's Tip

For Non-XP Users
The instructions in this chapter assume you are using the Windows XP operating system. If you prefer not to upgrade to Windows XP, or you are using another operating system, you can upgrade to older versions of the player, including Windows Media Series 9, by visiting the Windows Media Download Center at:
http://www.microsoft.com/ windows/windowsmedia/ download/default.asp.

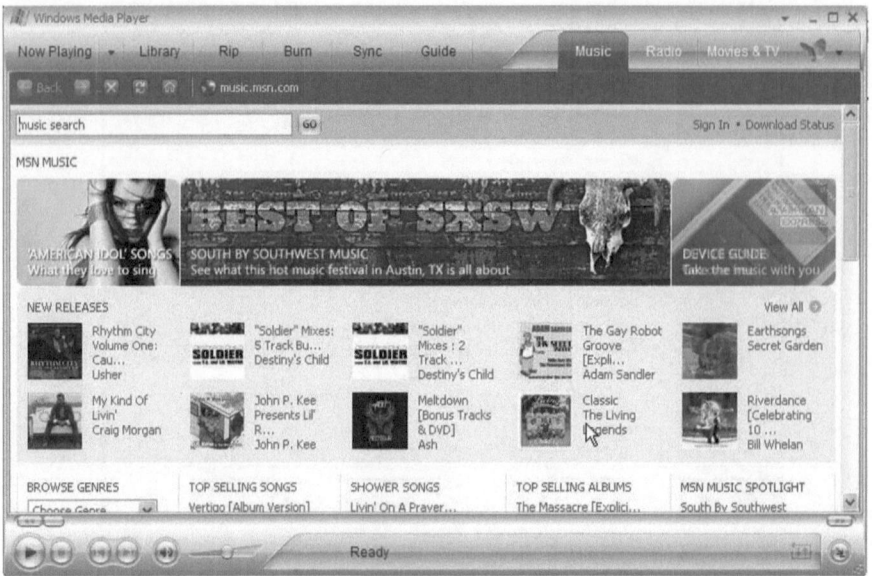

Figure 1-4
The Windows Media Player is a sophisticated media manager, as well as a streaming audio and video player.

Author's Tip

To change the visualization, click the down arrow next to the Minimize button in the upper-right corner.
Select View → Visualizations and choose one of dozens of choices.

Quick Access Panel
Nestled between the Now Playing and Library tabs is a down arrow. When clicked, it displays the Quick Access Panel, a handy way to select items from the personal media library that you create.

Library
The Library shows you all of the media files you've organized using your Windows Media Player.

Rip
The Rip feature enables you to copy tracks from your music CDs to your hard drive. The files are automatically converted from the CD audio format to Windows Media format. (More about formats in Chapter 5, Optimizing Your Audio and Video.)

Author's Tip

This book is focused on streaming media, so it won't show you how to build your own music library with Windows Media Player. For more information about these media management features, key F1 for help or visit the "Using Windows Media Player 10" page online at *http://www.microsoft.com/windows/windowsmedia/ mp10/usingplayer.aspx*.

Burn

Burn helps you make your own audio CDs from your Windows Media library. Burn converts the Windows Media formatted files on your hard drive to the CD audio format so you can play the CD in your car, home stereo, or certain portable devices.

Sync

The Sync feature synchronizes audio files and playlists created through Windows Media Player and devices such as portable media players that are compatible with Windows Media file formats. Sync also allows the transfer of files protected with Microsoft's digital rights management system.

Guide

The Windows Media Guide is a website for all kinds of streaming media content in Windows Media formats, from music to news to movie trailers, including downloadable files. The guide is updated frequently, so it's a good idea to check it out whenever you can.

MSN Music

You'll notice that the tabs change color slightly to the right. This is the online store section of Windows Media Player, which offers a variety of vendors selling everything from audio books to full-length movies. Microsoft's MSN service is shown by default, but there are nearly a dozen other stores. The following text explains MSN's main offerings to give you a sense of what's available in this marketplace of streams and downloads.

Music — The Music tab opens an interface to MSN Music, MSN's online site for sampling and buying music. You can listen to streaming samples of music in nearly all genres, buy individual songs or whole albums, and listen via Windows Media Player or via a Windows Media-compatible device.

Radio — Radio is MSN's free and pay-to-listen live broadcasting service. Many of the offerings don't cost a dime. Others give you access to specific genres of music or artists for a nominal fee.

Movies & TV — MSN's Movies & TV tab in Windows Media Player offers movie trailers, behind-the-scenes stories, and promotional spots for TV shows.

Other Important Features

Windows Media Player has several other important features related to streaming media that the book will touch on here, and explain in more detail later.

Properties

The Properties window under the File menu shows technical information about the file itself, such as the codec used to encode the file, as shown in **Figure 1-5**. It also shows copyright information, data such as the author of the content, and license information, if applicable.

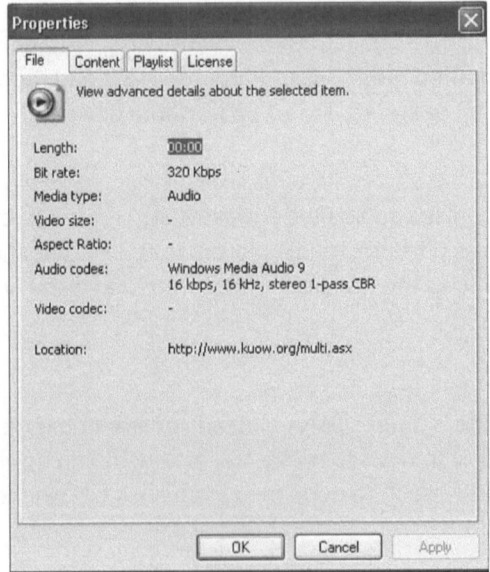

Figure 1-5
The Properties window under the File menu gives you important information about the file you're playing.

Statistics

The Statistics window under the View menu shows important information about your connection to the Internet and the stream as the data arrives, which can help you diagnose problems.

Captions

New rules under the Americans with Disabilities Act require some media producers to include features that make their content accessible to the hearing impaired. Windows Media Series has features that enable compliance, but they are switched off by default. Hit Ctrl + Shift + C or Play → Captions and Subtitles → On to switch the feature on.

Prepare Your Media File for Encoding

If you've worked with audio or video files at all, you're probably familiar with the **.wav** or **.avi** extension. These are industry-standard formats for audio (**.wav**) and video (**.avi**). But most of these files are far too large to send through the Internet, especially **.avi** files, even in these days of high-speed broadband. It's also important to remember that many home users prefer dial-up connections. Sending large files through these connections is like pouring Niagara Falls through a straw.

Streaming media technology solves this problem by converting **.wav** and **.avi** files into smaller files that retain most of the sound and picture quality of the originals. The word "most" is important, because the quality of the encoded files depends on several variables, which the book discusses in Chapter 6, Encoding for Windows Media. Because this chapter is designed to get you going quickly, the book will skip the details and get right to using the Windows Media Encoder.

Inside the Industry

 Encoding in streaming media technology refers to the process of converting certain audio and video files into smaller, compressed files optimized for transmission over a computer network.

Find Your Audio or Video File

Remember the assumptions at the beginning of this chapter? For the following instructions to make sense, you'll need a **.wav** or **.avi** file to encode. Even if you're not on a deadline, you should find one to practice on. There's a couple of ways to do this:

- Use the Search in your operating system to find a file. Search for the extension with a wild card, a la "*****.avi**". Be sure to include all your folders, including system folders.
- Check installation CDs for other kinds of software you have. Companies often include media files that play during installations.
- Search the Internet for files with the **.wav** or **.avi** extension. Government sites are good to mine, because the files usually aren't protected by copyright.

Find a file of at least a couple of megabytes. Then put it on your hard drive in a place where you can find it later.

Install a Windows Media Encoder

The following section walks you through the installation of a Windows Media Encoder, the software that converts "raw" **.wav** and **.avi** files into files suitable for streaming. (For information on minimum recommended system requirements, see Chapter 3, Get Ready to Capture Audio and Video.)

You'll notice immediately, especially if you've installed Windows Media Player 10, that the encoder is called "Windows Media Encoder Series 9." This is the latest version of the encoder software as of this writing. Should Microsoft update the encoder to a new version by the time you read this, the procedures below should still work.

1. Load the Microsoft Windows Media Encoder webpage in your browser, as shown in **Figure 1-6**:

   http://www.microsoft.com/windows/windowsmedia/9series/encoder/default.aspx

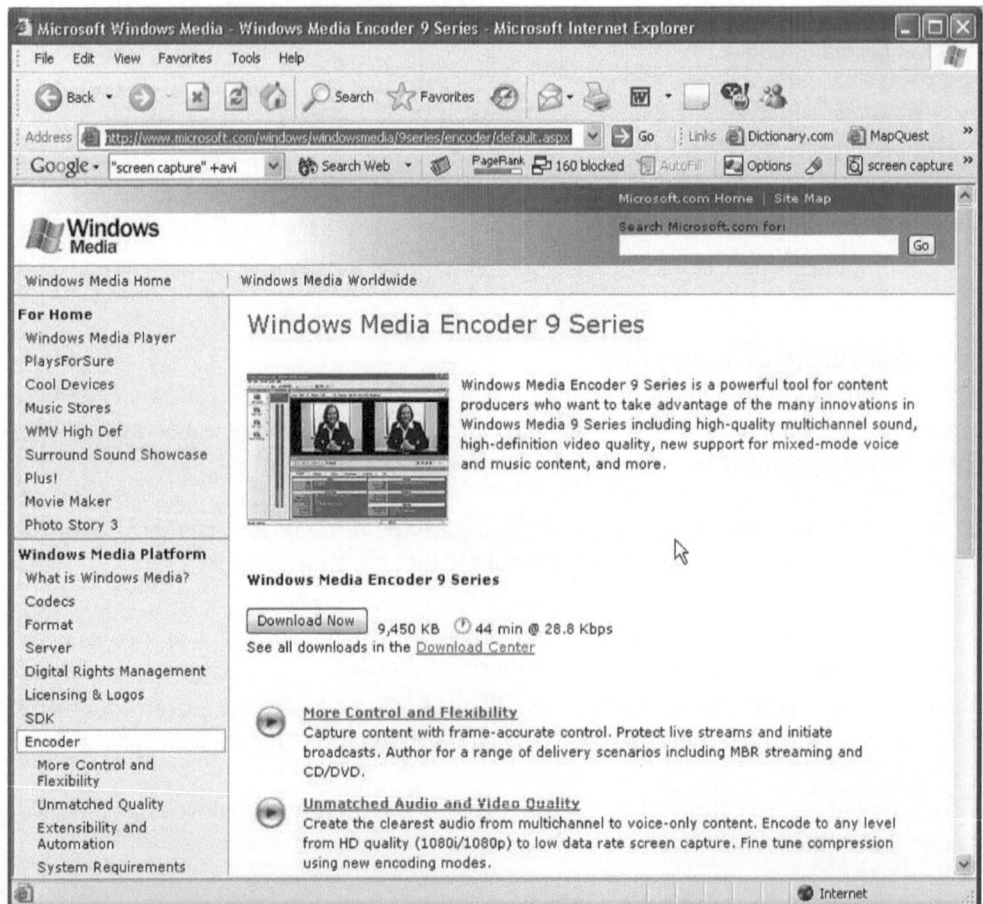

Figure 1-6
The Microsoft Windows Media Encoder Series 9 webpage. You'll download the encoder from here.

2. Click the Download Now button and then click Save, placing the file in a convenient spot on your hard drive.

3. Click Start → Run... → Browse..., find the directory where you put the installer, select it, and click OK.

4. When the Windows Media Encoder Series 9 Setup Wizard appears, click Next.

5. Accept the terms of the End User License Agreement.

6. Accept the suggested installation folder by clicking Next.

7. Click Install.

8. When installation is complete, click Finish.

Unlike most other programs, clicking Finish doesn't actually start the program to give you a chance to see what you've accomplished. You'll see the encoder in action in the next section.

Encode Your Media File

Now's the time for some real interesting stuff! You're going to convert your original file into a streaming media file. Step-by-step instructions follow.

> **ALERT** For the rest of this chapter, you'll work with an **.avi** (video) file. But most of the steps also work on **.wav** (audio) files.

1. Start the Windows Media Encoder by clicking the encoder icon on your desktop or selecting Start → Programs → Windows Media → Windows Media Encoder. Note that on startup, the encoder's New Session Wizard appears. This helps you walk through a simple encode.

2. Select the "Convert a File" option and click OK, as shown in **Figure 1-7**.

3. Click the "Browse..." button under Source File, locate your **.avi** file, and click OK. Note how the wizard automatically puts a location and a filename with the extension in the Output File box, as shown in **Figure 1-8**. Feel free to modify this information to taste.

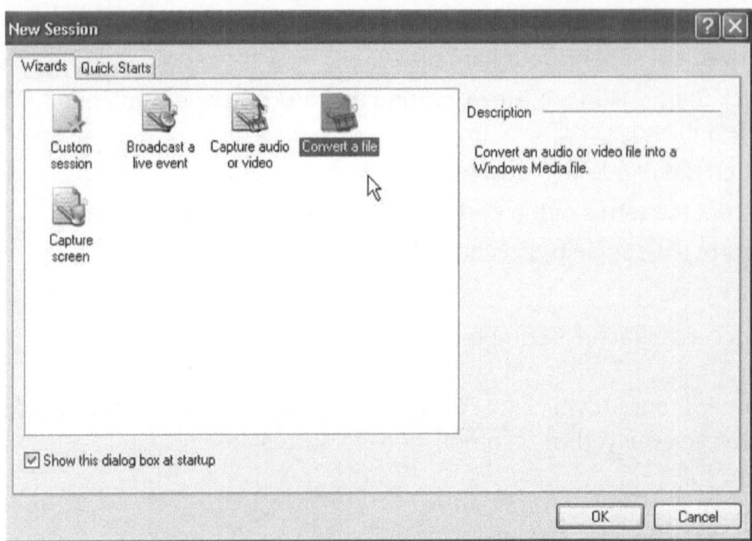

Figure 1-7
Select the "Convert a file" in the Windows Media Encoder New Session Wizard.

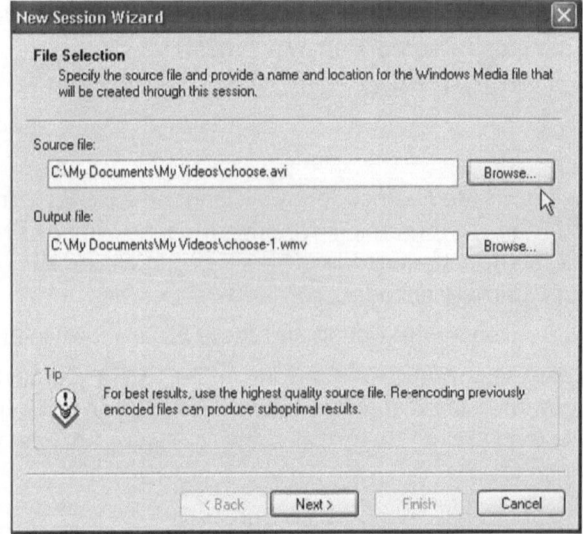

Figure 1-8
When you select the file to be encoded, the Session Wizard automatically assigns an output path and file name to the source file.

4.   Click Next.

5.   In the box labeled "Content Distribution," select "Windows Media Server (streaming)," as shown in **Figure 1-9**.

6.   Click Next.

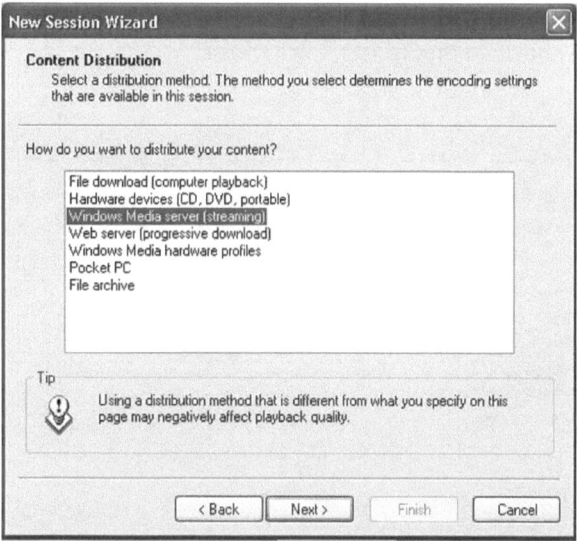

Figure 1-9
Choose "Windows Media Server (streaming)" as your Content Distribution option.

7. In the "Encoding Options," you can ignore most of the gobbledygook for now. However, take a moment to scroll down the box with the checkboxes until you find the checked box or boxes, which tell you the target bandwidth for the file, as shown in **Figure 1-10**. (More on these options in Chapter 6.)

8. Click Finish.

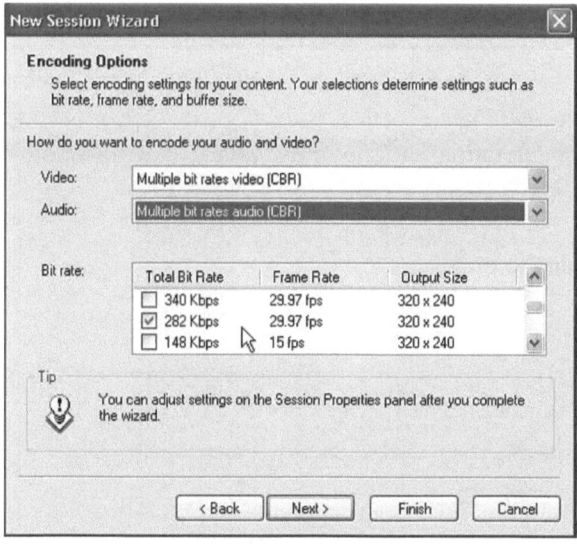

Figure 1-10
Scroll down the "Bit Rate" box to see the default bit rate for video encoding in the Session Wizard.

9. After the encoder completes its work, it shows you some statistics describing the results, as shown in **Figure 1-11**. Click Close.

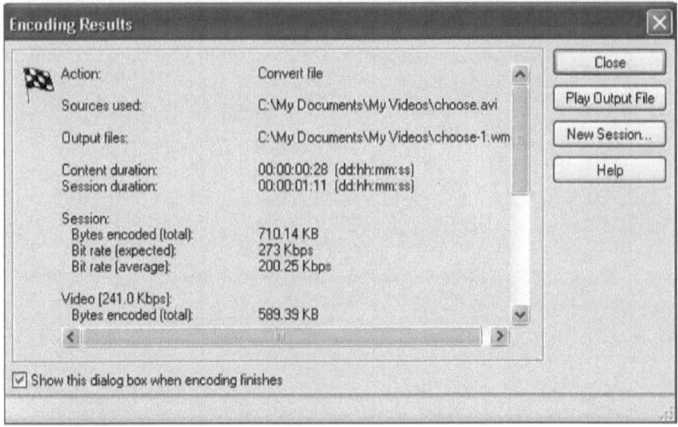

Figure 1-11
When the encoder finishes, it shows you some statistics about the encoded file.

You've successfully encoded your video file.

View the Encoded File

To view the encoded video, use the following procedure.

1. Start your Windows Media Player by clicking Start → Programs → Windows Media Player.
2. Click the down arrow in the upper right corner.
3. Select File → Open and find the output location of the encoded file you set in the encoder wizard.
4. Look for the file name with the **.wmv** (video) or **.wma** (audio only) extension.
5. Select the file, and click Open.

The encoded file begins to play.

Publishing Your Windows Media File

For the highest quality user experience, you should stream your newly encoded file with Windows Media Services, which is software designed specifically to deliver streaming media files. You have two main options for media serving:

- Place your encoded file on your Windows Media Server.
- Place your encoded file on a Windows Media Server provided by your Internet service provider (ISP).

Each option requires somewhat different skills and knowledge. To keep this chapter brief and to the point, the instructions assume you have access to your own Windows Server 2003 with Windows Media Services installed. That enables the following section to make use of two wizards that speed up the media publishing process.

Unfortunately, the book's assumption that you'll have access to a Windows Server 2003 running Windows Media Services isn't very realistic, especially if you're not part of your company's networking team. But the assumption does allow the book to use Microsoft's publishing wizards to illustrate the ease of publishing Windows Media files.

ALERT Note carefully where the book tells you to Stop! what you're doing before finishing the publishing points task just ahead. You need to do so before moving on to the next task.

Inside the Industry

 Within Windows Media technology, you'll sometimes hear the labels "Windows Media Services" and "Windows Media Server." The former is Microsoft's name for a set of technologies and tools for delivering and managing streaming media, such as managing content licenses and log files. The latter is just one of the Windows Media Services.

Create a Publishing Point

When a Windows Media Player requests a file to play, it uses a URL, similar to the URL of a webpage. The streaming URL points to a virtual location at the Windows Media Server, which redirects the request to the true location of the streaming file.

You create the virtual location by setting up a *publishing point*. The following instructions explain how:

1. At your Windows Server 2003 computer, open the Windows Media Services Administration Tool by clicking Start → Programs → Administrative Tools → Windows Media Services.

2. With your mouse, highlight "Publishing Point" in the left panel, as shown in **Figure 1-12**.

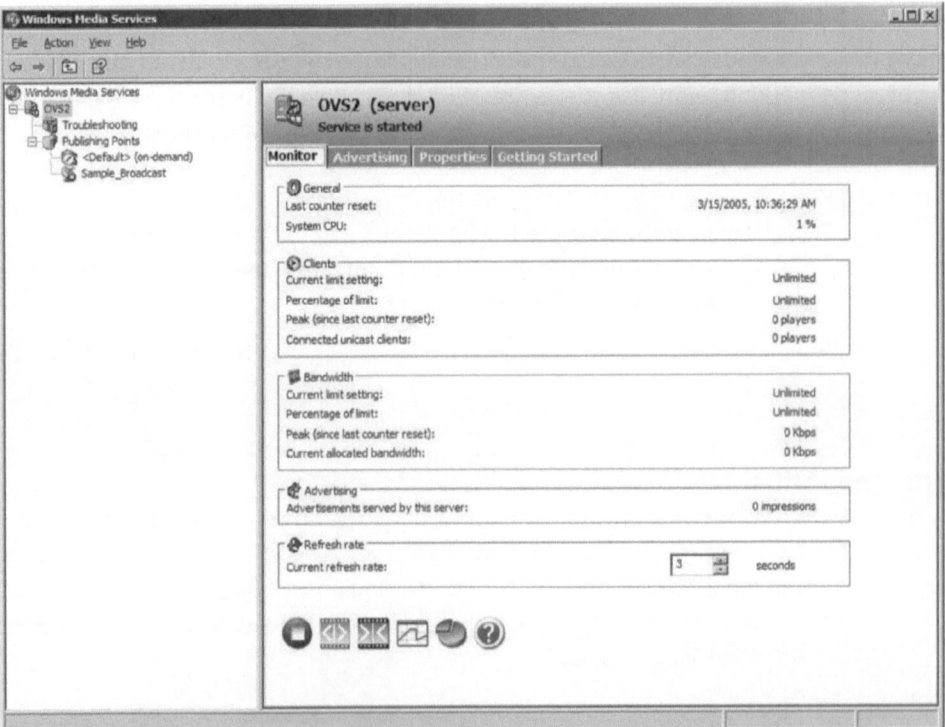

Figure 1-12
The Windows Media Services Administration Tool. Note the Publishing Points branch in the directory tree.

3. Right click, select Add Publishing Point Wizard, and click Next. This starts the wizard, a shown in **Figure 1-13**.

4. Create a Publishing Point name, if you don't want to use the default, and click Next, as shown in **Figure 1-14**.

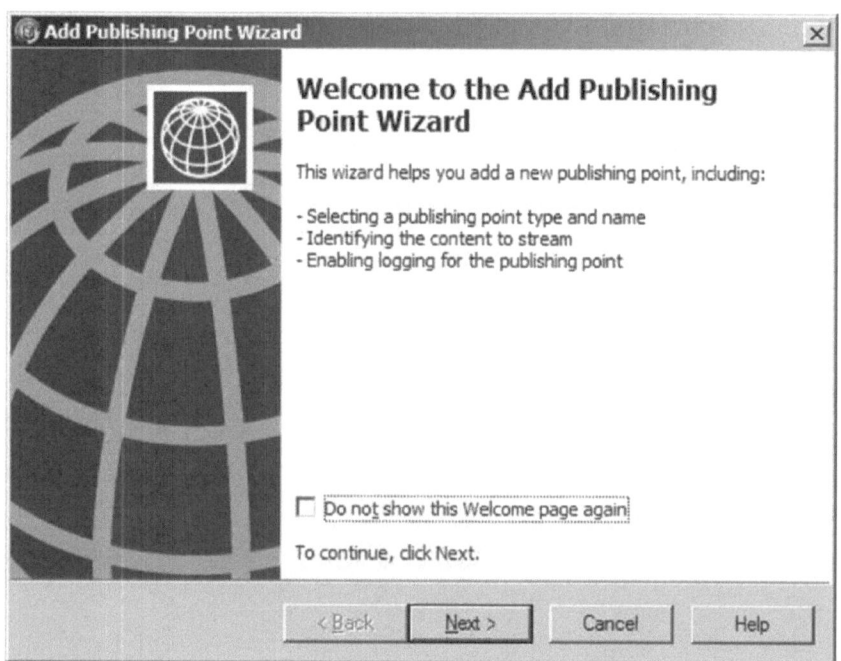

Figure 1-13
The Add Publishing Point Wizard.

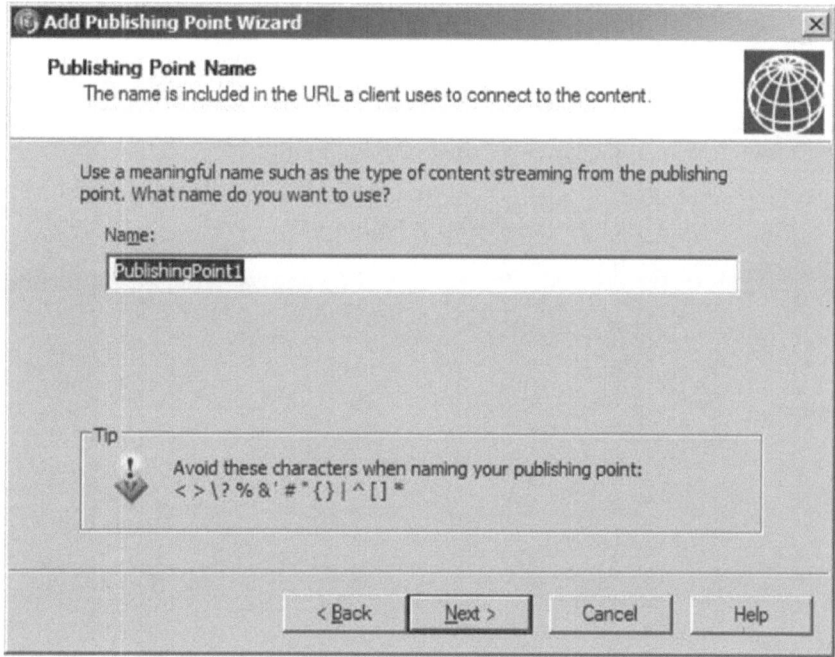

Figure 1-14
Create a name for the publishing point, if you decide not to use the default.

5. In the Content Type box, select the "One File" radio button, and click Next, as shown in **Figure 1-15**.

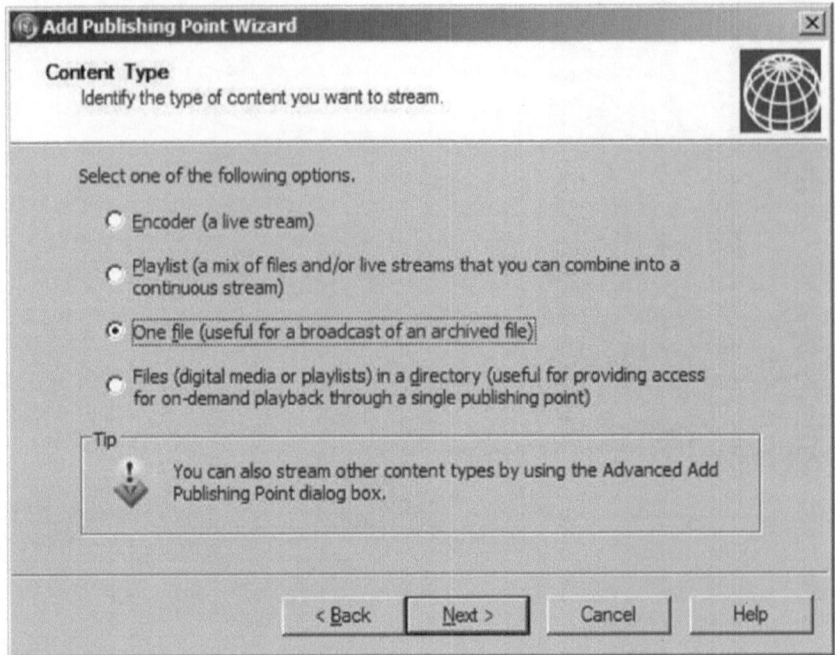

Figure 1-15
Select the "One File" option.

6. In the Publishing Point Type box, select the "On-Demand Publishing Point" radio button, and click Next, as shown in **Figure 1-16**.

7. In the Existing Publishing Point box, select the "Add New Publishing Point" radio button, and click Next, as shown in **Figure 1-17**.

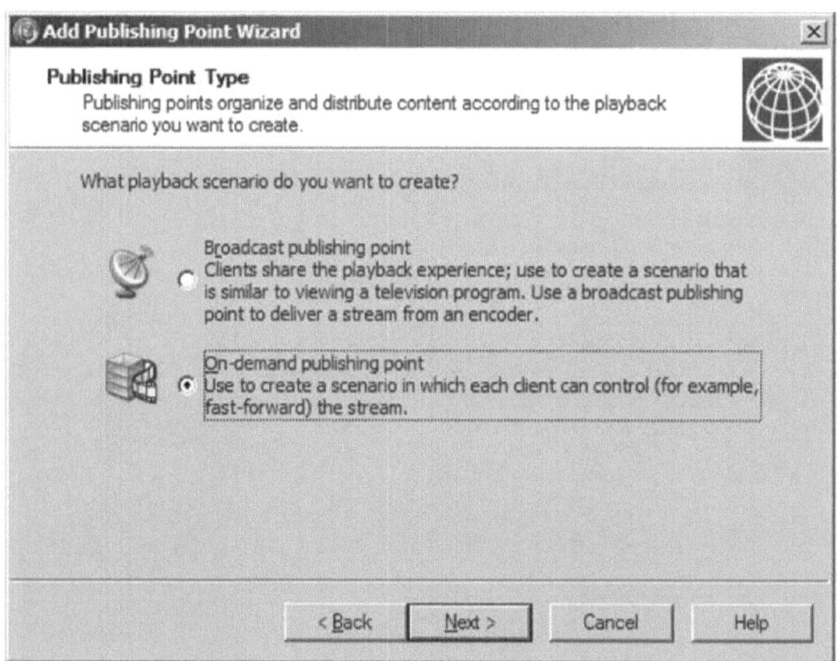

Figure 1-16
Select the "On-Demand Publishing Point" option.

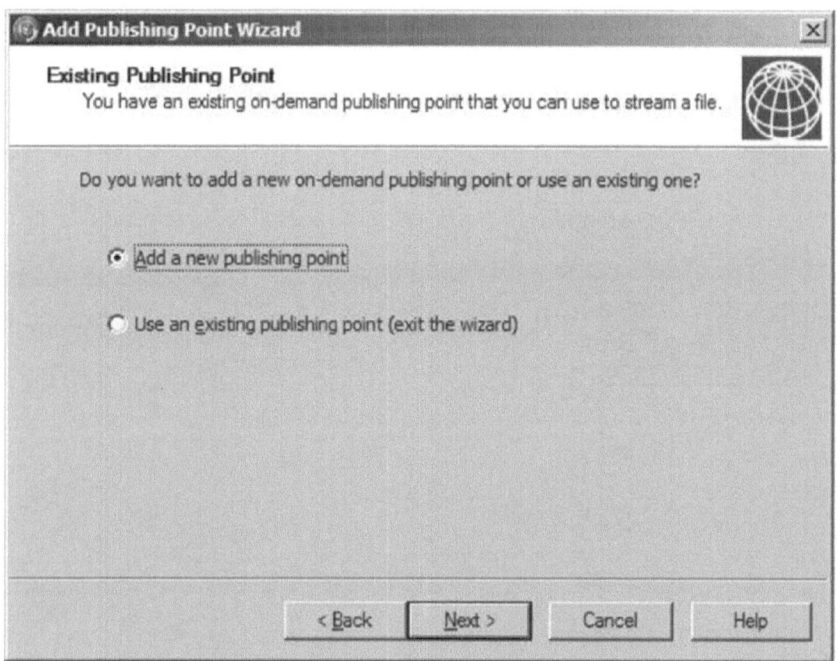

Figure 1-17
Select the "Add New Publishing Point" option.

8. In the File Location box, click the Browse... button, find the location of your media file, highlight it, click Open, then click Next, as shown in **Figure 1-18**. (See also QuickTip below.)

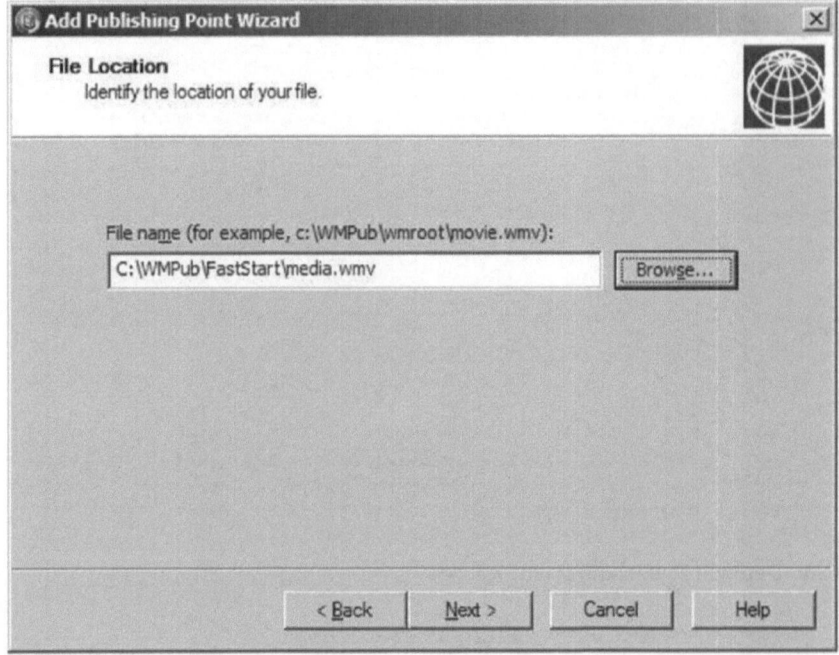

Figure 1-18
Place the location of your media file in the File Location dialog box.

9. In the Unicast Logging box, click Next, as shown in **Figure 1-19**.
10. Review the Publishing Point Summary box, and click Next, as shown in **Figure 1-20**.

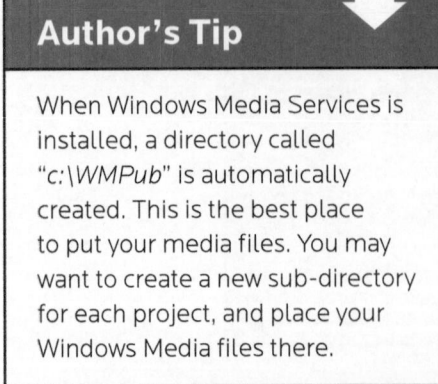

Author's Tip

When Windows Media Services is installed, a directory called "*c:\WMPub*" is automatically created. This is the best place to put your media files. You may want to create a new sub-directory for each project, and place your Windows Media files there.

Now you're ready to create an announcement file.

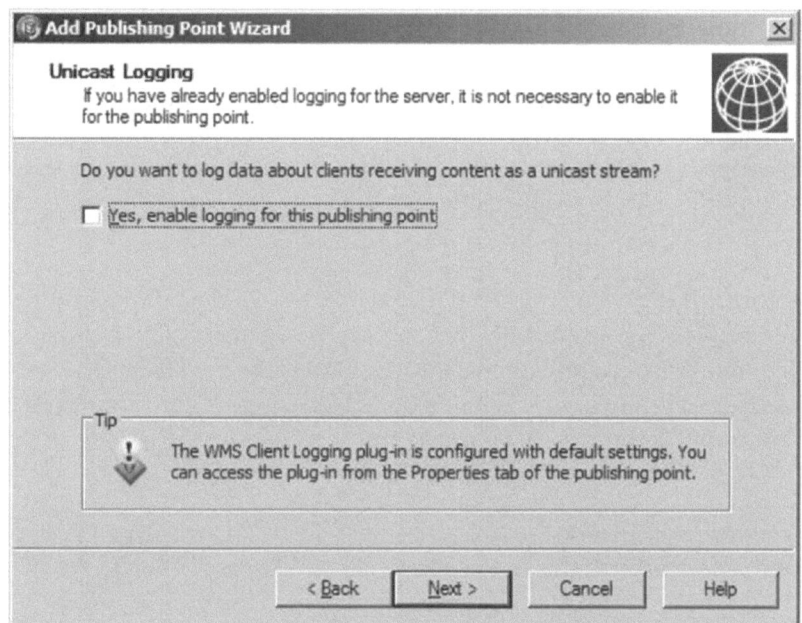

Figure 1-19
Leave the Unicast Logging box unchecked.

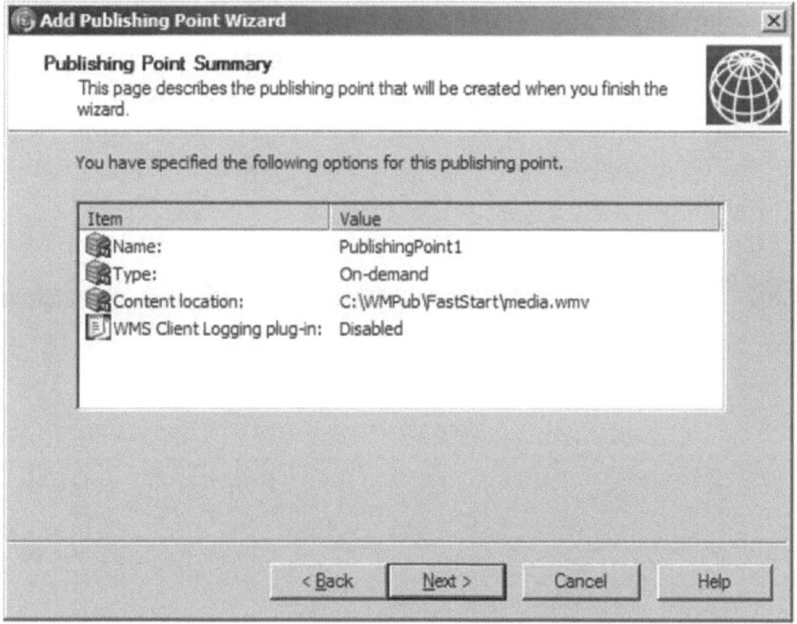

Figure 1-20
The "Publishing Point Summary" tells you what you've just accomplished. Stop here! A box appears saying "Completing the Add Publishing Point Wizard." Don't click Finish yet. We're going to use the next wizard in the next step via this box.

Create an Announcement File

You're probably familiar with how to go to a specific address on the World Wide Web: You type the location in the location bar of your browser, starting with "*http://*". You can do something similar with your Windows Media Player, but most links to streaming media files are found on webpages. That means you have to add an extra step to the process, a link on your webpage to a metafile, or as Microsoft calls it, an *announcement file*.

Inside the Industry

 A metafile is a small text file that contains the location of your streaming media file. Your webpage links to this file. When you click the link, the browser downloads the file and gives it your Windows Media Player. The player opens it, finds the location of your media file, and plays it.

Here's the procedure for creating the announcement file using the wizard in Windows Media Services. Afterwards, the book shows you how to link to it in your webpage.

Remember when you were told to Stop! in the previous section? Let's start at the same place, the "Completing the Add Publishing Point Wizard" dialog, as shown in **Figure 1-21**.

1. In the "Completing the Add Publishing Point Wizard" dialog, check the checkbox "After the wizard finishes," and select the radio button "Create an announcement file (**.asx**) or webpage (**.htm**)," as shown in **Figure 1-21**.

2. The "Welcome to the Unicast Announcement Wizard" appears, as shown in **Figure 1-21**. Click Next.

3. In the "Access the Content" dialog, click the "Browse..." button, locate your media file, highlight the file, and click Open, as shown in **Figure 1-22**.

4. In the same dialog box, replace the server name with the full domain address of your server. Click Next.

Figure 1-21
The "Unicast Announcement Wizard" helps you create announcement files.

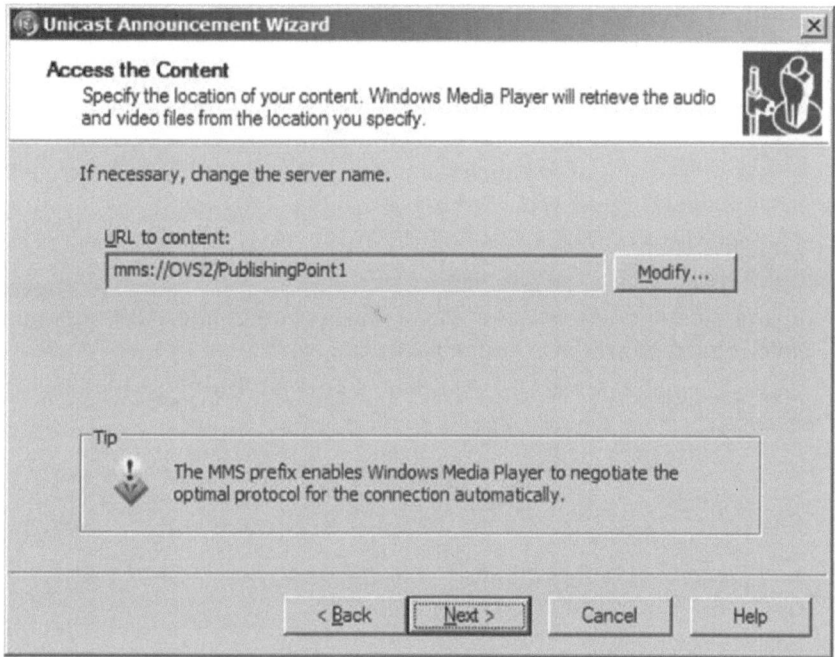

Figure 1-22
Tell the announcement wizard the location of your media file.

5. In the "Save Announcement Options" dialog, note the suggested location for your announcement file, which has the extension **.asx**, as shown in **Figure 1-23**.

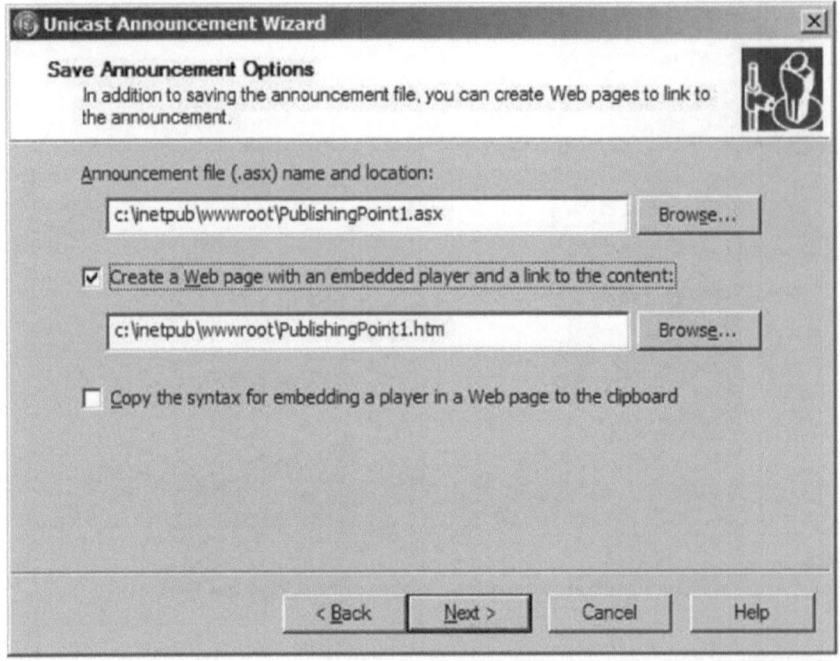

Figure 1-23
Note the suggested locations of your announcement file.

6. In the same dialog (see **Figure 1-24**), check the option "Create a webpage with an embedded player and a link to the content." (You won't use this webpage, but let's take the opportunity to create this code, which you'll use later in the book.)

7. Click Next.

8. In the "Edit Announcement Metadata" dialog, enter title, author, and copyright information, as shown in **Figure 1-24**. Click Next.

9. In the "Completing the Unicast Announcement Wizard" dialog, check the "Test" box, as shown in **Figure 1-25**. Click Finish.

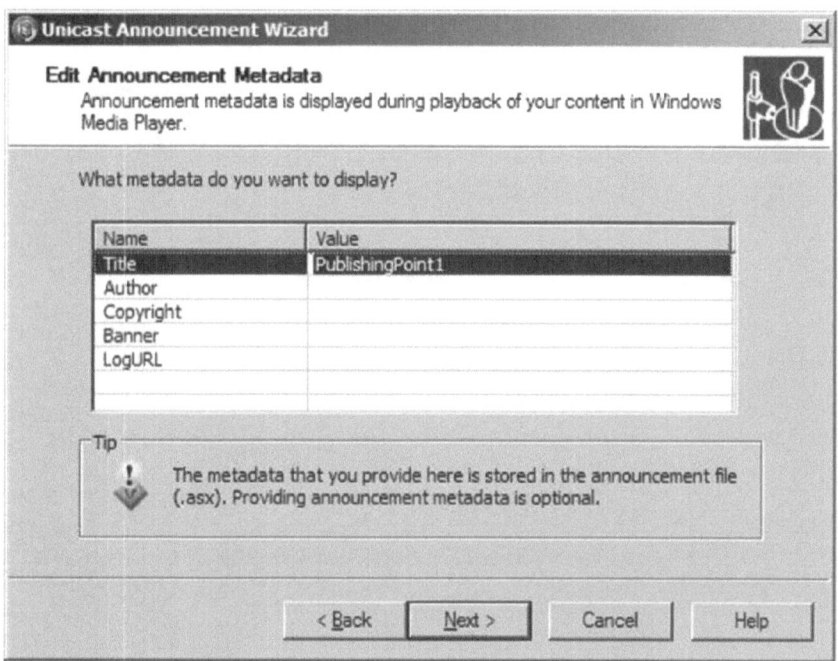

Figure 1-24
Title, author, and copyright information will be stored in the announcement file.

Figure 1-25
The final dialog in the announcement file wizard offers an opportunity to test your file.

10. A "Test Unicast Announcement" dialog appears with two buttons, labeled "Test," as shown in **Figure 1-26**.

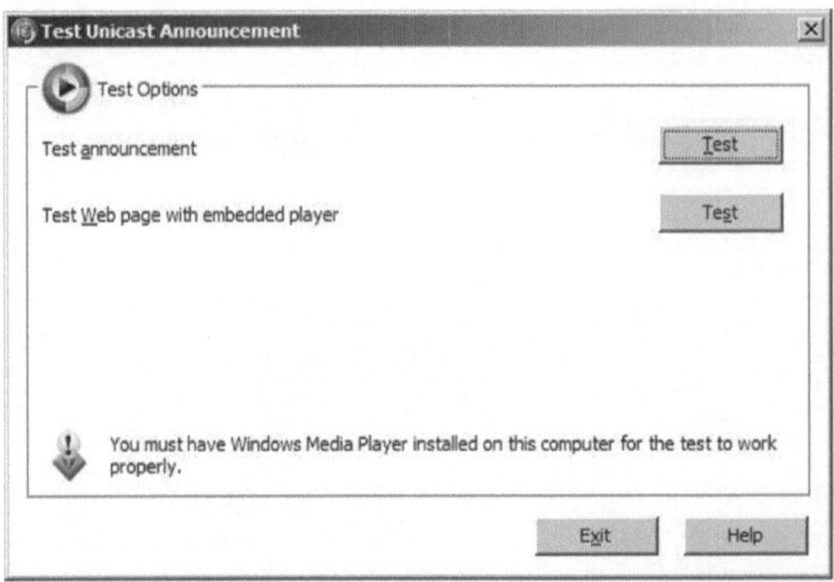

Figure 1-26
Click the "Test" buttons in this dialog to check whether the announcement files work.

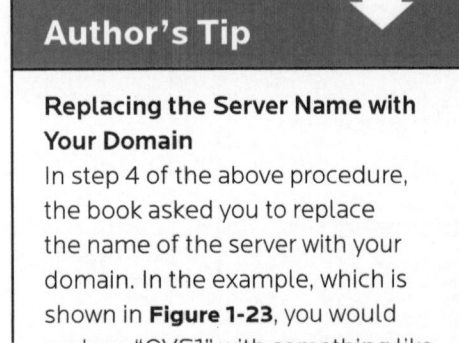

Author's Tip

Replacing the Server Name with Your Domain
In step 4 of the above procedure, the book asked you to replace the name of the server with your domain. In the example, which is shown in **Figure 1-23**, you would replace "OVS1" with something like "*www.mydomain.com*." Do NOT put an "*http://*" in front of the domain. The "*mms://*" serves that purpose. (More on this in Chapter 8.)

11. Click the upper Test button. Your media file should start playing. But don't be dismayed if your file doesn't start playing. Playback is somewhat dependent on how your network is configured, a subject beyond the scope of this book.

You're now ready to link to your media file via your webpage.

Link to Your Announcement File via Your Webpage

As noted previously, most websites link to a streaming media file by first pointing to an announcement file. To do this, you need to know some of the basics of hypertext markup language (HTML). Specifically, you need to understand hyperlink tags. If you're unsure, pick up a good, basic HTML book, or review the excellent free tutorials at W3 Schools, *http://www.w3schools.com/*.

First, you need to place your **.asx** file on a web server, most likely where your website lives. It's probably not the same server as your Windows Media Server.

Uploading and Testing Your Announcement File —
Contact your network administrator or ISP to obtain the address, username, and password for your FTP access. (In some networks, you may only need a directory location.) With your FTP client, upload the **.asx** file to your web server. For example, your website address may be *www.mydomain.com*. If you use an ISP, there's a good chance your FTP address is *ftp.mydomain.com*. Try this with your username and password.

Author's Tip

What about that announcement file with the **.htm** at the end? It's not actually an announcement file, but a webpage with a player embedded into the code. Save the location of this file somewhere handy. You'll refer back to it in Chapter 8. In the meantime, it's safe to click Test, and watch it in action, if you like.

Author's Tip

To move your files from place to place, nothing beats a good file transfer protocol (FTP) program. WS_FTP Pro is the author's favorite, followed by FTP Commander and CuteFTP. To try these, check out the links below.

WS_FTP: *http://www.ipswitch.com/downloads/*
FTP Commander: *http://www.internet-soft.com/ftpcomm.htm*
CuteFTP: *http://www.globalscape.com/cuteftp/*

Once you're logged on, create a directory called "metafiles" under your site's root directory to distinguish your Windows Media announcement files from webpages that may contain announcements in the more common sense of the word. Upload your **.asx** file to the "announcements" directory.

To test the file, load the site address, path, and file name in your browser's location bar. A typical address would look like this:
http://www.mydomain.com/metafiles/myvideo.asx

Hit Return on your keyboard and the video should start playing.

Putting a Link in Your Webpage — Now comes the last step in this chapter, creating a link to your Windows Media file all the world can see. Using your favorite HTML editor, add a set of anchor tags containing the path to your file. Here's one way to do it:

```
<html>
        <body>
                <a href="http://
http://www.mydomain.com/metafiles/myvideo.asx">
        Audio/Video</a>
        </body>
</html>
```

This code actually creates a small webpage. It might be a good idea to create a small test page with your link and check the path for yourself before releasing it to your users.

Inside the Industry

Why metafiles and what do they do?
Web browsers are designed to handle static kinds of data, such as text and photographs. Audio and video, however, change dynamically over time; one sound follows another, an image dissolves into the next. The browser needs what's called a *helper application* to handle this data.

When you click a metafile/announcement file link, the browser downloads the file, reads the **.asx** extension, and matches the extension against a list of extensions in its configuration file. When it sees a match between **.asx** and Windows Media Player, the browser hands the **.asx** file to the player, essentially saying, "Help me play this data." Windows Media Player opens the **.asx** file, reads the contents, including the URL to the audio or video file, requests the file, and starts playing it.

Troubleshooting

If you've followed all the instructions in this chapter closely, you're well on your way to mastering streaming media technology. But you're bound to run into problems. This chapter won't go into every conceivable issue that could crop up. However, three problems cause the bulk of headaches.

1. **Error in the path to the .asx file**: This is actually an issue with your HTML in the webpage. Your web browser will complain that "**the page could not be found**" or something similar. To troubleshoot, check the URL you placed in the anchor tags. It could be something as simple as a misspelling. If you used a relative path, instead of the full or absolute path, your reference to the "metafiles" directory could be broken.

2. **Error in the path to the media file**: In this case, Windows Media Player will show you an error message, such as the one in **Figure 1-27**. You need to look inside

the **.asx** file, using a simple text editor, such as Notepad, and see if you put it in the right location for your media file. Like the preceding problem, it could be something as simple as a misspelling of a directory name or the file itself. Once you've discovered the error and fixed it, upload the repaired **.asx** file to your web server and try to play the file again.

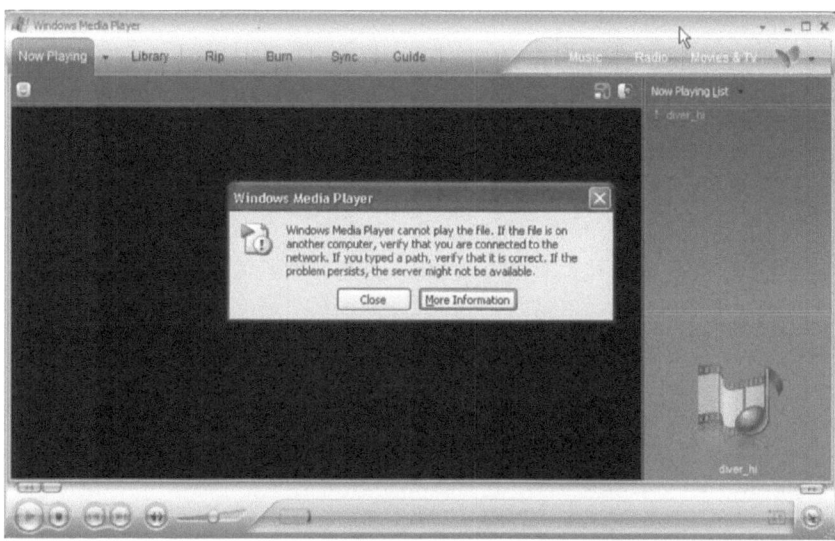

Figure 1-27
An error message from your Windows Media Player usually means the path to your media file and/or the media file name referenced in the **.asx** file has an error.

3. **Windows Media Server unavailable**: This error likely means the Windows Media Server is shut down for some reason. If you're certain that your paths and filenames are correct, restart the Windows Media Server or ask your network administrator to restart it for you.

Other explanations for problems include a corrupt media file, which would require you to re-encode it, or a networking issue, which means you should contact your network administrator. The vast majority of issues can be fixed quickly and painlessly.

Conclusion

This chapter showed you how to update and install a Windows Media Player from scratch, and explained some of the program's basic features. The chapter then took you through the steps for downloading and installing a Windows Media Encoder. The instructions demonstrated how to encode a simple video file. The chapter included information on publishing your media file on a Windows Media Server, and linking to the file with HTML on your webpage. The last section explained some basic troubleshooting.

The next chapter gives you a foundation in streaming basics.

CHAPTER 2

Streaming Media Basics

You've successfully encoded your first media file, and you're excited to learn more about streaming media technology and production. As with all new information and skills, you need to start with the basics. This chapter discusses the fundamental concepts behind streaming media and introduces you to streaming's four steps: capture, encode, distribute, and playback. In addition, you'll learn about the two main kinds of streaming: live and on-demand.

This chapter will also discuss your audience, the most important component in any kind of communications activity. You'll evaluate your audience's needs and how well you can meet those needs with streaming media. You'll also evaluate your content, that is, the media you want to deliver, in relation to your audience and how you use your tools. The chapter outlines the advantages and disadvantages of Windows Media versus other vendors. Finally, this chapter underlines the importance of cooperation between creative people and technical people when making and delivering streaming media. By the end of this chapter, you will:

- Understand the definition of streaming media
- Learn streaming fundamentals
- Follow the four steps of streaming
- Know the difference between live and on-demand streaming
- Begin to evaluate your audience
- Understand your own content in relation to streaming
- Compare Windows Media with other technologies

Streaming Media Defined

Streaming usually refers to the predictable transfer at a consistent rate of data with a time-line, most often audio and video. But other types of data can be streamed as well, including text and static images. Most kinds of streaming media are interpreted by a software application called a *player*, as in the case of the topic of this book, Windows Media Player.

Occasionally, you'll see the term *streaming* applied to other kinds of data that updates frequently, such as stock quotes, which this book does not address. Streaming is often used incorrectly when the speaker or author really means *downloading*, which is the process of saving data at one location to some kind of permanent storage device in another location, such as a hard drive. (Confusingly, some speakers and writers use downloading when they really mean streaming.) The streaming experience, especially live streaming, is much like radio or television: here for the moment, but transitory and ephemeral.

 ALERT One type of streaming media is called *progressive download*, which is a hybrid of streaming and downloading. More on this in Chapter 8, Delivering Windows Media to Your Audience.

Streaming Fundamentals

Streaming media technology is built on the client/server model. A *client* requests data via a network from a server, which fulfills the request and manages delivery. As the data arrives, the client interprets the data and displays it in readable form. In streaming media, the client, in this case, Windows Media Player, contacts a Windows Media Server, which locates the requested file and sends it to the player.

Unlike many other client/server applications, such as web browsers and web servers, streaming media clients and servers constantly communicate with each other during the streaming session. The audio and video data flows one way, from server to client, but the client tells the server how things are going, and request changes to delivery as conditions evolve. To oversimplify, it's akin to a pilot asking air traffic control to repeat a message or switch frequencies. The technological back-and-forth is an attempt to overcome the Internet's fickle mood; a connection can be good one moment and terrible the next. Without this communication, a video frame may be lost or a word garbled, and the frustrated user walks away.

The Four Steps of Streaming

The basic streaming media process contains four steps: capture, encode, distribute, and playback, as shown in **Figure 2-1**. Each step is discussed in detail in the following pages.

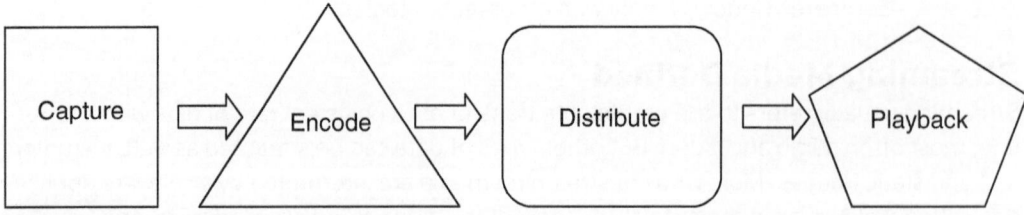

Figure 2-1
The four steps of streaming: capture, encode, distribute, and playback.

Capture

Step one of streaming media, capture, involves the conversion of analog or digital signals into a form that can be converted into a streaming media file. Think of scanning a photograph. The scanner passes over (actually under) the image, converting the analog information into digital bits that a computer can manipulate. In the context of streaming, capturing is similar. You play a video tape in a tape deck and send the signal to a computer, which converts the signal into "1s" and "0s," the building blocks of digital media, and stores it in digital form on a hard drive or other storage device.

This assumes your original content, such as video, starts out in analog form. However, more and more original content starts out in digital form, such as DVDs or digital tape. That means that capturing these days often means moving content from one form of digital media to another form, usually a file that sits on a hard drive.

Inside the Industry

Analog and Digital

The term *analog* describes data that flows in a continuous, often variable mechanical or electrical signal. Analog devices include the phonograph or early tape recorders.

Digital refers to data that is broken into binary information, those familiar 1s and 0s. Recording and playback devices built around computer chips are digital.

Encode

Most files created in the capturing step, especially video files, are far too large to send through the Internet. A 60-second video can hold several megabytes worth of information, depending on a number of variables. Even with a high-speed connection, downloading the file could take longer than playing it once it arrives.

Thus the need for the second streaming step, *encoding*, often called *transcoding*, the process of converting the captured audio or video file into a compressed file far more suitable for sending over the Internet. Encoding requires a special application called an *encoder*. In the case of Windows Media, you use the Windows Media Encoder.

Encoders make use of *codecs*, short for COde/DECode or COmpress/DECompress. Codecs are special algorithms that remove unneeded information to make files smaller, as illustrated in **Figure 2-2**. Codecs also fall into two general categories of *lossless* and *lossy*. Lossless means no data is lost during the transcoding. Lossy means that some portion of data, a little or a lot, is removed.

Streaming codecs also arrange the data in the file a certain way that optimizes them for transfer over the Internet. Microsoft and third-party companies write codecs for different

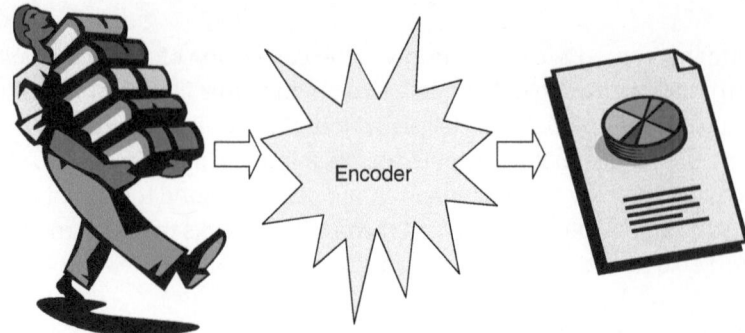

Figure 2-2
A streaming media encoder, including Windows Media Encoder, removes unneeded or repetitive data to make audio and video files smaller and more suited to streaming over the Internet.

types of content, such as music or voice, and different network conditions, such as dial-up or broadband.

Distribute

Once your audio or video file is encoded, you need a way to deliver it to the world. Similar to radio or television, streaming media requires a transmitter to distribute the information. In this case, the transmitter is Windows Media Server, one of a set of applications under Windows Media Services.

The most basic function of the server is responding to requests from Windows Media Player for streams of audio or video. But Windows Media Services performs several other key tasks as well:

- Manages requests from dozens, sometimes hundreds of clients simultaneously
- Works with other Windows Server applications and Windows Media Servers to balance the workload
- Authenticates and/or authorizes users to make sure only the people you want to see your content see it
- Works with licensing applications and services to protect your intellectual property
- Logs server activity so you can understand your traffic patterns and monitor the server for security issues
- Inserts advertisements, limits connections and bandwidth usage, manages play-lists, and a host of other functions

Most content producers naturally focus on the user experience in Windows Media Player and the encoding parameters in Windows Media Encoder. Thought it's a bit more arcane, Windows Media Server is just as critical a component in the streaming media system as the other two.

Playback

Playback is the last step in the streaming media process. Turning again to the radio and television analogy, the player is the receiver converting unseen signals into sounds or images humans can enjoy.

In some ways, the Windows Media Player is the most important variable in the streaming equation. It's your handshake with the user, and as such, you have some control over how you present yourself. You can leave the player as it appears on most desktops, or you can customize it to suit your own needs.

Embedding the Player — You may have come across a streaming video that plays directly in a webpage, instead of a standalone application, such as Windows Media Player. In fact, you're still looking at the player, or rather pieces of it, embedded in the HTML code that defines the page. You can show as little as the video image only, or add the controls, such as play, pause, and stop, and even add other visual elements, such as author, title and copyright. Embedding is the simplest and easiest way to manipulate the player.

Skins — A more sophisticated, and more complex, method of customizing the player is designing "skins," essentially putting new clothes on the framework that makes up the player. Skin creation requires graphic arts skills, a good understanding of user interface design, access to the Windows Media Player Software Development Kit (SDK), and some knowledge of programming. It's not for the faint of heart.

But skins are often spectacular feats of design. Entertainment companies are wizards at creating skins that help them promote music, movies, or games. The magic of skin design is beyond the scope of this book, but nothing beats them for eye candy that's also functional.

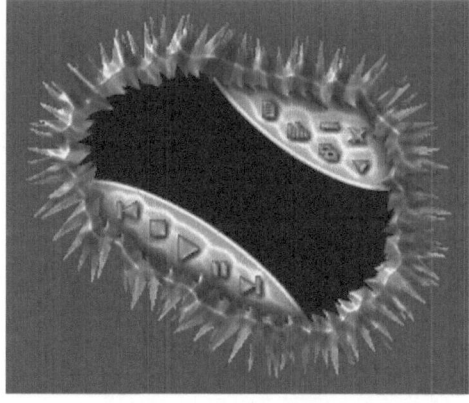
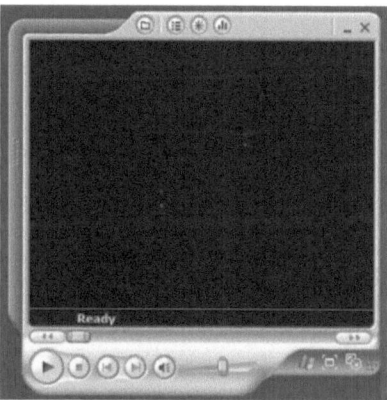

Figure 2-3
Skins add a wonderful visual dimension to the Windows Media Player experience. The skin on the left is called "Anemone." The skin on the right is the compact version of the player. You can download and install more skins by selecting View → Skin Chooser from the main menu and clicking "More Skins."

Live or On-Demand

Most of the discussion in this book focuses on creating *on-demand* streaming experiences, similar to putting a DVD into a hardware player and pushing play. You request the information from an archive in the same way you click a link to an archived stream from a webpage. You can learn almost all you need to know about streaming by working with recorded material.

However, sending a just-captured audio or video signal live over the Internet to thousands of people is streaming media's greatest strength. Broadcasters have known about the power of "live" for years; seeing something happen as it happens is far more compelling than watching a recording, hence the penchant for television news operations to send you "live" to the scene of a disaster or a crime. There's an edginess and tension to a live broadcast that a recording can't match.

However, live streaming is more resource intensive than on-demand streaming. The book explains live streaming in more detail in Chapter 10, Encoding and Distributing Live Webcasts, including whether a live broadcast is right for you. For now, it's enough to know that you need specialized equipment and know-how to pull off a live stream convincingly with a high-quality result. So be careful before you dive into the world of "live."

Inside the Industry

 Streaming media is a relatively new technology, so the terminology is still evolving. In the streaming industry, you'll often see the term *webcast* or *webcasting*, which is similar to "broadcasting." The older word generally refers to all types of radio and television broadcasting, including recorded material. But in some quarters at least, webcasting refers only to live streaming broadcasts. The terms *on-demand* or *archived* refer to recorded material available as streams.

Evaluate Your Audience

As you get further along in the streaming media process, you will make critical technical decisions that will affect the quality and impact of your results. But how do you make these decisions?

Professional media producers always start with the audience. Who is the man, woman or child you want to reach? What are their characteristics? Are you aiming at a mass audience or a niche audience? What makes your target audience different from the general audience? Once the audience is identified, the message is tailored to resonate as strongly as possible with the target.

Streaming media producers also start with audience. But they have to ask some very specific questions related primarily to the audience's capability to hear or view the content they produce. Put another way, television producers don't have to worry whether the family TV can show the video of the week. That's because television technology is just about the same everywhere. But the capabilities of office or home computers and their Internet connections differ wildly. Streaming producers have to take these variations into account.

Here are some variables to evaluate as you decide which streaming media platform(s) work best for your situation.

External versus Internal

You can roughly divide the entire universe of streaming media users into people external to your organization or internal to your organization. You have virtually no control over the types of hardware, software, or Internet connections of external users. These users could include a bored receptionist at her desktop computer surfing the Internet for entertainment or information. External users also can be a very specific group of people, such as receptionists at laser eye surgery centers. Whether it's a mass audience or a niche audience, you'll have to keep in mind a wide variety of computer configurations and Internet connection types.

You have much more control over an audience internal to your network, at least in theory. Most large organizations try to limit the configurations of desktop and laptop computers for ease of maintenance. The receptionist's office computer at the laser eye surgery center is likely to be very similar to the lead surgeon's in that company. And connectivity within an organization is likely to be similar across the network.

Figure 2-4
You have no control over your network delivery conditions once the data enters the Internet "cloud."

Internet versus Intranet

The Internet has been described as a vast, undifferentiated cloud between the starting place of data and the destination. This means you have zero control over the network conditions at any given moment of your streaming media broadcast to an external audience. Some people have used the term *net weather* to describe the capricious nature of Internet conditions. One minute you may have summer sunshine, the next, a winter blizzard. You simply have to accept this fact when streaming to large numbers of external users. You can take some comfort in the fact that streaming media systems are designed to cope with unpredictable conditions.

You have more control over conditions on an intranet, much like you have control over the heat and air conditioning in your house. Network administrators set the rules and parameters for network conditions on an intranet. This is especially true for single buildings or corporate campuses.

Operating Systems and the Media Player

Consumers and corporations have only two choices for desktop/laptop operating system environments if they want to stream with Windows Media: Microsoft Windows and Apple Computer's operating systems. And Microsoft overwhelms Apple in terms of deployment in the marketplace.

But Microsoft operating systems out in the real world have a lot of variability, especially in the home market. There have been six major versions of Windows: Windows 3.1, Windows 95, Windows 98, Windows ME, Windows 2000, and Windows XP. That's not even counting the "Home" and "Pro" versions of Microsoft's operating systems. All are still in use somewhere, though newer versions tend to replace older versions over time. And Microsoft engineers are coding more versions of Windows. Apple® also has several versions of its operating system still in use. And its latest product, Mac OS® X Tiger™, is a radical departure from previous Apple operating systems.

These upgrades over the past ten years or so create enormous headaches for the streaming media producers, especially those who want to reach a large external audience. You don't have to worry so much about the operating system itself. But you do have to worry about the media players that work on that system. Almost the same variability applies to Windows Media Players as applies to Windows itself, as shown in **Figure 2-5**.

Here's an example. Windows Media Player 6.4 was *bundled*, that is, included, with Windows 98. But the streaming video quality of those days was poor, compared to today's video quality. However, if you think you need to create video for those players, you may have to settle for inferior video quality, potentially alienating users with later versions of Windows and Windows Media Player. If you decide to cater to later versions of Windows/Windows Media Player, you may alienate users of Windows Media Player 6.4 by forcing them to upgrade.

Inside the Industry

 Microsoft also released a codec package called Windows Media 9 VCM (Video Compression Manager), which allows Windows Media Series 9-encoded content to be played back on the Windows Media 6.4 player.

Before you down another dose of your ulcer medication, consider your audience. Let's say you want to reach an audience of corporate executives at Fortune 500 companies in the United States. It's a virtual certainty that these men and women are using the latest version of Windows, or at least the one right before the latest. That means Windows Media Player 7.1 is installed and possibly Windows Media Series 9.

Here's the lesson: carefully analyze your audience for clues that can help you reduce the chance that your streams are incompatible with an individual audience member's operating system and media player.

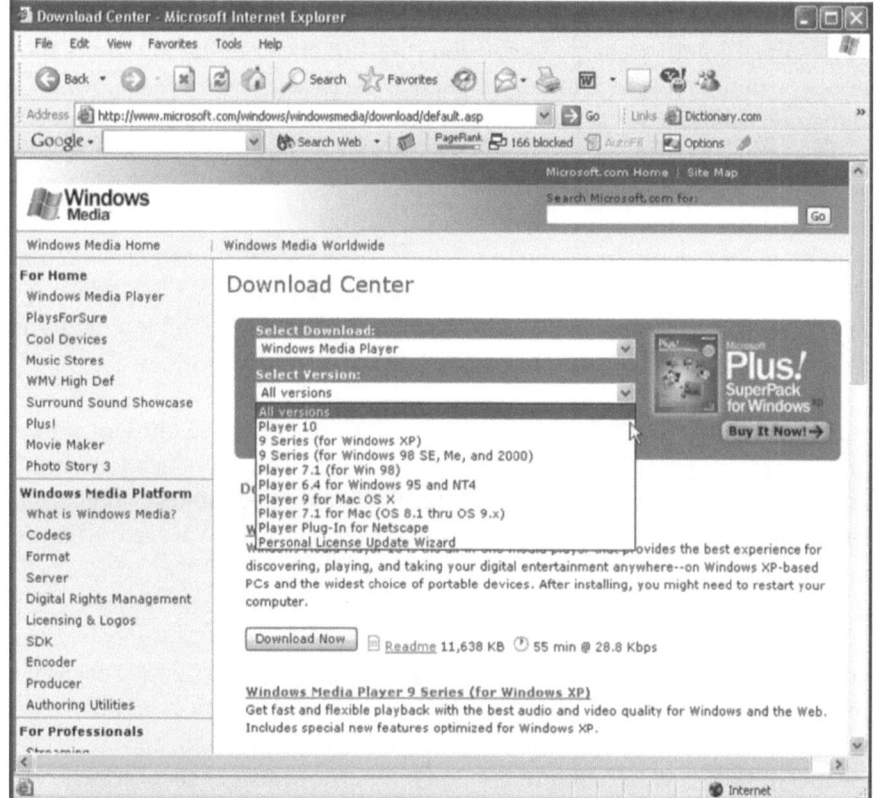

Figure 2-5
You have little control over the Windows Media Player version installed on your audience's computers, especially if they are a general public audience. You'll make a trade-off between quality and audience reach.

Early Adopters versus Late Adopters

Various technology observers divide people who adopt new technologies into four groups: innovators, early adopters, the early majority, and laggards. These categories can help you choose streaming formats that cater to your audience's attitude toward the online experience.

For example, you may determine that your audience is made up of gaming crazy, extreme sporting uber-geeks who think last week's product is so last week. Chances are they have the latest streaming media player running on the newest version of Windows or OS X. They probably have high-speed connectivity at home. You could take the risk of using the latest streaming codecs and high-bandwidth delivery. Using codecs from 1996 would definitely turn off this audience.

If you know your audience and their preferences well, selecting encoding and delivery options is easy.

High Bandwidth versus Low Bandwidth

The amount of bandwidth available to you and your audience may be the single most important factor determining your streaming production decisions. The more bandwidth on your side and the end user's side, the more likely you can satisfy your audience's expectation for a radio or television-like streaming experience. This is especially important if you want to reach an external Internet audience.

The trends are in your favor. According to Arbitron/Edison Media Research's *Internet and Multimedia 2005* report, 48% of all Americans have broadband cable or digital subscriber line (DSL) access at home. That's up from 12% in January 2001. Streaming media usage and adoption tends to follow the broadband deployment trends.

Of course, the flip side is that 48% or so of external users access the Internet via a dial-up connection, most likely at 56 kilobytes per second. The audio experience for this audience is acceptable, but the video experience is terrible. If you decide your target audience is primarily on dial-up, your audio options are decent, but your video options are extremely limited.

If you're focused on an audience within the boundaries of a corporate network, you have more options. Many small organizations with 10 megabit Ethernet networks have more bandwidth than they can use, and you could take advantage of that extra capacity with streaming. You may face a different limitation: The number of people you can serve at one time. For example, if you have a 10 megabit local area network (LAN), and your boss will only accept high-quality video streams taking up 250 kilobytes per second each, you're limited to 40 simultaneous users. (It's really closer to 20; 40 simultaneous 250K streams would essentially freeze the entire network.)

Organizational Relationships

Each and every organization depends on relationships with other organizations to thrive. An educational institution may depend on a particular set of major enterprise-funded foundations for annual support. A single individual donor may be the life-blood of a community not-for-profit. The lion's share of a small business's revenue may come from a single customer. If your target audience includes people who form a key business relationship, it makes sense to check that group's streaming capabilities. If you choose Microsoft's technology, and you later found out your key customer or client prefers RealNetworks' or Apple Computer's technology, you could be in deep trouble.

Author's Tip

Audience Evaluation Scenarios

External Audience
You volunteer for a youth sports association in a community with a high percentage of technology workers. The sports association has received a generous technology grant from a locally-based Fortune 1000 company that is a close partner with Microsoft. The association's board has accepted your proposal to record its annual awards ceremony for archiving on the Internet. About half the town's residents have broadband connections at home. You decide that the most likely viewers are parents and friends of team members, and your informal telephone survey of parents shows they run Windows 98. How do you use this knowledge to design your streaming?

Player Version: Windows Media 7.1

Streams: One audio stream for dial-up users. One 225K video stream for broadband users.

Internal Audience
You work for a healthcare company that depends on video training. About 1,000 employees work in several small buildings connected with a high-speed LAN. Most of the employees are comfortable with computers, but they are not technology workers per se. A few workers sometimes have trouble understanding things beyond simple printing or e-mail. Your chief financial officer spent 10 years at Microsoft before starting at your company last year, and he's okayed spending for a desktop/laptop operating system upgrade to Windows XP Pro. The upgrade project manager and the human resources director like your idea of providing video training online, and they're willing to upgrade the Windows Media Players on the company's computers. How do you use this knowledge to design your streaming project?

Media Player Version: Windows Media Player 10

Streams: One 225K video stream

Making a Decision

You've done a careful analysis of your audience and your resources. But you're still having trouble deciding which options to choose for your audience. Take a look at the form, labeled **Figure 2-5**. It puts all your thinking into one place by listing all the important criteria discussed previously and asking for some estimates. Once you've filled it out, you can refer to it as you make decisions further down the road.

Evaluate Your Content

Just as it's important to analyze and understand the characteristics of your audience, it's also important to analyze and understand the nature of the material you are about to send over the Internet. It's not quite as complicated as your audience, but taking a few moments to think objectively about your content will save time and headaches in the long run, especially when you encode raw media files into streaming media files. The encoder will give you choices for codecs that apply to specific situations.

Here are a few questions to ask about your content.

- **Audio Content**: What kinds of sounds are in your audio? Is the audio recording or video soundtrack voice only, music only, or a combination of the two? If you have music, what type is it? Classical, folk, rock and roll, or something else?
- **Video Content**: What kinds of images make up the majority of the video? Talking heads, such as a news report or a seminar? Some action with a moderate amount of editing, such as a documentary? Or lots of action and movement in the frame, such as a movie trailer?

Understanding the nature of your content will help you make good codec choices that result in the highest quality user experience.

Windows Media and Microsoft's Competitors

This book is focused solely on helping you get up to speed on Windows Media technology. But it's important to give a nod to the other manufacturers in the streaming media marketplace: RealNetworks, Apple Computer, and recently, Macromedia. Knowing about the other choices helps you understand your choice better.

RealNetworks

Progressive Networks started the streaming media industry in 1995 when it released RealAudio 1.0. The audio-only product produced barely intelligible sound over a 14.4 modem (remember those?), but it was revolutionary. Founded by ex-Microsoft executive Rob Glaser, the company proved that geography no longer mattered in the world of media distribution, because you could now send your audio signal in real time to the entire planet.

The company changed its name to RealNetworks when it went public in 1997, and it became one of the darlings of the Internet bubble. But when the bubble popped in 2001, RealNetworks managed to survive. It took the lead in developing new business models for Internet media distribution, though it still struggles to make a consistent profit.

It's important to note a file encoded with one vendor's codec usually won't play in another vendor's player. However, RealNetworks' server will support the transmission of Windows Media files to Windows Media Player. The same cannot be said for Microsoft's Windows Media Services.

Apple Computer

Apple Computer developed the QuickTime® file format for video, which became the standard throughout the entertainment industry and other creative markets. But Apple never really got started in the streaming game, despite its sleek QuickTime player, built in the same design tradition that runs from the Apple II personal computer to the iPod.

Furthermore, Apple Computer's server products are also-rans behind Microsoft, Linux, and other server software specialists. Without a complete streaming system (despite taking the open-source Darwin server under its wing), the company is unlikely to gain significant traction in the streaming niche. However, its entrenched place in tools related to digital audio and video production mean other vendors must cater to Apple enthusiasts.

Macromedia

Macromedia, the makers of Flash animation technology for websites, stepped into the streaming melee in 2002. Better late than never, supporters say, because Flash is probably one of the most ubiquitous and interesting tools available to the web designer. Whole careers have been built on Flash animation design and execution. Macromedia's Flash MX incorporates a low-level type of streaming media, and Macromedia offers a streaming server tool as part of its Communication Server product. So far, however, streaming professionals have stuck to other vendors' solutions.

Ownership

Microsoft owns a large chunk of the streaming media marketplace; just how big is a matter for debate. It all depends on how you slice the pie. If the pie is all installed media players, Microsoft dominates, because Windows Media Player is installed on virtually all Windows computers. However, if the pie is streaming player usage, Microsoft gives ground to RealNetworks in particular. For example, many agencies of the federal government prefer RealNetworks' products because the law precludes them from buying products from companies that the courts have labeled a monopoly.

Relations between the Media Department and the IT Department

One of the revolutions engendered by the invention of the World Wide Web in the early 1990s was the sudden need for media professionals to cooperate closely with computer professionals. Before the Web, even before streaming, the only time an audio or video producer talked with an information technology professional was when the Mac or PC broke down.

But when the Internet became a distribution medium for audio and video via streaming media and downloading, media professionals suddenly found themselves in greater need of the geeks in the basement who run the network. However, the two groups come from entirely different worlds, so relations are sometimes strained.

The answer is communication. Delegate someone to act as liaison between the two departments. Yeah, it's more meetings and incessant e-mails. But you need to do this. Media people, be careful not to antagonize your networking guys, because they help you by getting your work out to the world. You need them frankly more than they need you. And computer gurus, be patient with the media people. They don't know a NIC from a NAT, but they're producing some pretty cool storytelling, and if it goes out to the world on time and wows the planet, you'll look good, too.

Conclusion

Before you can dive into the details of streaming media, you needed to learn some of the technology's fundamentals. In this chapter, you learned about the foundation of streaming media technology, the client/server model of computing. You learned the four basic steps of streaming: capture, encode, distribute, and playback. The chapter discussed live webcasting, contrasting it with on-demand access to streams. The chapter suggested that you evaluate your audience before deciding how to deliver your content. And that content should also be evaluated. The chapter gave a nod to Windows Media competitors in the streaming marketplace, and finally, the chapter urged media pros and computer pros to get along. The next chapter discusses how to plan your production with streaming in mind, some recording equipment considerations, and a basic workstation.

CHAPTER 3

Get Ready to Capture Audio and Video

The best opportunity for creating high-quality streaming media starts at the beginning of the creative process. Someone may simply hand you a tape or DVD and say, "Stream this!" But it's better to get involved before the tape deck records the first sound or camera takes the first frame. In fact, you may even be asked to produce the whole thing from start to finish, which can be very exciting! The book doesn't have space to get into all the details of planning and preparing a production, but the text will lay out some of the basics. (To learn more about audio and video production, the author recommends *Single-Camera Video Production*, by Robert Musburger, published by Focal Press.)

This chapter also gives you insight into the kinds of audio and video equipment best suited to streaming production, whether you have to rent it or buy it. And the chapter will offer guidelines on building your own Windows Media capturing and editing workstation.

By the end of the chapter, you'll have a basic grasp of:

- Pre-production planning
- Audio and video inputs
- Portable audio recorder and video camera options
- Options for support equipment
- A Windows Media capturing and encoding workstation

Pre-Production Planning

Planning audio and video productions is about *risk management*—that is, thinking ahead and reducing the potential for upsetting surprises. The following section reviews a few of the pre-production basics for any audio/visual production. These include:

- A script
- A budget

- Location scouting
- A schedule
- Connectivity
- Expecting the unexpected

Author's Tip

The Microsoft Office website offers a Word template for the standard screenplay format.
Visit *http://office.microsoft.com/templates/*.

The Script

The best productions start out with a well-written script. Take the time to put down in words what you want the audience to hear and see. A script can be as simple as a one-page general description of the words and actions laid out in one or more scenes (the concept of "scene" applies to audio, too). Or it can be hundreds of pages of dialog and instructions. Your script is your most important planning document.

Budgets

Once you're happy with the script, work out a budget. Again, it can be as short as a single spreadsheet page. If you're renting equipment, include a line item for each piece. Labor is always the most expensive commodity; estimate the number of hours you'll need to plan and execute your script. But keep your scale in mind. You don't need to spend weeks working on a budget for a one-minute announcement by the CEO. You may not need a budget at all.

Author's Tip

Video producers should consider storyboarding their script. A storyboard is a series of drawings that help you plan each video shot. A storyboard is akin to a visual outline of your video. It's an invaluable planning and time-saving tool.

Location Scouting

Scout out the location or venue for your production. This is especially vital for live production, because you typically won't have time to postpone production to fix problems with a site or find another site. Visit the place physically, even if it's an unused office down the hall. Here are some questions to ask:

- Do you have enough physical space for cameras, microphones, tripods, and other equipment that takes up floor space?
- Do you have enough physical space for props, such as a desk and a chair?
- Do you have enough grounded power outlets nearby?
- Do you have access to the physical space during off hours for setup purposes?

Scheduling

A detailed schedule is especially important for coordinating with people in leadership roles, such as corporate executives. Can the CEO show up for your recording session? Plan your production far enough ahead so you can fit his/her schedule. And keep in touch with his/her staff as recording or shooting approaches so you can revise the schedule as needed.

Inside the Industry

Hiring Actors and Crew

If you've got the budget to hire actors, take some time to learn about federal and state laws governing contractors. Your human resources department or your state department of labor are great places to start. It's also wise to research rules governing the use of union and nonunion labor. The American Federation of Television and Radio Artists, the union representing many video and audio workers, has an excellent website at *http://www.aftra.com/*.

Connectivity

If you plan to stream something live, you will need a solid physical connection to the Internet at your venue. Ask the events manager how much bandwidth is available and where the network jacks are located. If no high-speed bandwidth is available, find another venue. At minimum, you need DSL or cable. Keep in mind, however, that your actual bandwidth varies with the specific type of DSL/cable connection. Ask the events manager or the bandwidth provider how many kilobytes per second you have going to and coming back from your server. Do you need an account of some kind to connect to the local network? Be sure to have all these details in place before shooting begins.

Even if you're not planning a live broadcast, you may need to quickly upload encoded files to a server back at the office. Or you may simply need to check last-minute e-mail. A method for connecting to your corporate network remotely could save you time and frustration.

ALERT   **Wired is Better for Streaming**

Wireless is all the rage in the Internet world, but it's deadly for streaming media production. In other words, don't rely on a wireless connection for streaming purposes. Wireless Internet is simply too unreliable to handle the data loads and quality needs of streaming media production. (Just ask yourself how many times the cellular carrier has dropped your calls.) However, wireless is fine, if you need it for more run-of-the-mill purposes, such as checking the streaming links on a webpage.

Figure 3-1
Do not use wireless connections in the streaming media production process. They are far too unreliable.

Be Ready for Anything

When sailors at sea prepare for a storm, they "batten down the hatches," meaning they prepare themselves for the inevitable problems. A mild form of paranoia is useful in the audio and video game, including the streaming scrimmages. In short, be ready to tackle any contingency. Good planning will see you through. (For more on this, see Chapter 9, Get Ready to Webcast Live with Windows Media.)

Audio and Video Inputs

Quality results require quality tools, and this section talks about the audio and video recording equipment you'll need for high-quality production. The text makes some specific equipment recommendations, although there are many more choices than those listed here.

Author's Tip

For Best Results, Buy the Best Gear
Don't skimp on equipment. You don't need to buy the very high-end, but you certainly want to avoid "consumer" level equipment. Consumer cameras, tape recorders, CD players, and so on, are designed to be cheap, almost throwaway. Consider your equipment an investment, not an expense. Also, be careful about so-called *prosumer* hardware, which has many of the features of professional equipment at a consumer price. Prosumer devices that record to a digital format, such as mini-DV, may work. But when in doubt, buy pro.

Portable Equipment Gets You Started

To get started quickly, you should select equipment that's easy to master and use. And it's not necessary to break your bank account. To meet these goals, focus on portable equipment, rather than equipment designed for studio use only. The good news is that most portable equipment can double as studio equipment in a pinch.

Digital versus Analog

Audio and video recording devices fall into two main categories: analog and digital. *Analog* tape recorders and cameras record light and sound as a continuously variable electrical signal, usually onto a magnetic tape wound in a plastic case, such as audio cassette or VHS. Analog devices store a virtually infinite range of sounds and color. On the other hand, even the best analog recorders are subject to the problem of "noise," which is extraneous information often introduced by the equipment itself. Noise can sometimes be filtered out during later stages of production.

Digital equipment, on the other hand, stores sound and light as binary "digits," often called *1s* and *0s*. The ordered combination of these values, when interpreted by a computer, results in what we perceive as sound and light. Like analog devices, digital devices record onto magnetic tape, such as DAT for audio and DV or mini-DV for video. (See **Table 3-1** for a list of video formats.) Digital devices are also less susceptible to the "noise" problem.

Because streaming relies completely on computers and computer networks, and computers only understand digital data, it makes sense to record and store sound and light digitally. Therefore, you should use digital recording equipment whenever possible. However, if your budget is tight, analog equipment will work, though getting the signal from the recorder to the computer may require more work. And the quality of the final output may suffer slightly, because analog equipment introduces more data that must be filtered out.

Format	Type	Quality
DigiBeta	Digital	Excellent
Betacam SP	Analog	Excellent
DV (DVCAM, MiniDV)	Digital	Good
Digital 8	Digital	Good
S-VHS/Hi-8	Analog	Avoid
VHS	Analog	Avoid

Table 3-1
Whenever possible, record your material onto digital media, though analog will also work.

Inside the Industry

Is Digital Really Better?

Many people still debate the relative advantages of digital recording over analog recording, despite the ascendance and dominance of digital. Here's a list to help you make up your own mind.

Advantages
- More precise recording than analog
- Copies are exact, without data loss when copies are made from copies
- Easier to edit and manipulate
- Cheaper to design and build digital recording and editing equipment

Disadvantages
- Exact copies make piracy, that is, theft easier. (With analog, copies of copies look worse than the original.)
- Digital video files are large and awkward to work with
- Some audiophiles believe digital recordings lack a certain warmth and smoothness

Portable Audio Recorders and Cameras

Here are some recommendations for portable audio recorders and video cameras. These are only recommendations; you should shop around for something that meets your specific needs and budget.

Analog

Marantz PMD-222 — The Marantz PMD-222 analog tape recorder is the standard portable cassette tape recorder for radio stations all over the world. It's inexpensive, rugged, and full-featured. It also has an all-important XLR microphone cable connector. (More about cables below.)

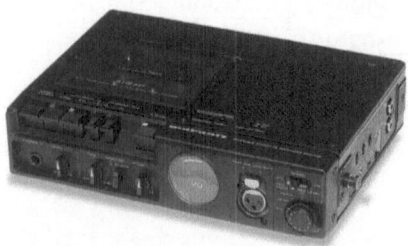

Figure 3-2
Marantz PMD-222 analog tape recorder.

ALERT You may have to buy or construct a special cable to get audio signal from the tape deck to your computer, depending on the audio inputs to the sound card. The cable needs an RCA connector on one end and a "mini-plug" (one-eighth inch) connector on the other.

Sony BVW-200 — The Sony BVW-200 analog video camera with built-in recorder is a broadcast standard that records in Beta SP format. The camera uses a charged-couple device (CCD), a chip that transforms light into analog electrical signals. The camera is relatively inexpensive compared to its digital counterparts.

Figure 3-3
Sony BVW-200 analog video recorder.

Digital

Tascam DAP1 — The Tascam DAP1 digital audio recorder is also used by broadcasters for field recording. It can record in stereo as well as mono, and it uses digital readouts for elapsed time and other information.

Figure 3-4
Tascam DAP1 digital audio tape recorder.

Canon GL-2 — The Canon GL-2 is a solid entry-level, multiuse digital video camera. It's pricier than some others, but affordable. The camera records in MiniDV format.

Figure 3-5
Canon GL-2 digital video camera.

Inside the Industry

NTSC and PAL
Video recorders are designed to record for either the NTSC or PAL standards. National Television Standards Committee (NTSC) is the standard used in the United States. Phase Alternation Line (PAL) is the standard used in many European countries. NTSC delivers 525 lines of resolution at 60 half-frames per second, whereas PAL delivers 625 lines at 50 half-frames per second. Although neither standard affects streaming media directly, you should make sure all your recording equipment uses one standard or the other, especially if you plan to use it for other purposes than recording material for streams.

Support Equipment

Good audio and video production requires dozens of small items that you never seem to use, except when there's a crisis. A list follows. To save money, you can rent some of these items or buy them used. Other items you'll use primarily in the studio.

Recording Tape

Magnetic recording tape varies in quality from manufacturer to manufacturer. Use a brand name and stick with it. It's also a good idea to use 60-minute blanks. The tape itself is thicker and more durable than tape in a 90-minute or two-hour blank.

Microphones

Next to the recorder, the microphone is the most important tool in your audio kit. Never rely on microphones built into the recorder, whether audio recorder or camera. Their quality leaves a lot to be desired. Following are three suggested hand-held microphones:

- Electrovoice RE-50
- Shure SM-58
- Audix om7

And here's a couple of clip-on Lavalier mics for video work:

- Audio Technica AT803B
- Shure MX183

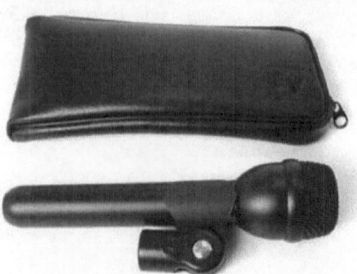

Figure 3-6
An Electrovoice RE-50 microphone with clip and carrying case.

Microphone Stand

The microphone stand is an often-overlooked piece of equipment. Putting your handheld mic on a stand reduces the chance you might introduce noise when you move the mic around. It's also easier to point it toward a sound source, such as an actor's mouth.

Figure 3-7
A typical microphone stand with a weighted base. Other stands have tripods and booms, which can extend several feet.

Camera Tripod
Just as a microphone needs a stand to keep it steady, so do cameras. Avoid flimsy consumer tripods, which can fall over at the drop of a hat, perhaps ruining your camera. Invest in a heavy duty tripod that will prevent the camera from jiggling when you walk past or when swaying in a wind.

Lighting Kit
Good video requires good lighting. A professional lighting kit starts with two lights and a carrying case. You may also want to purchase a diffusion sheet or diffusion umbrella to soften your light sources. Diffusion equipment also reduces harsh contrasts and shadows.

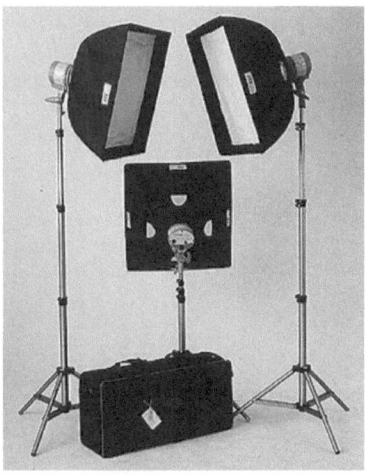

Figure 3-8
JTL T-1500 lighting kit.

Headphones

You should always monitor your audio via a good pair of headphones. These tell you what the microphone is picking up, allowing you to adjust placement of the microphone or the volume levels. Be sure to buy headphones with ear cups that cover the entire ear, not just part of it. That keeps out room noise. Here are suggestions for headphones.

- AKG Acoustics K141M
- Sony MDR 7506

Figure 3-9
Sony MDR 7056 headphones.

Cables/Connectors

Cables get your information to and from devices. Connectors need to be strong enough to cope with the constant banging, jiggling and pulling they experience. Cables should be balanced and shielded to avoid the introduction of noise from nearby electronic devices. Use XLR connectors whenever possible. These are the strongest available.

The main types of cable connectors ranked by quality are:

- SPDIF/Digital
- BNC
- XLR
- RCA
- Quarter-inch
- Mini (one-eighth inch)

Here's a ranking of audio and video cabling by type:

- HDMI/DVI/IEEE 1394 (audio and video)
- Component (video)
- S-Video (video)
- Balanced (audio)
- Unbalanced (audio)

ALERT  Don't step on cables! There are smaller cables inside the sheathing, and stepping on them could rub off insulation, causing a short, and even break one in two.

Audio Mixing Desks

Mixing desks blend multiple recordings of audio into a single whole. For example, you can mix voice, music and natural or ambient sound onto a single track.

These can be used for an audio-only production or for creating a highly produced audio track in a video. (By the way, you can mix audio in software.) Two good mixing desks are:

- Behringer MXB1002
- Mackie 1202 VLZ-Pro

Figure 3-10
Behringer MXB1002 audio mixing desk.

Video Tape Recorders

You'll use a video tape recorder (VTR) primarily for video tape playback, rather than record-ing. Like portable tape recorders and cameras, VTRs come in analog and digital flavors. Make sure you get one compatible with your other choices. And make sure your VTR has a FireWire/iLink connector. (Firewire is only available on digital decks. More on FireWire later.) The main drawback with VTRs is cost. New ones can cost $50,000 to $100,000. But you can get used VTRs in good condition for a tenth of the price of a new one, even less. A couple of good VTR choices are:

- Sony DVR-20 (analog)
- Panasonic AJ-D650 (digital)
- Sony DSR-11 (digital)

Figure 3-11
Sony DSR-11 digital video tape recorder/player.

Author's Tip

If your camera has a FireWire connector, you can take the video/audio feed directly out of the camera and send it to your computer workstation that has a FireWire card. However, if someone else takes the video and hands you a tape, you'll need a VTR.

Compressors and Proc Amps

Compressors help you manage the volume levels in your audio. Most professional sounding audio is compressed. Here's a couple of equipment options:

- Presonus Blue Max
- FMR RNC1773

A *proc amp*, (short for *processing amplifier*) cleans up video signals coming out of a camera. Options include:

- SignVideo PA-100 (single-channel)
- SignVideo PA-200 (dual-channel)

Figure 3-12
SignVideo PA-100 single channel proc amp.

Equipment Bag or Rack

Invest in a set of sturdy portable equipment cases with wheels if you have lots of equipment and need to set it up quickly. Cases also make hauling equipment on airplanes much easier. (More on portable racks in Chapter 9.)

Odds and Ends

A few odds and ends like these will come in handy:

- Duct or gaffer tape
- Connector adapters (RCA to XLR, mini to 1/4 inch, etc.)
- Extra cabling
- Extra batteries and extension cords
- Pencil and paper
- Small toolkit (Phillips and flathead screwdrivers, sharp knife, scissors, pliers)
- A credit card to buy the things you forgot

Places to Buy Equipment

You can buy most, if not all, of the equipment you need online. Here's a few suggestions:

- Broadcast Supply Worldwide (audio),
  http://www.bswusa.com/
- The Broadcast Store (video),
  http://www.bcs.tv/
- B & H (audio and video),
  http://wwwphotovideo.com
- Online auction sites (Some people swear by these for mining good deals.
  Caveat emptor!)

> **Author's Tip**
>
> If you go out on location, find out where the nearest electronics store is, such as a Fry's Electronics or a Radio Shack. This will save you time if you discover you've forgotten a connector or you need batteries.

A Windows Media Capturing and Editing Workstation

Now that you've purchased or rented your audio and/or video equipment, it's time to talk about building a capturing and editing workstation. You can spend tens of thousands of dollars on nonlinear editing hardware and software packages. You can also spend a lot less by building your own out of off-the-shelf parts and packaged software. You have to pay particular attention to some of the parts, notably the hard drive. But if you don't mind tinkering with computers, you can build an excellent workstation at no more than half the cost of a package deal. Note that your capturing/editing workstation doubles as a streaming media encoding workstation, though you can separate the two functions on two different computers.

The main points of difference between the hardware of a standard desktop computer you buy at a retail store and an editing workstation are:

- Processing power
- Memory (RAM)
- Storage (more than one hard disk)
- Video capture card
- Support for two monitors

A rule of thumb for a capturing/editing workstation: More is better. Buy or assemble the most powerful equipment you can afford. See **Table 3-2** for some requirements and recommendations.

The hard drive recommendations in **Table 3.2** are actually pretty dinky. They'll get you started, but you're better off getting the biggest hard drive you can afford. And try to get a SCSI (pronounced *scuzzy*) hard drive, not the standard IDE hard drive. SCSI drives are more expensive, but they perform better under the demanding conditions of audio and video editing. SATA and ATA 133 drives, which fall somewhere between SCSI and IDE, are good options as well.

Inside the Industry

Nonlinear Editing

"Nonlinear" editing refers to moving elements of video and audio around via an editing software package. It's very similar to cutting and pasting words, sentences or paragraphs in a word processor. Before computers, most editing happened in a linear fashion, that is, physical film clips or audio tape clips were assembled one after the other.

Minimum Requirements	2.4 GHz Pentium 4 Hyperthread
	512MB of RAM
	Dual 40 GB hard disks
	16-bit sound card and speakers
	24-bit color video display
	Dedicated video memory
	Firewire and USB support
	10/100 Ethernet NIC
	Microsoft Windows XP Pro
Recommended Requirements	Fastest Pentium 4 processor available
	800 Mhx Front Side Bus (FSB)
	2 GB of DDR RAM
	Dual 100 GB hard disks
	32-bit sound card and speakers
	24-bit color video display
	Dedicated video memory
	Gigabit Ethernet NIC
	Firewire, Firewire II, and USB 2.0 support
	Windows XP Pro

Table 3-2
Minimum and recommended personal computer hardware and software requirements for a do-it-yourself nonlinear capturing, editing and encoding workstation. Be sure to purchase name brand hardware only.

Audio and Video Cards

Analog signals from analog audio recorders and cameras have to be converted to binary 1s and 0s before a computer can manipulate them. Specialized hardware in the form of a *capture card* does this work. You'll need to install one or more of these cards before you can work with your audio or video. The following are some recommendations on audio and video cards:

- **Audio Cards**
    - Minimum: Factory installed sound card
    - Recommended: Creative Labs Sound Blaster® Audigy® 2 (See **Figure 3-13**)
- **Video Capture Cards**
    - Minimum: ViewCast Osprey 210 (audio and video combined)
    - Recommended: ViewCast Osprey 500 DV

Author's Tip

Audio Card/Sound Card

Most off-the-shelf personal computers include a sound card, which can double as an audio capture card. These are enough to get you going, but they can pick up noise from disk drives and other equipment. If you plan a large audio project in which sound quality is critical, upgrade to a professional level audio card.

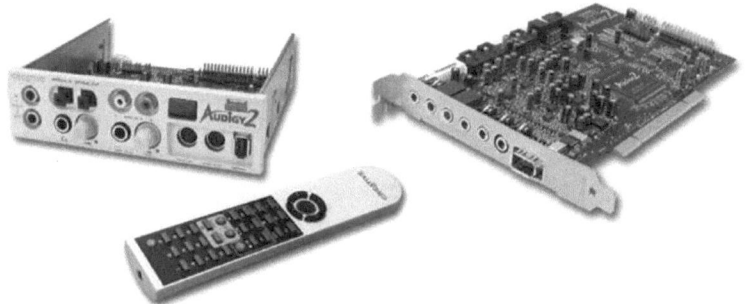

Figure 3-13
The Creative Blaster Audigy 2 Platinum sound card package comes with a remote control and a controller unit, which can be mounted into an empty 5-inch drive bay.

Editing Software

Editing software lets you manipulate your audio and video files by cutting and pasting portions of audio or video from the same file or different files. You can have an almost unlimited number of audio and video tracks. The software filters out certain kinds of audio-destroying noise or adds video effects, such as fades. Here are a few choices:

- **Audio Editing**
    - Adobe Audition (formerly Syntrillium Cool Edit Pro)
    - Sony Sound Forge (formerly Sonic Foundry Sound Forge)
- **Video Editing**
    - Adobe Premiere Pro
    - Sony Vegas (formerly Sonic Foundry Vegas)
    - Avid Express

A Studio Environment

It's true you can produce audio and video on your desktop computer in your office. But a quiet, well-organized work environment devoted to audio and video editing is best. Think about converting an unused office into an editing booth. Put sound baffles on the walls and weather stripping around the door. Organize your equipment so that everything is in reach, that cables and other equipment are properly stored, and you have a good chair. You'll probably spend a lot of time in here, so you might as well be comfortable.

Conclusion

This chapter reviewed some of the basics of audio and video production related to streaming media, including writing a script, budgeting, scheduling, and selecting a location. The chapter gave an overview of typical kinds of audio and video equipment that you can purchase or rent. And the chapter discussed how you might build your own capturing and editing workstation with off-the-shelf equipment. Next, the book discusses best practices for recording and capturing audio and video.

CHAPTER 4

Recording and Capturing Audio and Video

You may be coming to streaming media technology with a good understanding of how to record sound or shoot video with high-quality results. But the quirks of streaming media mean that some of the techniques you've learned may not work as well for the computer screen as they do for the television screen. This chapter reviews some of the fundamentals of audio and video production, and offers some tips for adapting video techniques you may already know to a streaming environment. This chapter also demonstrates how to capture audio and video to a hard disk, and we'll look at using Windows Movie Maker as a quick and dirty video production tool. By the end of the chapter, you'll understand:

- Best practices for recording audio
- Best practices for recording video
- Best practices for capturing audio and video
- How to capture with Windows Media 9 Capture free software
- How to edit with Windows Movie Maker

Best Practices for Recording Audio

Sound is an incredibly rich and rewarding medium, and most people associate audio production with music. But to put you on the right path immediately, we're going to focus on voice, because it's the simplest type of audio, and your first audio productions are likely to be voice only. You can build on these skills if you move on to music and other more complex types of recording.

Simple Steps for Professional Results

This book offers some simple steps for recording voice. You'll need some time to practice and get used to working with your recording equipment. But you'll be surprised how fast you catch on.

First, write a script, that is, write down what you want to say. Compose it on your word processor, and print it double-spaced and in all capital letters. That makes it easier to read while speaking.

Author's Tip

The Towel-Over-the-Head Trick
Finding a quiet place to record will be harder than you think. Once you close the door, plug in your headset and listen to what the microphone picks up. If you're in an office, you might hear the whirr of your computer's cooling fan, the whoosh of the air conditioning, or the buzz of fluorescent lights. If you can turn off these gadgets, go ahead. Also, if your room is next to the street, your mic may pick up traffic noise or wailing sirens. Try hanging curtains or blankets on the walls. You also can buy sound-muffling foam panels.

If you have trouble finding a quiet room, try this trick. Get a light blanket or a large beach towel. Put it over your head and your microphone, as if you were in a tent. Then listen. Hopefully, the ambient sounds of your makeshift studio will be gone, or at least muted. This will lead to better sounding recordings, though your friends and co-workers may avoid you for awhile.

Next, find a quiet place for recording. Any place where interruptions are few will work, though a studio is best. Set up your equipment so that all of it is within arm's reach. And make sure you can read the volume meter, for reasons we'll explain later. (Check your recorder's manual to locate the volume meter, if you're not sure.)

Check that all your connections, such as your mic cable, are tight. A slight jiggle on a loose cable could cause a momentary loss of signal. Put on your headset and plug it into your recorder. You'll hear everything coming through the microphone and going on the tape. Neatly coil the extra cable and place it where you won't kick it or step on it.

Put your microphone on the mic stand near your mouth. The best distance is usually three to six inches. Place the mic at a slight angle to your lips. When people say the letters "p" or "t," they tend to make extra noises with their lips and teeth. The mic at an angle reduces this problem.

Inside the Industry

The text uses the abbreviation *mic* for microphone, pronounced *mike*.

Volume Levels
The most important concept in audio recording is volume levels. A volume "level" is a measure of the power of the signal reaching the recording heads of the recording device. (The *head* is an electromagnet that rearranges metal oxides on the physical tape.) Too little level means that background noise caused by electronics and other factors could overwhelm the sound you really want to hear, your voice. Too much level could result in irritating distortion. Ever hear someone scream into a microphone? That grating sound you hear is distortion.

Monitor your levels by watching the volume meter on your tape deck. See **Figure 4-1** for an illustration of volume meters (sometimes called a *VU*, for volume unit, meter) you're likely to encounter.

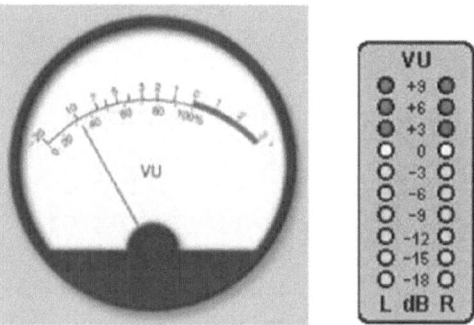

Figure 4-1
Two types of simple volume meters. The left VU meter is found primarily on analog equipment. The right one, often called an LED (light emitting diode) peak meter, is usually on digital equipment.

Depending on your equipment, you need to react to the readings differently. On analog equipment, keep the needle out of the red zone as much as possible. A little bit is ok. If the needle barely nudges, your level is too low. On digital equipment, lights will be green, yellow and red. Say a few words, and if the red lights blink a lot, your volume level is too high. If just a couple of green lights blink, the volume level is too low. If you see lots of green lights, with a smattering of yellow lights, your level is just right.

On both digital and analog equipment, use the adjustment dial to modify your volume level up or down. Experiment and you'll find the right place. You might even turn your level down just a bit before you read your script. Some people increase their voice volume slightly when they actually start recording. By the way, ignore all the numbers and minus signs. Those are for experienced pros to figure out.

ALERT The most expensive equipment in the world is no match for the human ear attached to a thinking brain. Use metering to check against your ears and perception. If what you're hearing doesn't "sound right," despite what the meter says, you may be onto something. In other words, don't let metering overrule your own good judgment.

Author's Tip

If you feel tense while you're reading your script, try reading while standing. This lets you move at least one of your hands around, as if you were having a conversation. You probably already do this when you talk on the phone to a friend. It's the same principle.

Start Your Recording

If everything looks correct, and you feel comfortable, push the record button (or the "play" and "record" buttons together), take a good breath, not too deep, and start reading your script. You're likely to rush through it the first time. This is a common problem for the inexperienced. Next time, cut your reading speed by half. It'll feel odd at first. But when you play it back, it'll sound normal and easy to understand.

Read your script several times and stop recording. Rewind and listen to all the takes. If you don't like any of them, read a few more times. When you're satisfied with a take, note its location on the tape, and remove the tape from the deck. Put it in a safe place and neatly store your equipment for later use.

Best Practices for Recording Video

When streaming video came along in the late 1990s, many long-time film and video producers assumed they could use the same editing techniques, shot compositions, special effects, camera movements and other common elements of visual language. They were disappointed when these creative options didn't automatically translate to the streaming medium.

Video communication over a digital network is not the same as throwing a tape into a VCR or sending a video signal over the air. Think of streaming video as a new canvas with a different palette. Once you understand streaming, you can create compelling stories.

Audio Caveats

Before we get into the video only material, you might review the audio section above. All the suggestions and techniques for audio-only recording apply to audio recording for video with a few variations. Microphones are a potential problem. You can use your audio-only microphone on a mic stand, but they are large and distracting. In the case of video, a Lavalier mic is a better choice. These small devices clip on to a blouse or tie and produce a high-quality audio signal. Don't forget to check your audio levels! A great picture with bad sound is worse than a great picture with no sound.

Lighting Is Everything

Light is critical to video recording. Cameras aren't as sensitive to light as you might think. The real reason shots look good, other than good framing and composition, is the extra light thoughtfully cast on the scene. This helps you capture all the details, the correct colors, and the correct contrast between light and shadow. You definitely need extra light indoors. And you may need it outdoors as well.

Lighting a scene for video is an art in itself. Most techniques start with the classic "three-point" system, as shown in **Figure 4-2**. Three lights bathe the subject in enough light for good color, contrast and definition. Here are the elements for the three-point system:

- **Key light**: The key light is the main light source placed above the camera. It highlights the contours of the subject and throws deep shadows.
- **Fill light**: The fill light is softer than a key light, and "fills" some of the shadows. The fill light lowers the contrast between areas lit by the key light and shadows caused by the key light.
- **Back light**: The back light throws light behind the subject, and gives the subject a three-dimensional look by bringing the subject out of the background.

If you shoot outdoors on a day with heavy overcast, you may need to add artificial light. On a clear day, the sun provides plenty of light, but the shadows may be harsh. A simple solution is a "bounce board," a large flat panel painted white that reflects sunlight to fill in shadows.

Figure 4-2
Captured audio as it appears in CoolEdit2000. (CoolEdit2002 was recently purchased by Adobe and renamed Adobe Audition.)

Composition for Streaming

Moving graphics, whip pans, fast dissolves, and soft focus have become part of our visual language. Unfortunately, most of this phraseology doesn't work with the current level of streaming technology. Why? Each time something moves in the frame, data is added to the total amount of information. To be displayed, this data has to be transmitted over the Internet. But the pipes that carry data over the Internet are still far too small to manage all the information contained in a video designed for display on a television. Therefore, you have to pare down your visual language. This doesn't mean you're limited to putting the camera on the tripod and locking it down. But it does mean you need to scale back some of your creative options and expectations.

Inside the Industry

The Importance of Bandwidth

As discussed in Chapter 3, Get Ready to Capture Audio and Video, you should get a good understanding of your audience's capabilities as you plan your streaming project. In video production, bandwidth is probably the single most important variable. If you think your audience will watch the video primarily at dial-up speeds, that is, 28.8 Kbps or 56 Kbps, you are severely limited in your visual language. The data pipes are tiny, and simple visual changes from one shot to the next adds enormous amounts of data. Fortunately, dial-up is slowly giving way to DSL and cable at home. And most medium-sized businesses and large corporations have faster speeds. This gives you more flexibility in your language choices. **Table 4-1** gives you a sense of your creative flexibility in relation to bandwidth.

Bandwidth	Flexibility
28.8 Kbps Dial-up	Severely Limited
56 Kbps Dial-up	Limited
DSL/Cable Modem	Moderate to good
T-1	Moderate to good
OC3	Good to excellent
Gigabit LAN	Excellent

Table 4-1
The greater the bandwidth, the more creative flexibility you have.

Good and Bad Techniques

Here are some techniques that translate well to streaming and some that don't. Good writing and storyboarding will help you get the most out of the techniques that work.

- **Good**
  - Close-ups
  - One and two shots
  - Solid clothing colors with a contrasting background
  - "Cool" colors, such as light blue
  - Simple, static backgrounds
  - Simple editing, including cutaways
  - Slow camera movements
  - Large font text and graphic elements with minimal detail

- **Bad**
  - Bright colors, especially whites, reds, and yellows, which tend to bleed
  - Group shots
  - High-motion, such as fast pans, wipes or cinema verite
  - Quick cuts, i.e., too many shots in a brief period of time
  - Available light, unless full sunlight
  - Small text fonts or small graphic images
  - Moving graphics
  - Fast dissolves
  - Backgrounds with motion, such as rolling surf or flapping flags

Author's Tip

PowerPoint Slides in Streaming Video

Corporate executives love Microsoft PowerPoint®, and many corporate video producers are shooting speeches or demonstrations that feature PowerPoint presentations, which add visual variety to a stream without adding tons of digital information. Here's a simple technique:

1. Record the speech and get the PowerPoint file.
2. Have a graphic artist extract the slides as JPEG image files. Or try the "Export to web" command in PowerPoint.
3. Using your video editing tools, drop each JPEG image into appropriate spots in the video, keeping the audio track underneath.

Now you have a video with switches between the talking head and their slides. It's much more engaging than just watching the speechmaker. (Another method of webcasting a Microsoft PowerPoint presentation is described in the appendix, Streaming PowerPoints with Producer.)

A Final Word about Audio

It's a fact that many experienced video producers dislike streaming video. The technology is limited and often clunky. Well, you could wait a decade for the technology to catch-up to your visual storytelling skills, or you could respond to the growing demand for streaming right now. How so? Think about your audio. You can deliver very high quality audio even at low bandwidths. And you don't have to worry as much about the data implications of multitrack recording, sound effects and so on. So consider spending extra resources on an award-winning audio track. It might make a dull visual experience a richer multimedia experience.

Best Practices for Capturing Audio and Video

One of the most critical tasks you'll undertake as a streaming media producer is *capturing*. This is the process of moving data from your audio or video recording device to your computer workstation's hard drive. It's important to do this well, because after you've captured the data, it's much harder to fix problems that may have been introduced by poor capturing technique.

Much of the capture procedure is driven by the particular hardware and software you use. Read the instruction manual for both the audio and/or video capture hardware. Hardware manufacturers often bundle simple editing software packages with their cards. These give you a chance to experiment with the hardware, though the software is rarely up to professional production standards. If you have purchased editing software, be patient while you learn the software's intricacies. Fortunately, most editing software uses familiar concepts such as Play/Pause/Stop and Record for basic tasks.

Optimize Your Workstation

You may want to optimize your workstation before capturing, especially if you've been doing some other intensive work. Here's a checklist:

- Defragment your hard drive
- Turn off network access and file sharing

- Close all other programs, especially those that access your hard drive, including virus scan.
- Monitor your system resources to ensure the computer has enough power to keep up with the work it has to do.

ALERT You may have noted with some trepidation the suggestion that you turn off virus scanning programs before capturing audio or video. Here's why: Virus scanning programs, just like any program, accesses the disk drive for routine work. It also uses some of the main processor's resources. The same goes for e-mail programs, web browsers, and so on. When you capture audio or video, the computer is using processing resources and writing data to the disk as intensively as it ever will. If the virus scanner or other program interrupts things for even the smallest fraction of a second to get the processor to perform a calculation or read data from the drive, there's a chance the capture process could be compromised, resulting in dropped frames, audio samples, or even a corrupted file.

Inside the Industry

 Video Sources Matter

As always, the original source of your video affects the final quality of your stream. The rule of thumb is start with digital, but even that rule has some sub-sections. Here's a list of video sources, starting with the most desirable and ending with the least.

- **Serial digital interface (SDI) video capture cards**: The data remains digital through the process, from beginning to end. (See the previous chapter for more information and recommendations on video cards.)
- **Component video**: Found on DVDs.
- **S-Video**: Found in S-VHS, DVD, and Hi-8 video cameras.
- **DV video**: Found in digital video (DV) devices, such as MiniDV cameras using FireWire.
- **Composite video**: Found in most analog video devices, such as cable television. You should avoid this source whenever possible.
- **Video over coaxial cable**: Coaxial cable combines the audio and video signals into a single signal, which creates extra noise in both picture and sound.

Prepare to Capture

Hook up all your equipment to your workstation and make sure you can monitor output from your recorder via your computer during setup. That way, you'll hear and see the same thing that's about to go on the hard drive. Once you're satisfied, turn off the preview function of the capture software to save processor resources and disk usage.

Disk Space Needs

You'll be stunned at how fast your hard disk fills up when you start capturing video, especially if you use uncompressed video. Bottom line: The greater the sample frequency and larger the bit rate, the larger the file. To avoid the dreaded "disk full" error, here's a quick formula for calculating how much disk space you'll need for a given clip.

(pixel width) × (pixel height) × (color bit depth) × (fps) × (duration in seconds) / 8,000,000

You'll know most of these values from your configuration for the capture. Or check the feature that displays properties for the session you're in. This varies from one software application to another. Duration in seconds depends on the length of the clip you intend to capture. Here's a potential calculation for a two minute clip:

320 × 240 × 24 × 30 × 120 / 8,000,000 = 829.44 megabytes

ALERT　**File Size Limitations**

Be aware that some older file systems, notably FAT, and older types of AVI formats, limit individual file sizes to 2 GB (2,048 megabytes). That means if you have a long production, you have to either reduce certain parameters, such as color depth, or use editing software that can support file sizes greater than 2 GB. If you have a very long video, you may be able to glue individual pieces together after encoding with Windows Media utilities.

Audio and Video Capture Settings for Windows Media

This section discusses some common capture settings for audio and video.

Audio — Let's assume you have some tapes in front of you. Find the specific sections you want to capture. Don't capture the whole thing; that wastes time and disk space. Now choose some capture settings. This is critical! If you don't capture at the right settings, you could have trouble later when you encode. You may have to experiment some, but here's some basic audio capture settings:

- **Bit depth**: 16-bit
- **Sample rate**: 44.1 kilohertz
- **Format**: WAV (**.wav**)

You should also set audio levels in the editing software. These usually take the form of peak level meters. (See the earlier section on volume levels.)

Video — Following are some basic video capture settings:

- **Frame size**: 320 × 240
- **Frame rate**: 30 fps (frames per second)
- **Compression ratio**: Lowest available
- **Format**: AVI (**.avi**)

Video capturing offers a few other parameters to consider.

- If you use a video monitor, adjust the SMPTE color bars (a standard color gauge in television and video production) and then adjust your computer monitor to match using a high-resolution computer bitmap of the SMPTE bars.
- Adjust your video capture levels (hue, saturation, and brightness) so that the picture matches the video monitor.
- You may need to tell your capture card whether the video meets the NTSC or PAL standards. NTSC covers video produced in the United States and Canada. PAL covers Europe and parts of Asia.

ALERT **FireWire and Video Frame Settings**

If you use FireWire, you don't need to worry about setting frame sizes, frames per second (fps), and so on. The technology automatically transfers the digital video data at full-frame size and 30 fps using the built-in digital video compression.

Inside the Industry

The Importance of Pixel Formats

Digital video stores color and related information in a number of ways, known as *pixel* formats. (A pixel, or *picture element*, is the basic unit of composition in a digital image.) Pixel formats fall into two main types: RGB (Red Green Blue) and YUV, which refers to the luminance and chrominance of the three primary colors.

RGB uses the full range of color in the visible spectrum. However, the human eye cannot perceive the full range, so there's no need to store that information and waste hard disk space. However, YUV takes advantages of the eye's sensitivity to the intensity of a color, while storing less data. The downside is that sampling video via YUV means a video signal with slightly lower quality.

Microsoft recommends sampling video with YUV settings, such as YUY2, as noted above. Other YUV settings include IYUV/1420, YV12, and UYVY.

And...Capture

Now that you're ready to capture, click "Record," and the hardware converts the analog signal from the recording device to the 1s and 0s that computers understand. The software applies its settings and stores the data on your hard drive. In a few moments, you'll have your source audio or video file, all ready for encoding.

Common Source File Formats

You'll come across a variety of file formats as you work with computer audio and video. *Source* file formats, for the purposes of this book and as shown in **Table 4-2**, are formats used to store audio and video in a computer before they are transformed or *encoded* into streamable formats. (A format is simply a way to organize data on a storage medium.) To keep things simple, we like to think of these formats as *raw* formats, just like the raw materials that a foundry uses to make steel.

Name	Type	Extension
AIFF	Audio	.aif, .aiff
AU	Audio	.au
MIDI	Audio	.mid, .midi
MOD	Audio	.mod
VOC	Audio	.voc
WAV	Audio	.wav
AVI	Video	.avi

Table 4-2
Common source data file formats you'll encounter in the world of digital audio and video. You'll transform files in these formats to streaming media formats.

Capturing with Windows Media 9 Capture

Now that you've reviewed best practices for recording and capturing video, it's time to actually capture some video to a file. There are several software programs on the market for this, among them Adobe Premiere® and Microsoft Movie Maker, which we'll use later to edit the video. Whatever capture program you use, most, if not all the settings, will be the same.

Follow these steps to capture a video. The instructions assume you are on a workstation with an SDI video capture card installed and using a digital Betacam camera. It also applies to some digital cameras and tape decks connected to a card via Firewire.

1. Select File → Set Capture File and specify the name and location of the new AVI (**.avi**) file.
2. Select your video capture card as the source for both audio and video.
3. Select Options → Preview to display the source video in the capture utility. This helps you configure the video settings.

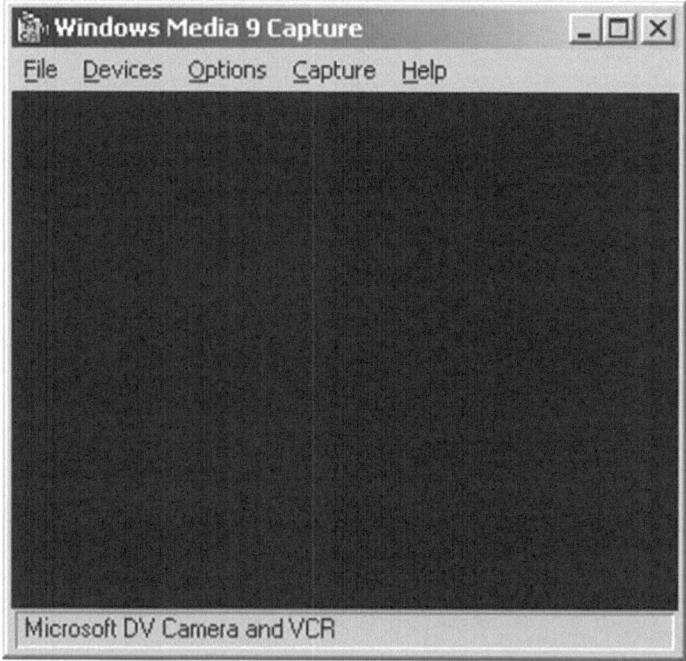

Figure 4-3
Microsoft Windows Media 9 Capture utility. To download and install, visit the Windows Media download page and look for the utility in the Encoder area.

4. Select Options → Video Format to display the properties you'll set in the next step.

5. Click the Source tab.

6. Under Input, click SDI.

7. Under Video Settings, select Bypass color correction.

8. Under Video Standard, select NTSC-M. (Check your documentation for PAL settings.)

9. Click the Format tab.

10. Under Color Format, select YUV12 planar (1420). This is Windows Media Series' standard format.

11. Under Proportions, select CCIR601. This reproduces the image with the same proportions as the original image.

12. Under Video Size, select Full. This captures the image at a resolution of 720 × 480.

13. Click OK.

> ## Author's Tip
>
> As the capture progresses, watch the Windows Media Capture 9 status bar. Note the number of frames captured and dropped. If you see several dropped frames, the computer is not keeping up with the data transfer. Too many dropped frames will reduce the quality of your streaming media. To solve this problem, either start over or adjust the utility's settings.

14. Select Options → Audio Format. Configure the format for PCM audio, 48 KHz, 16-bit, and stereo. This will match the data already on the digital tape.

15. Open Microsoft Volume Control by double-clicking the speaker icon in the taskbar. Select Options → Properties and click Recording to open Microsoft Recording Control, as shown in **Figure 4-4**.

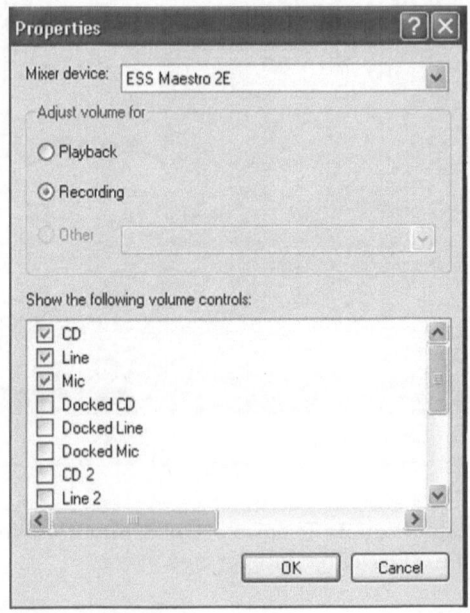

Figure 4-4
Windows Recording Control, which is accessed via the Windows Volume Control.

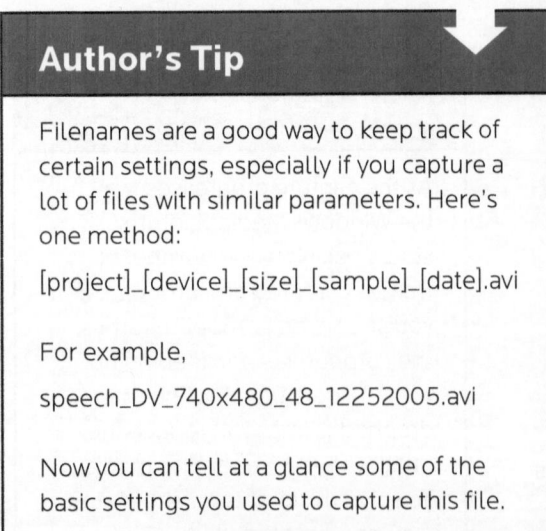
16. Select the Mixer device under Properties and make sure the AES/EBU digital audio input is enabled. Click OK.

17. Returning to Windows Media Capture 9 utility, select Capture → Set Frame Rate and deselect Use Frame Rate.

18. Select Capture → Start Capture.

19. After the Ready to Capture dialog box appears, click OK.

20. Press Play on the Betacam deck.

21. To stop the capture, press ESC on the computer keyboard. Press Stop on the tape deck.

22. Give the newly captured file a unique name, making sure it has an **.avi** extension.

Editing with Windows Movie Maker

In most film and video productions, the actors or possibly the director gets most of the glory. But it's the editor who often has the most fun. They take the individual shots taken by the director and assemble them into a story. This book won't go into the details of the language of film, but you may be called upon to perform some elementary editing. To get started, you'll use Windows Movie Maker, which is installed with Windows XP. (It's not available for older Microsoft operating systems.)

The instructions assume you have captured a number of shots from a video source to AVI format. They all have the same capture parameters, such as image size and audio sampling rate.

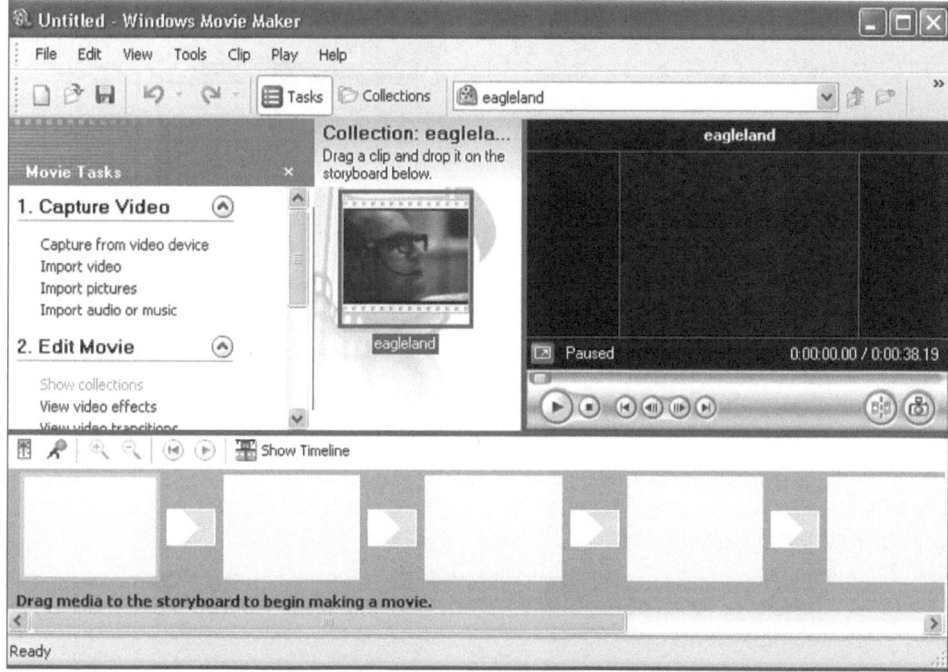

Figure 4-5
Windows Movie Maker with an imported AVI clip.

Getting Started

Get started by adding your first clip to Movie Maker.

1. Open Windows Movie Maker by clicking Start → Programs → Windows Movie Maker.
2. In the Movie Tasks pane, click Import Video and find the location of your clips on the hard drive.

3. Select a clip and click OK. The clip name and a thumbnail of its first frame appear in the Collections pane.

4. Select the clip, drag it to the beginning of the storyboard pane, and drop it. The visible frame now appears in the first box, as shown in **Figure 4-6**.

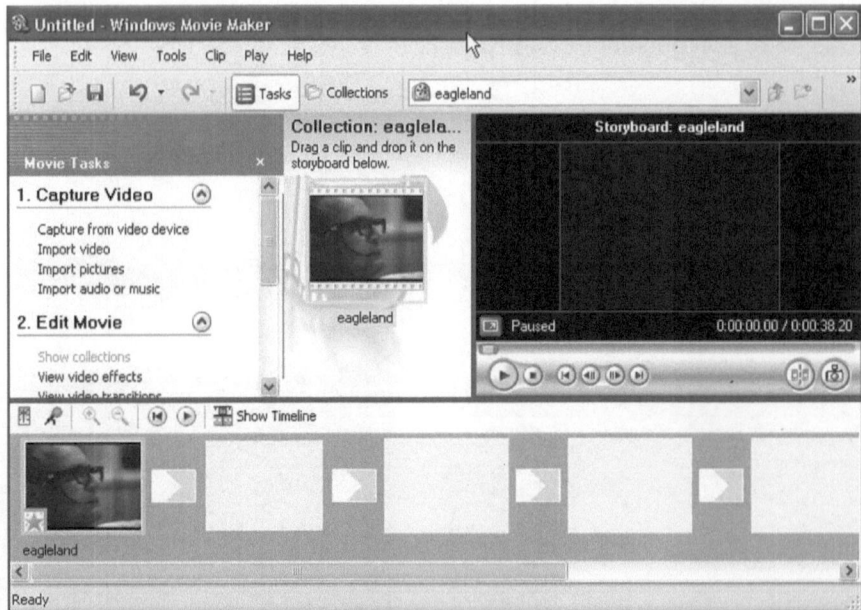

Figure 4-6
Windows Movie Maker with the first shot placed in the lower-left of the storyboard pane.

Add a Shot
Add a new shot to the storyboard.

1. Via the Movie Tasks pane, find your next AVI clip and import it as you did in the preceding procedure.

2. Drag-and-drop the second clip into the storyboard. The thumbnail of its first frame appears next to the first shot, as shown in **Figure 4-7**.

Correct an Error
Let's say you meant to put another shot between the first two.

1. Via the Movie Tasks pane, find your clip, and import it.

2. Select the new clip, and drag it *between* the first and second clip, and drop it. The new clip is placed in correct order, as show in **Figure 4-8**.

3. Check your work by clicking the Play button in the Storyboard pane.

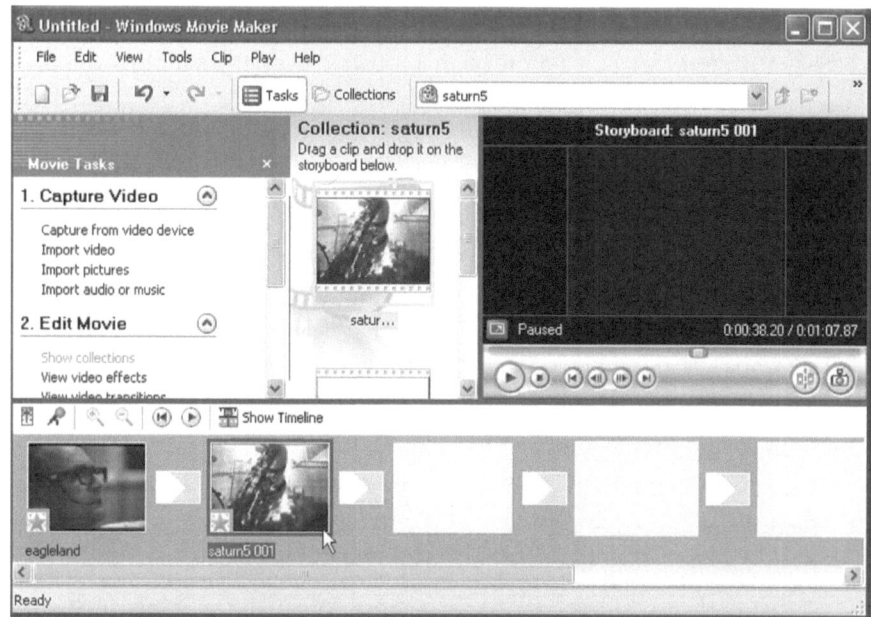

Figure 4-7
Drag and drop the second AVI clip to the storyboard, and another thumbnail appears.

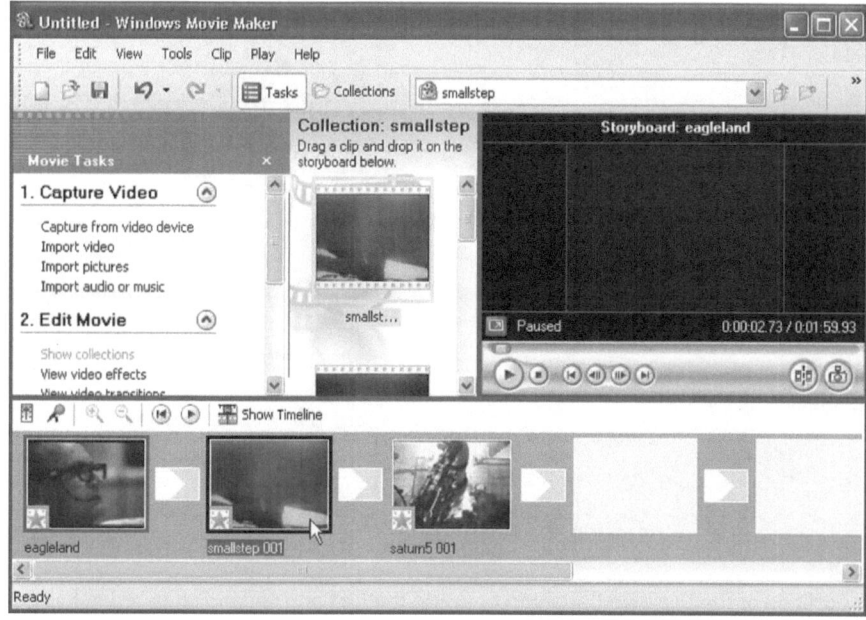

Figure 4-8
The Storyboard pane with the third clip inserted between the first and second.

Add Effects

Special effects such as fades add a professional touch to even the simplest videos.

1. To add a fade-in from black to the beginning, click the Movie Tasks pane.
2. Click View Video Effects.
3. In the View Video Effects pane, find "Fade In, from Black."
4. Select the effect, drag it over the first video clip, and drop it.
5. To add a transition effect, click View Transition Effects in the Movie Tasks pane.
6. In the View Transitions Effects pane, select "Dissolve." (Preview the effect by clicking Play in the Video Player.)
7. Select the effect, drag it to the square between the first two shots, and drop it.
8. Repeat step 7 for the second transition.
9. To add a fade-out to the end, click View Video Effects in the Movie Tasks pane.
10. Find "Fade Out, to Black"
11. Drag the effect over the last clip in the sequence, and drop it.
12. Click Play in the Storyboard pane to check your work, as shown in **Figure 4-9**.

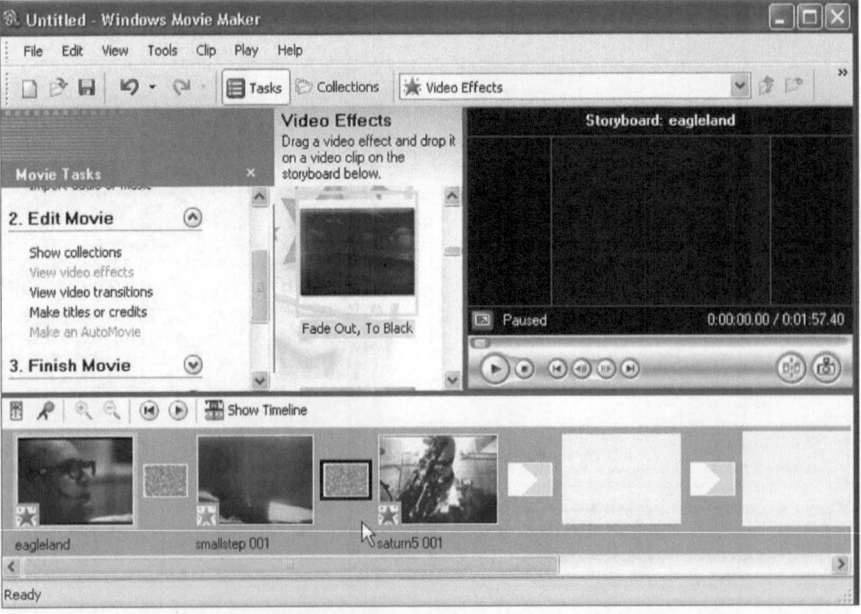

Figure 4-9
Note the addition of the Dissolve transition between the first and second shot, as well as the second and third shot.

Add a Title and Credits

A title and credits helps others identify your work.

1. Under the Tools menu, select Titles and Credits.

2. Click "Add title to the beginning of the movie."

3. Add the title and author information. (Note the automatic preview in the Player pane.)

4. Click "Done, add title to movie."

Figure 4-10
The title and author slide appears in the lower-left before the first shot.

Save Your Work

To save your work for posterity, implement the following steps.

1. To add title, author and copyright information, select File → Properties and enter the data. The data is stored as metadata, that is, data describing the file, within the edited video.

2. To save the project parameters in a file for later use, click File → Save Project and create a file name. For convenience, save the project file in the same folder as your clips.

3. To export the clips, effects, and transitions into completed file, select File → Save Movie File... and select the destination. Enter a file name at the appropriate prompt.

Saving the movie make take several minutes depending on its length and complexity.

Conclusion

Capturing audio and/or video to a hard disk is a critical step in the streaming media production process. In this chapter you learned best practices for recording audio and video files, noting that standard types of production and composition may not always work for streaming. You also learned best practices for capturing audio and video to .**wav** and .**avi** files for encoding. The book discussed capturing with the Windows Media Capture 9 utility, and simple editing techniques with Windows Movie Maker. Next, the book will discuss optimizing your captured and edited audio and video in preparation for encoding.

CHAPTER 5

Optimizing Your Audio and Video

Recording and capturing high-quality audio and video are the first steps toward building a killer streaming media production. But the captured files need more work in order for you to increase your chances of a successful outcome. Before you encode with Windows Media Encoder, you need to *optimize*, that is, get the most out of your raw media file. You can do this with your editing program or Windows Media Encoder. This chapter goes over some of the fundamentals of optimization to prepare you for the next major step, encoding. By the time you finish, you'll know how to:

- Optimize your audio
- Optimize your video

Optimize Your Audio

The following sections gives you background about the properties of recorded sound. It also discusses some of the parameters you modify to achieve best sound quality before converting the audio file to a streaming media file.

The Nature of Digital Audio

Humans perceive sound as a complex set of vibrations in a medium, usually air, with differences in frequency, tone and volume over time. These vibrations can have infinite variety, although the perceptible range is limited. Our ears convert these vibrations into analog electrical impulses. Our brain interprets and applies meaning to these impulses.

The first recording devices stored sound as variations in a continuous groove etched on a metal or wax cylinder or plate. To play the sound back, a motor powered by a spring or electricity turned the cylinder or plate at a constant speed. A diamond needle placed in the groove vibrated with the variations and transferred this mechanical energy to an amplifier. (Later devices used a magnet to rearrange and/or read the magnetic patterns of iron oxide crystals on Mylar® tape.) The amplifier drove an electromagnet, which vibrated a rubber or paper cone. The cone's vibrations were transferred to the air, which we hear as reproduced sound. The sound can be represented as a wave, as shown in **Figure 5-1**.

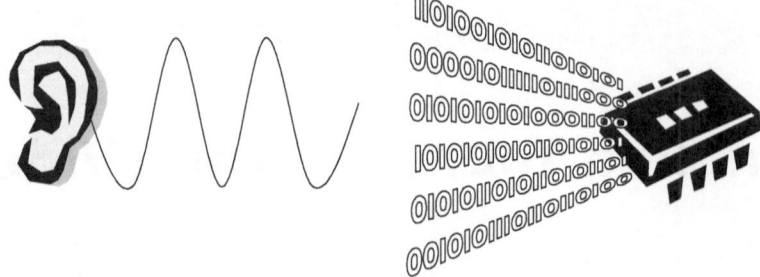

Figure 5-1
The human ear perceives sound as a continuous vibration in the air, which can be represented as a wave. Computers interpret sounds as electrical impulses broken into binary digits, that is, 1s and 0s.

In the digital world, an electromechanical device (the microphone) picks up sound and converts it into analog electrical impulses, much like our ears. But when the sound goes into a computer, the specially designed semiconductor chips in the sound card take "samples" of the sound. It's somewhat like the sampling done in surveys or polls. If you take a large enough sample from the general population, you can extrapolate the opinion of the entire group.

Audio sampling is no different. You can set your sound card to take just a few samples of the incoming signal, or you can tell it to take a lot. More samples mean more information and a better representation of the sound as a whole. The number of samples you take of a signal is called the *sampling rate*. The rate is expressed in hertz, a measurement of how often you take samples per second. Most samples fall in the range of 8 kilohertz ("thousands" of hertz) to 44.1 kHz, sometimes up to 48 kHz. Sample rates for DVDs can go as high as 196 kHz.

A second factor affects the amount of information gathered by the sound card. The *bit depth* determines the amount of detail gathered from the sample, sometimes called the *range of detail*, resolution or depth. Typical bit rates for digital audio include 8-bit, 16-bit, and 32-bit. (CD quality audio is 16-bit.)

Inside the Industry

The Difference between Voice and Music

It's important that you understand the basic difference between voice and music from an audio engineering standpoint. Audio pros talk about the difference using the term *dynamic range*, which can be thought of as the span of volume from quiet to loud of all the sounds in a particular file. Music, typically, has a wide dynamic range. Think of Tchaikovsky's 1812 Overture. In the space of a few seconds, the music can go from the quiet of a few wind instruments to cannon fire. The music has a wide dynamic range.

Voice normally has a narrow dynamic range. The next time you have a lengthy conversation with your best friend, listen for the range of quiet places to loud places. Unless your friend likes to yell a lot, the dynamic range will be fairly narrow. Have you ever noticed how terrible music sounds over the telephone, while your best friend's voice can sound almost next door? That's in part because telephone lines are designed to handle the narrow dynamic range of the human voice, not the wide dynamic range of music.

Audio Optimizations

Even the most experienced streaming pros find problems with audio after it's been captured. For example, you may not have noticed the quiet buzz caused by an overhead fluorescent lamp. The whoosh of air conditioning may be particularly loud. Or the presenter has a few too many "aahs" and "umms." You can fix these problems in the editing software. Furthermore, the software can manipulate the entire audio file to make the final encoded product sound even better.

It's best to perform these tasks in a certain order, such as the one suggested in this section. Here's a quick checklist:

- ✔ Editing
- ✔ Equalization
- ✔ Compression
- ✔ Normalization
- ✔ DC offset
- ✔ Noise reduction

Author's Tip

The Windows Media Encoder contains a feature called "Pause Removal" that automatically removes pauses in voice tracks. This can help make a speech, for example, more listenable and shorter by removing long pauses. However, use the feature carefully. Having the encoder edit your work automatically risks unwanted effects. That pregnant pause may be needed!

Editing — Audio editing tools exist to compensate for the problems caused by long pauses, backtracking, coughs, cleared throats, and other distracting mistakes by public speakers. Experiment with your editing software to remove these errors, not just to make the speaker sound better, but to make the audio more "listenable." It's hard to listen to a presentation constantly interrupted by "aahs" and "umms." And don't forget that when you remove these things, you should listen to the change and fiddle with it if it sounds odd. Software editors are "nondestructive." You can always Undo.

Equalization — The experts trust their ears. Sometimes the file just doesn't sound right. You may discover, for example, that the speaker sounds "muddy." That's when there's a lot of lower frequency sound, but not a lot of higher frequency sound to give each word definition. One way to solve this problem is *equalization* or *EQ'ing*.

Equalization is the process of turning up (*boosting*) or turning down (*attenuating*) small frequency ranges within audio. In the case of a muddy sounding voice, you can try turning up the higher frequencies and turning down the low frequencies. Try attenuating frequencies below 100 Hz and boosting frequencies in the 1 to 4 kHz range.

Your audio editing software should have a graphic equalizer, along with some presets, similar to the one shown in **Figure 5-2**. Again, don't hesitate to play with the settings and learn what works best. But work with moderation. You'll find that small adjustments go a long way.

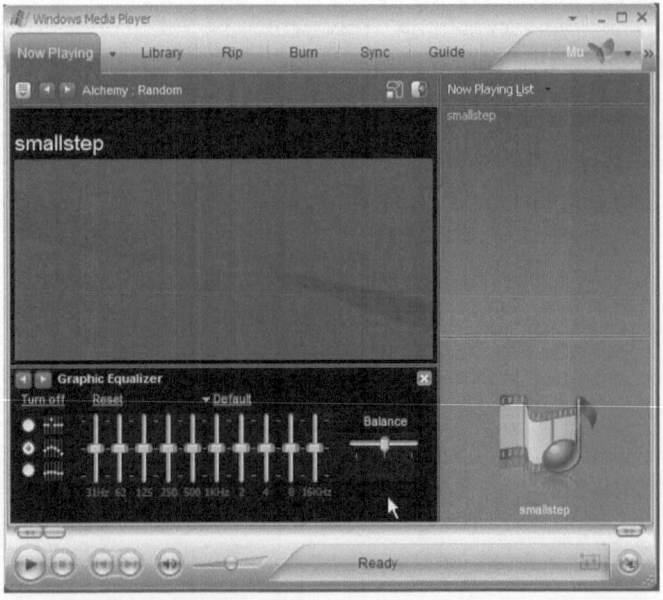

Figure 5-2
The graphic equalizer in Windows Media Player 10. All professional audio editing programs and video programs have a built-in graphic equalizer to let you adjust audio quality.

Dynamic Range and Compression — *Compression* is one of the most important optimizations you perform on audio files. Beginners sometime confuse audio compression with encoding, which is sometimes called compression as well. However, encoding removes data from a file to make it smaller and streamable. Compression in the context of audio optimization means turning down the loudest portions of the file, in effect narrowing the dynamic range according to parameters set by the engineer, which means you. Compression lessens the chance your audio may sound distorted at the loudest points.

Open up your audio editing software and the audio file you captured in the previous chapter. It will show a *waveform*, a graphical representation of the sound, as shown in **Figure 5-3**. Find the function called Compression, or sometimes called Dynamics Compression. To apply it, you'll probably need to highlight all or portions of the waveform. Most editing software packages offer compression presets, so you don't have to spend a lot of time figuring out the right settings. If you want to experiment with these settings, try these:

- **Threshold**: –10 dB
- **Ratio**: 4:1
- **Attack and Release**: 100 ms
- **Input level**: 3 dB of compression
- **Output level**: 0 dB of compression

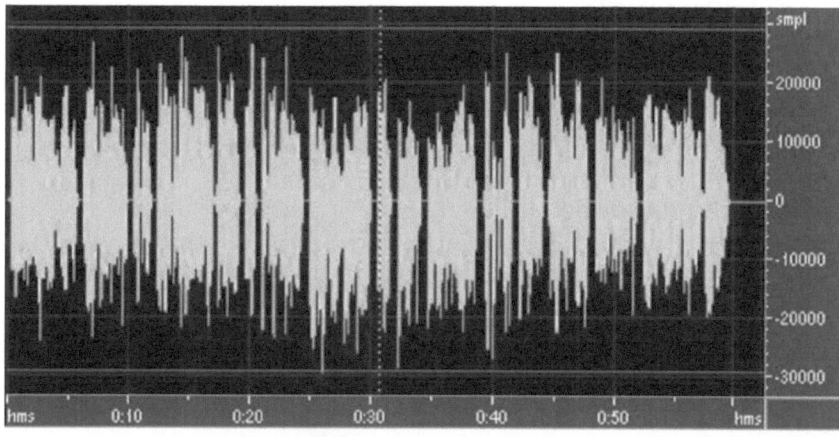

Figure 5-3
A typical waveform in audio editing software. The waveform is a graphic representation of the sound in the audio file.

As always, use your ears to judge the results. If you don't like them, change the settings, or go with a preset. And always remember to listen to your results in headphones that block outside noise. At least listen to the results in high-quality speakers.

Normalization — *Normalizing* your audio file turns up the volume on the entire file to a point just before distortion occurs. Streaming audio files sound best when they are loudest without distortion, sometimes called *clipping*. Check your audio editing software for a Normalize function and normalize the file to about 95%, or −0.5 dB. Keeping normalization just under 100% or 0 dB gives the editing and encoding software a bit of wiggle room.

DC Offset — When recording equipment isn't grounded properly, inaudible noise is sometimes introduced into the audio. It sometimes manifests itself by clicks and pops. You can fix this with your editing software's *DC Offset* function. Some software packages can remove this problem as you capture audio. Check your manual.

Noise Reduction — Many people have heard of *noise reduction*. Many people associate Dolby Laboratories with noise reduction, because the company has set industry standards for quality. In simplest terms, noise reduction (Dolby's and everyone else's) identifies unwanted audio frequencies, and through complex calculations attenuates them (turns them down) without affecting the rest of the audio. Check your editing software manual for the specifics.

 ALERT   To get anything useful out of noise reduction features, you need some fairly advanced understanding of acoustics. It might be better to just stick to equalization.

Optimize Your Video

Just as audio files need to be tweaked to get the best results in the encoding process, video files need the same kind of nudging. Remember that video is actually audio and moving images. Apply the preceding information to your audio track. The following material applies to your video track only.

The Nature of Digital Video

Video starts with light. Another word for light is *electromagnetic radiation*, or more precisely, waves of energy moving through space. Light waves travel at different wavelengths. Scientists measure a wavelength from the crest of one wave to the crest of the next, analogous to the waves caused by dropping a pebble into a pond. The wavelengths of light, as shown in **Figure 5-4**, are measured in billionths of a meter. The range of electromagnetic wavelengths is enormous, but humans see only a small portion of it, known as *visible light* or the *visible spectrum*.

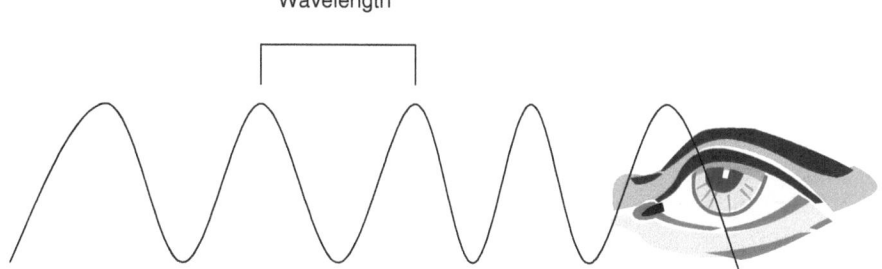

Figure 5-4
One way scientists measure light is by its wavelength, which is the distance from one crest of the light wave to the next.

Light is measured as a frequency, similar to sound, and the human eye perceives different frequencies as color. Color frequencies range from 430 trillion hertz (red) to 750 trillion hertz (violet). Light travels through the iris of the eye into a flexible lens, which focuses it on the retina. Cells called rods and cones transform the light waves into electrical impulses that travel along the optic nerve to the brain. The 120 million rods in the average eye pick up dim light and motion. The six million or so cones specialize in color reception.

Inside the Industry

 A Light Prediction Gone Awry
The first artificial light gathering and storage device appeared in 1826, when a French inventor named Joseph Nicéphore Niépce made a picture of the roofs of some houses in his neighborhood. He gathered light using an old device called a *camera obscura* and stored the image on a pewter plate coated with a chemical akin to asphalt. Photography advanced to the point in 1895 when fellow French-man Louis Lumiere invented a camera that could take photographs quickly one after the other on a long roll of cellophane film. (Lumiere's invention could also process and project the film.) One of the men credited with inventing motion pictures, Lumiere predicted the movie industry would never amount to anything.

In the early 20th century, inventors started experimenting with sending wireless images. An inventor named Philo T. Farnsworth found one method in the 1920s. He scanned the surface of a light-gathering device (called a *pickup*) and converted the signal into electrical impulses. Think of how you read a page in this book. You start at the top left, go across the page, and start again at the next line and repeat the process to the end of the page.

A camera does this "reading" work at nearly the speed of light. A television reverses this process. You see an image because the scan happens so quickly. It's the same principle, known as *persistence of vision*, that makes the millions of images on film appear as one moving image.

Farnsworth's analog methods dominated video technology until the 1980s and the advent of the digital camera. A digital video camera measures light in tiny pieces called *pixels*, assigns a value to each, and converts the value into "1s" and "0s." Like digital audio, digital video samples the video signal at a given rate and a given depth in bits.

However, digital cameras gather far more information than we can store efficiently. Therefore, electronics in the camera or elsewhere *compress* or remove some of the redundant information. To display the video information, the computer reverses the compression or *decompresses* the signal stored in the digital video signal or file and illuminates individual pixels on the monitor, somewhat like the drops that create an image in a Jackson Pollock painting.

Video Optimizations

Video capturing is an inexact science. At the very least, the video probably doesn't start or end exactly where you want. You may see black bars along the edges. You may discover unwanted artifacts or other problems with the video image. Or the video seems too dark or too bright.

Unfortunately, video has fewer "fixes" available to it than audio. This is why a correct capturing technique is so important. But there are a few things you can do.

As with audio, you should follow a certain order in your video optimizations to get the most out of them. The order isn't hard and fast, though.

- ✔ Editing
- ✔ Cropping
- ✔ Video processing
- ✔ Filtering
- ✔ Resizing
- ✔ Rendering

Editing — Unlike audio, editing video is not as simple as removing an "ahh" or an "umm." When you take out an "aah," the two pieces of audio on either side simply come together and the listener is none the wiser. But when you cut out a piece from a moving image, you wind up with something called a *jump cut*. Even if the change is slight, the eye will notice that something was missing. Viewers will be distracted, and then you've lost their full attention.

To solve this problem, use *cutaways*. When you're shooting your video, spend a few minutes recording some of the visual information around you. These could include shots of the audience, other participants in an event, or the general scene where the action takes place. These are called *covering shots*. At your workstation, capture some of this video, using the same settings as your main video. When you come across a jump cut, take a piece of a covering shot, and "cover" the jump cut with the visual image, as shown in **Figure 5-5**, while maintaining the original audio. This takes some practice, but the transition will be much smoother and less likely to confuse the audience.

Figure 5-5
Cover a video edit with a shot of something else to mask the jump cut. The result is a smoother transition.

Inside the Industry

Cover Shots and Local News
Covering shots are a mainstay of TV news packages. Next time you watch the evening news, look for a story about a speech or a press conference. You might see video of the speaker delivering an announcement or answering a question. Suddenly, the shot changes to a shot of all the cameras and their operators recording the event. Then the shot changes to the speaker again. The editor probably used a covering shot of the cameras to mask a jump cut and give the scene some visual variety.

Use the video editing process to add simple effects, as demonstrated in the previous chapter's section on Windows Movie Maker. For example, insert a fade up from black at the beginning of a video, and a fade down to black at the end. This transition signals visually the beginning and end of a video. You can also add simple titles, called *slides*, to the beginning and credits at the end. However, you should avoid the temptation to add a lot of effects that introduce too much information to the video file, such as wipes, whip pans, fast dissolves, and so on. These generally don't translate well to streaming media, especially at low bit rates.

Cropping — Photographers are familiar with cropping. If you're not a professional photographer, you may have removed parts of your family photos to make them smaller or remove irrelevant information, as shown in **Figure 5-6**.

Figure 5-6
Use your video editing software's cropping function to remove unwanted material from the video image. Be sure to maintain your original pixel ratio, usually 4:3 or 16:9.

Streaming media producers use the cropping functions of video editing software to solve two problems, overscan and letterboxing.

Overscan — Black bars around the edges of a video image often appear after capturing, especially after capturing analog video. These bars, called *overscan*, are normally covered by the plastic casing around a television's picture tube.

To solve this problem, use your editing software's cropping function. In many editing tools, video cropping works very much like the cropping tool in photograph manipulation software. Simply draw a rectangle inside the video image that leaves out the overscan area.

Letterboxing — Movies shot in a widescreen format such as Cinemascope are sometimes shown on TV in their original aspect ratio. This means black bars appear on the top and bottom of the image. This is called *letterboxing*, as shown in **Figure 5-7**.

Figure 5-7
Overscan and letterboxing. In the left illustration, overscan is the black area around the actual image.

In terms of streaming, these bars are just extra information you don't need to transmit over the Internet. Your viewers are better off without them. Use your video cropping tool to draw a square or rectangle inside the actual image and lop off the unneeded bits.

ALERT   Maintain Your Pixel Ratios

When you crop video to remove overscan or letterboxing, you need to make sure that the pixel dimensions of the new rectangle match the original video dimensions, usually 4:3 for a standard television or 16:9 for widescreen. This means for every four (or sixteen) pixels you shave off the width, you need to take three (or nine) pixels off the height. Otherwise, your video could suffer distortion later in the process.

Video Processing — Like the audio proc amp discussed in the previous chapter, video processors enable you to manipulate an incoming video signal. If you don't have a hardware proc amp, there's a good chance you can perform similar manipulations using your video editing software. And while hardware proc amps don't offer fine-grained control, software processing lets you change individual shots, even frames. The trick is to limit your urge to fix to the amount that gets the job done without introducing more problems.

Author's Tip

Occasionally, you'll see a video artifact called *tearing*, which is noise that appears on the edge of the video image. You can remove this with the cropping tools of your video editing software.

The most likely change you'll make is brightness, mostly because video often looks darker on a computer screen than a video screen. As you play with it, you may notice your blacks moving closer to gray. You'll just have to fiddle with the settings until you like what you see. Check your editing software manual for specifics.

Author's Tip

Before capturing video, be sure to match your computer monitor to the video monitor using the SMPTE color bars. In the case of a computer monitor, display the color bars with a high-resolution bitmap of the bars.

Filtering — Hardware and/or editing software packages offers filters that take out certain artifacts or distortion introduced or highlighted by the capture process. The filters we'll talk about are *deinterlacing*, *inverse telecine*, and *noise reduction*.

Deinterlace — TV monitors display visual data differently than computer monitors. Video equipment records data in a way meant for display on televisions, usually in an interlaced fashion. An interlaced video frame has two fields that overlap. If you imagine a TV screen as a set of vertical lines stacked one on the other, one field in the frame contains the odd numbered lines, the other holds the even numbered lines. As shown in **Figure 5-8**, the lines of one field are shown first, and the second a moment later, although the human eye can't see the change.

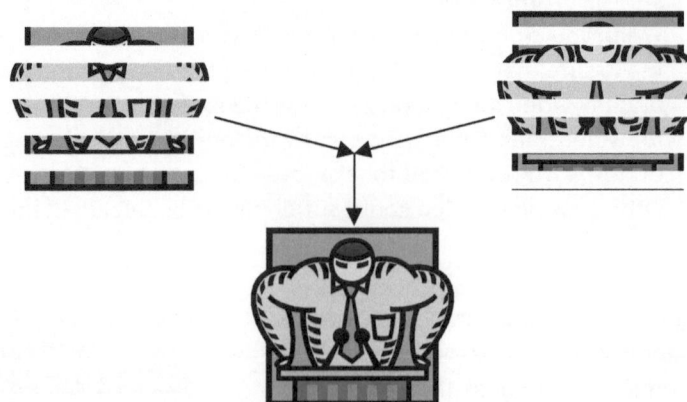

Figure 5-8
Televisions interlace two fields of lines to create a frame. To avoid artifacts created by this, use your editing software's deinterlacing feature.

When the data is displayed on a computer screen, artifacts are introduced under certain circumstances, especially when image sizes are larger than 320 × 240 and there's a lot of movement in the frame. Use your editing software's deinterlacing filter to remove these artifacts.

Inverse Telecine — Motion picture film is usually shot at 24 frames per second (fps). Video is shot at 30 fps (29.97 fps to be precise). When film is transferred to video, the process introduces extra fields to make up the extra six frames per second, as shown in **Figure 5-9**. This is redundant information you don't need for streaming. Use your editing software package's inverse telecine filter to remove these extra frames. Then render the video as *nonprogressive*. This removes the problem from the final video file.

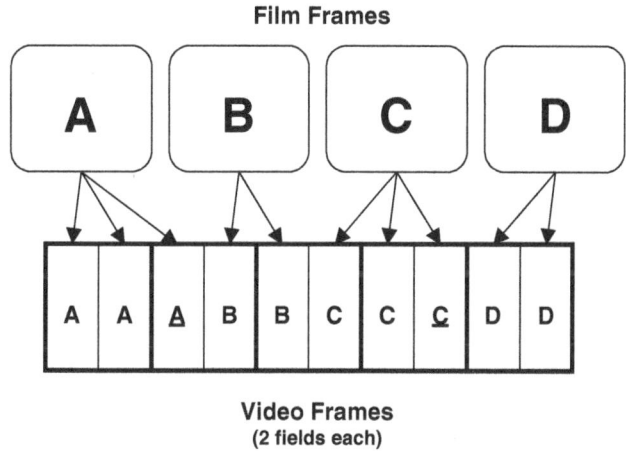

Figure 5-9
The telecine process, which creates extra fields (the underscored letter). This creates artifacts in video which are fixed with the inverse telecine process.

Noise Reduction — The previous chapter recommended that you purchase professional quality cameras and recording equipment. This reduces the chance for noise in the video, which can appear as lines, snow, or any other unwanted electronic glitches. If you're trapped into using a cheap consumer video camera, you may be able to clean the image up a bit with your editing software's noise reduction. However, poorly applied noise reduction may blur the image, introducing more problems than it solves.

Rendering — The final step of video optimization is *rendering*, in which all the edits and other changes are saved to an AVI file that becomes your final encoded file. Before rendering, you choose an image size, the final size you want for the streamed image. A large image is

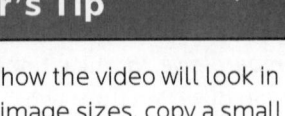

Author's Tip

To check how the video will look in different image sizes, copy a small portion of your video into a new file, render it, and view the results. That will save time and energy.

closer to the TV experience most users expect. A smaller image size might mean a sharper image. You may render two files, one with a small image size and one with a larger image. The type of content you have, for example, talking heads or fast action, may also influence your decision. As discussed previously, ensure your image dimensions are in a ratio of 4:3 or 16:9. Here are some standard streaming video image sizes with a 4:3 ratio:

- 640 × 480 (recommended only for very high-bandwidth streaming)
- 320 × 240
- 240 × 180
- 176 × 132 (this is the standard size from streaming over mobile networks to cell phones)

Depending on the length of the video and the power of your workstation, rendering could take 30 minutes or more.

Conclusion

In this chapter you learned how to improve, or optimize, your WAV and AVI files in preparation for encoding. For audio, the chapter included information about editing, equalization, compression, and other processes. The section on video optimization also included a discussion of editing, as well as cropping, overscan and letterboxing. These optimizations lead to a higher-quality encoding result. In the next chapter you learn how to encode with Windows Media Encoder.

CHAPTER 6

Encoding for Windows Media

Now that you've recorded and optimized your raw audio and video files, it's time to get into the meat of streaming media: encoding. You'll convert the raw files into compressed files specially designed for distribution and playback over the Internet in real time. In this chapter, you will:

- Revisit your audience evaluation
- Choose the right codec
- Encode audio and video with Windows Media Encoder
- Encode video with Windows Media Encoder
- Customize a Windows Media Encoder session
- Learn about Windows Media Encoder utilities

Revisit Your Audience Evaluation

Before you get too far into the mechanics of encoding, you should revisit your audience evaluation in Chapter 2, Streaming Media Basics, and review your streaming audience evaluation form. Familiarize yourself with the details of your audience's capabilities, especially with regard to bandwidth and the version of Windows Media Player they likely have installed.

You should also be sure you fully understand the type of audio and video you have; in other words, is it action-packed, talking heads, or something in between. And if you haven't done so already, touch base with your IT department and bring the networking gurus up to speed on your plans. Their help will be invaluable, especially as you get ready to deploy your work.

Choose the Right Codec

Most people who've learned a little bit about streaming media understand the importance of codecs. In simplest terms, a *codec* is a mathematical formula that transforms source files to streamable files. The Windows Media Encoder applies these formulae to your optimized audio and video files.

However, codecs are also rather mysterious and slightly scary. People with high-level math and physics degrees design codecs. Microsoft and its competitors spend large amounts of money researching codecs or buying the rights to use them. Some people say the word stands for enCOde/DECode. Others say it means COmpress/DECompress. Even the word "codec" has a certain other-worldly feel to it.

It's important to keep codecs in perspective. You're correct if you understand the central importance of codec choice. But, hopefully, you've gathered from the rest of this book that codecs are only one piece of a bigger puzzle. Don't get hung up on them.

What We Perceive and What Codecs Do

Streaming media is just one of many ways producers can deliver sound and light to an audience. Professionals in every medium, from music to painting to filmmaking to codec engineering, start with research into the way humans perceive sound and light. Without this knowledge, codec design would be impossible.

Sound — Humans hear sound in the range of 20 Hz (low) to 20,000 Hz (high). Information on either side of this range is inaudible. Musical tones can take up a large portion of the audible spectrum. The range of a human voice is far narrower, from about 500 Hz to 2,000 Hz. Vowels tend to make up most of the low range. Consonants take up the higher frequencies. Audio codecs are roughly divided into music and voice because of the different characteristics.

Codecs work by removing information irrelevant to the perceptual experience of sound. These codecs are referred to as *lossy*, because information is "lost" in the encoding process. (Codecs that don't lose information are called *lossless*.) Lossy audio codecs first remove information below 20 Hz and above 20,000 Hz. Music codecs take out more information, but not as much as voice-only codecs. The latter can throw away large amounts of information because of the narrow range of human speech. Voice codecs were among the first truly successful codecs, because you could transmit very high-quality speech sounds over dial-up Internet connections.

Light and Motion — Light and color are central to the human experience. And our eyes are especially tuned to motion, which is one reason why action movies can be so riveting. The amount of data the millions of rods and cones in our retinas gather and send to the brain is almost beyond comprehension. In fact, the brain can't handle it all, and humans have evolved internal filters to help them decide which data to pay attention to and which to ignore.

Lossy video codecs attempt to do something similar. Because the Internet cannot handle the sheer number of bits in an uncompressed video file, codecs look for information that's redundant and gets rid of it. In conventional film or video, the information in each frame replaces the information in the previous frame. But much of this information is the same, frame to frame. Maybe it's the color of the sky or the lamp in the background. Instead of replacing all the information frame to frame, codecs replace only the parts that change. Every few seconds, a codec inserts a *key frame*, which becomes a reference point until another key frame appears. (The other frames are called *difference frames* or *delta frames*, because they only contain information different (the delta changes) from the key frames.)

Video codecs can be roughly divided into two kinds, low action and high action. Low action codecs are designed for video with little movement in the frame, such as a speech or a "talking heads" program. They have fewer key frames and large amounts of repeated information, such as a background blue screen. Low action codecs can work well at dial-up speeds. High action codecs, on the other hand, have more key frames and less repeated information frame to frame. These codecs are designed for music videos or movie trailers. They work best on high bit rate connections, at least DSL/cable.

Constant Bit Rate Encoding versus Variable Bit Rate Encoding

In the language of encoding, the bit rate is the amount of data available to the media player for playback. Data can flow at a constant rate or a variable rate, depending on the scenario.

Constant Bit Rate Encoding — In streaming media, almost all audio and video files are encoded for a constant bit rate, or CBR. This means that the data flows from the streaming server over the Internet to Windows Media Player at a steady, predictable rate. CBR encoding results in a better experience over unreliable Internet connections. However, because CBR encoding assumes that the type of content in a file remains the same over time, a change in the content may result in visual glitches. For example, if a boring news report suddenly switches to an exciting car commercial, the increased amount of data in the commercial (complex music, faster editing) may be lost and the impact diluted.

Variable Bit Rate Encoding — Variable bit rates actually reflect real life more closely. As suggested previously, a video image can instantly transform from slow and steady storytelling to quick and dynamic action. In variable bit rate encoding, or VBR, the codecs account for these changes in speed and timing. However, because current streaming media technology can't handle variable bit rates, VBR encoding is usually applied only to files that will be played back on devices, such as a compact disc player or a DVD player. See **Table 6-1** for more details about VBR encoding.

Types of Variable Bit Rate Encoding	
Quality-Based	Useful for archiving; best for guaranteeing the quality of encoded content; bit rate fluctuates according to content complexity; file size is unpredictable.
Bit Rate-Based	Often used if files are downloaded and played off a hard drive; allows highest possible quality while remaining within a predictable average bandwidth.
Peak Bit Rate-Based	Best when used for content that will be played off a CD, DVD or other device with a constrained reading speed; bit rate does not exceed a peak rate you specify.

Table 6-1
Variable bit rate encoding is used primarily for archiving or encoding content to be played off a hard drive or device. Content encoded for delivery via streaming media almost always uses a constant bit rate codec.

Inside the Industry

One-Pass and Two-Pass Encoding

Windows Media Encoder applies either *one-pass* or *two-pass* encoding to your files. In one-pass encoding, the encoder simply applies the codec from the get-go. In two-pass, the encoder analyzes the file for the most optimal application of the codec, and then applies the codec. Two-pass takes longer, but usually results in higher quality.

Windows Media Audio and Video Codecs

Microsoft offers six codecs in Windows Media Encoder. Each is applied to specific circumstances based on the type of content, as shown in **Table 6-2**. Each codec also accepts a number of settings via the encoder, which are discussed later in this chapter.

Author's Tip

Another mode of encoding, known as *multiple bit rate* (MBR) encoding, is discussed in the following section, Windows Media Audio and Video Codecs.

Windows Media Series 9 Audio and Video Codecs		
Codec	**Type**	**Application**
Windows Media Audio 9.1	Audio	Voice and music; backward compatible with Windows Media Player 6.4
Windows Media Audio 9 Pro	Audio	Voice and multichannel music; high-end home audio and commercial applications, such as gaming.
Windows Media Audio 9 Voice	Audio	Voice only; Suitable for low-bandwidth needs.
Windows Media Audio 9 Lossless	Audio	Not recommended for streaming.
Windows Media Video 9	Video	General-purpose video codec.
Windows Media Video 9 Screen	Screen	Designed for capturing and encoding screen activity on desktop/laptop computers.
Windows Media Video 9 Image v2	Stills	Slideshows.
Windows Media Video 9 Advance Profile	HD Video	High-definition video.

Table 6-2

Windows Media Series 9 codecs. Each codec takes a number of settings via the Windows Media Encoder.

Windows Media Audio 9 — The Windows Media Audio 9 codec is the most popular codec for encoding audio-only content, such as music. The codec is backward compatible to a wide variety of devices while improving the quality of the audio. Windows Media Players as old as version 6.4 can play audio encoded with this codec, though you may get better results with newer players.

Windows Media Audio 9 Professional — Windows Media Audio 9 Professional codec supports high resolution audio files with multiple channels. It's designed for high-end computer audio or home entertainment, such as gaming, or commercial applications, such as theatres. The codec is designed for broadband bit rates, starting at 128 kilobytes per second (kbps).

Windows Media Audio 9 Voice — Because the human voice has a narrow dynamic range, Microsoft has developed the Windows Media Audio 9 codec to create tiny files while maintaining high quality sound. This codec can squeeze the bit rate down to as little as 4 kbps, which makes it ideal for dial-up bandwidth situations.

Windows Media Audio 9 Lossless — Windows Media Audio 9 Lossless is integrated into the Windows Media Player and it is designed to facilitate CD copying. It is not intended for use in streaming media.

Windows Media Video 9 — Windows Media Video 9 is a general-purpose video codec that can be applied to a wide variety of bandwidths and content types. It supports all types of broadcast formats, including high-definition, and allows bit rates of up to 6 megabytes per second (DVD rates).

The decoding portion of Windows Media Video 9 also supports *interpolation*, also called *video smoothing*. The codec builds an intermediate video frame based on the data of two consecutive frames of video, increasing the frame rate during playback. This improves the video experience, especially at low bandwidths. (The feature is enabled by default within Windows Media Player in the Video Acceleration Settings.)

Windows Media Video 9 Screen — The Windows Media Video 9 Screen codec is designed for capturing activity on the desktop in real time. For example, you can record a tutorial on a new software application by showing menus and selections as you work with the application. Bit rates range from 28–100 kbps.

Author's Tip

Encoding Multichannel Audio

Most music and entertaining programs use multichannel audio, starting with stereo all the way up to 6-channel (5.1) and 8-channel (7.1) surround sound. The latter formats are designed for CD, DVD, high-definition television, and digital cinema audio programs. Windows Media Encoder can handle these formats, provided your source file meets the following criteria:

- *A single 6-channel or 8-channel file in wave_format_extensible format:* If you are sourcing from an 8-channel file, it is recommended that the sample rate and bits per sample of the source file and the encoded content match. For more information on wave_format_extensible, visit:

  http://www.microsoft.com/whdc/device/audio/multichaud.mspx.

- *Six single channel* **.wav** *files for 5.1 audio:* Use your audio editing program to create one file for each channel. In the encoder, create a source for each file and tell the encoder which file belongs with which channel. To create the files, use an audio editing program to fold down your audio to six files, one for each channel. Each **.wav** file cannot exceed 2 GB in size. (This option is not available with 7.1 audio.)

- *An AVI file:* The file can be audio-only or contain both audio and video. Audio-only AVI files do not have the file size limitation of WAV files. For multichannel use, the AVI file must have the wave_format_extensible audio header.

When encoding 5.1 audio, you control the fold-down distribution between the surround, center, and subwoofer channels on the Processing tab of the Properties panel.

Multichannel encoding requires either the Windows Media Audio 9 Professional codec or the Windows Media Audio 9 Lossless codec. In addition, your users must have Microsoft Windows XP and a player based on the Windows Media Format 9 Series Software Development Kit (SDK). Otherwise, the audio will be folded down automatically to two channels for stereo speakers.

Choosing the Right Codec

To choose the right codec, go back to your audience and content analyses. Look at expected players and bandwidths. What types of information does your content contain? Audio content is relatively easy to analyze: voice, music, or both. When you deconstruct video content, you'll analyze a video track and an audio track. The answers to the following questions should help you make a final choice.

- Is the audio primarily voice, music, or a mixture of voice and music? If it's a mixture, is the music just for variety or is it critical to the message?
- Is the video primarily one or two people speaking, such as a lecture or panel discussion, with only a few scene changes?
- Does the video contain numerous scene changes or lots of movement in the frame, such as music video or an action thriller movie?
- What Windows Media Players and Internet connection speeds do you expect for your target audience?

It's almost impossible to cover all the possible combinations of circumstances that might lead you to select one codec or another. Fortunately, the Windows Media Encoder makes codec selection relatively easy. It'll help with automatic selections for certain circumstances, and you should always experiment in unfamiliar situations.

The thing to remember is this: Codecs are just like wrenches in a toolbox. You have to apply brainpower to get any value out of them. Ultimately, you have to apply your own sense of what works and what doesn't work to the technology at hand.

Player Behavior and Multiple Bit Rate Encoding

Some behaviors of Windows Media Player can be frustrating, especially those that make users wait for something to happen. Fortunately, you can mitigate some of the frustration with good encoding practices. This section explains some of the behaviors and a suggested solution, called *multiple bit rate encoding*.

Pre-Roll — When your end user clicks a link to a streaming media file, Windows Media Player attempts to contact the streaming media server to get the stream. The player shows this by displaying a "Connecting to media..." or similar message. When the connection occurs, the player may then display "Buffering..." or "Loading..." This could go on for several seconds or longer, depending on the connection speed, the network conditions, and player settings.

Here's what's happening. The player is filling a reservoir of random access memory (RAM) with data from the stream, a process called *pre-roll*. When the reservoir is filled, the audio or video starts to play. In the meantime, the player continues to receive data from the Windows Media Server. It tries to keep the reservoir, also called the *buffer*, filled so that playback continues without interruption, creating a smooth user experience from the beginning of the clip to the end, as shown in **Figure 6-1**.

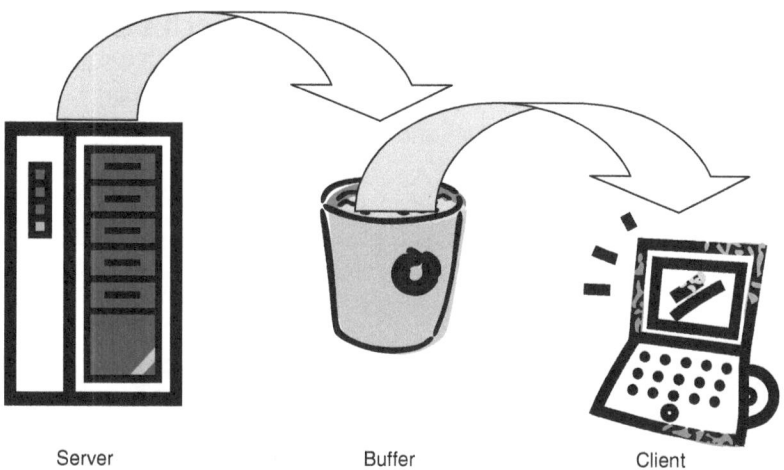

Server   Buffer   Client

Figure 6-1
A media player keeps a buffer of memory filled with streaming data to maintain a smooth user experience.

Rebuffering — The unpredictability of the Internet can sabotage a player's valiant attempt at smooth playback. One minute, network conditions may be perfect. The next minute, something in the great cloud goes haywire and the media player stops receiving data from the streaming server. The media buffer empties, and playback stops while the player asks the server for more data to refill the buffer. The player tells the user what's going on by redisplaying a "Buffering..." or "Loading..." message. As with pre-roll, *rebuffering* can seem to take forever.

Multiple Bit Rate Encoding — You can mitigate the buffering problem with multiple bit rate encoding. Normally, files are encoded with a single bit rate in mind, e.g., 125 kbps for a low-bandwidth DSL/cable connection. However, encoding for this bandwidth means people on dial-up have to wait extra to receive the file.

The solution is to combine several bit rates into a single encoded file. For example, if you combine encoding settings for a 56 kbps dial-up connection with settings for a 256 kbps DSL/cable connection, the player will ask the server for the version that fits the current network conditions. The player will shift up or down depending on its needs. Note that a downshift could cause a loss in quality because 56 kbps streams carry much less data than a higher bit rate stream.

ALERT	For multiple bit rate encoding to work, Windows Media Player has to know via its own settings that it's on a DSL/cable connection so that it can shift up or down as needed. If it's set to receive streams for a dial-up connection only, it will never ask for the 256 kbps stream.

Encode Audio and Video with Windows Media Encoder

This section takes you through a typical audio encoding session with Windows Media Encoder 9 Series. If you have not done so already, download and install the encoder now, as described in Chapter 1, Windows Media Series Quick Start.

The following procedures assume you have an optimized audio file in WAV format stored on your local computer hard drive. For the purposes of simplicity, the file is a voice-only file, but the basic procedures can be applied to music or voice and music combined. Most of the differences occur during the selection of codecs.

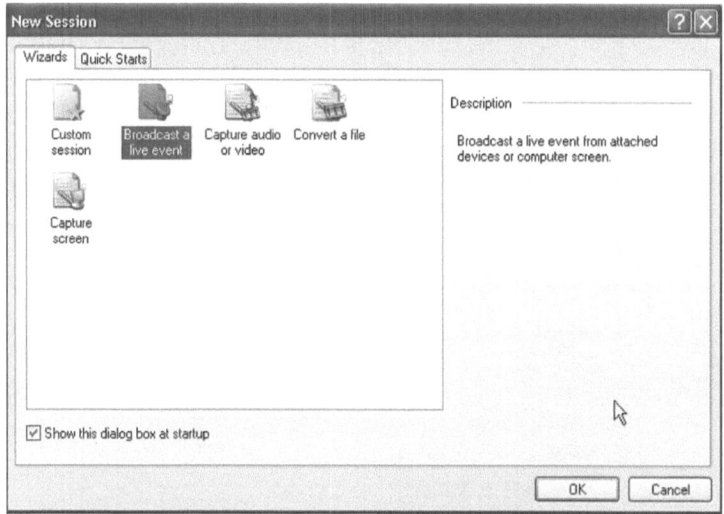

Figure 6-2
The New Session dialog box. The dialog appears at startup or when you click the New Session button in the encoder user interface.

Encoding Audio Step-by-Step

1. Open the Windows Media Encoder and select "Convert a file" in the Wizards tab of the New Session dialog. (If the dialog does not appear, click the "New Session" button in the upper left.) Click OK.

2. In the File Selection box, click "Browse" next to the "Source file" text box to locate the WAV file to be encoded, as shown in **Figure 6-3**.

Figure 6-3
Select the file you wish to encode. If you want the output file to be saved in a different directory, modify the "Output file" location.

3. The "Output file" location is automatically updated when you locate your source file. If you wish to save the output file to a different location, change the location here, as shown in **Figure 6-4**. Click Next.

4. In the Content Distribution box, select "Windows Media Server (streaming)," as shown in **Figure 6-4**. Note that the other listed distribution methods make use of different codecs as described in the preceding section, "Windows Media Audio and Video Codecs." Click Next.

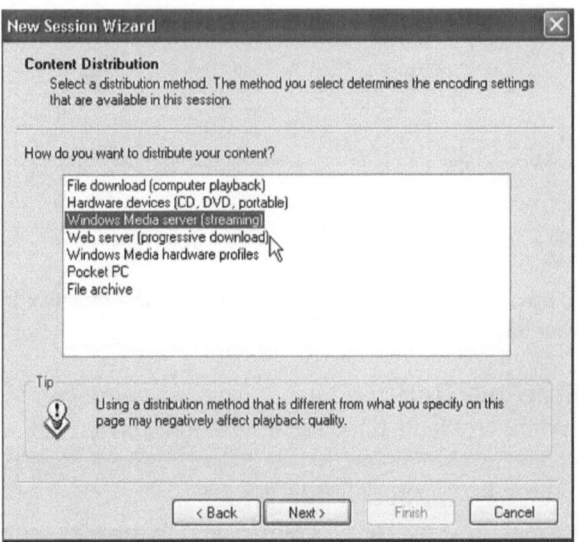

Figure 6-4
The Content Distribution box enables you to choose the correct codec by asking you how you want to distribute your content.

5. In the Encoding Options box, select the quality of the encoded file, as shown in **Figure 6-5**.

6. Stay with the Encoding Options box, and select the bit rates for your encoded file, as shown in **Figure 6-6**. (This assumes you chose "multiple bit rate (CBR)" in step 5.) Click Next.

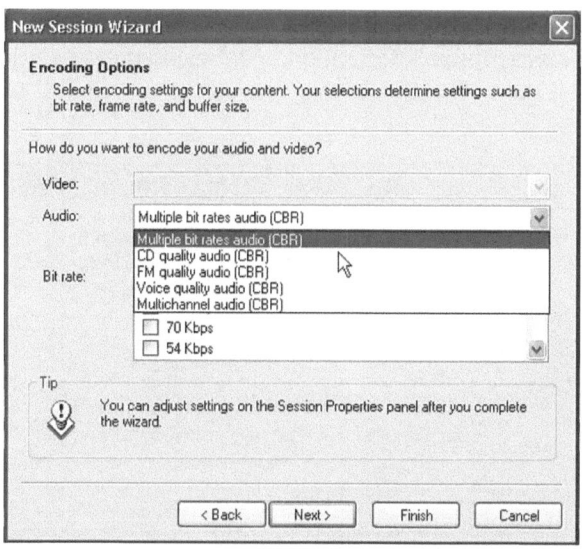

Figure 6-5
Multiple bit rates are the recommended selection for encoding quality. However, you can encode to a single bit rate by selecting another option.

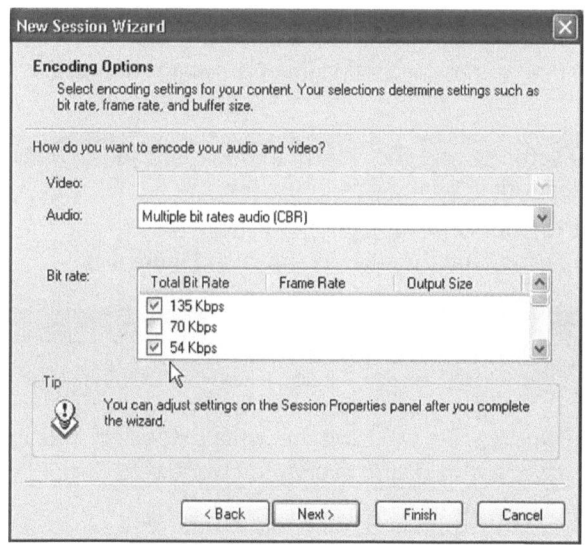

Figure 6-6
If you choose a multiple bit rate encode, choose two or more bit rates to target. Note the scroll bar on the right. Scroll down to see all your options.

7.   In the Display Information box, enter title, author, copyright, PICS rating (see below), and description information for indexing purposes, as shown in **Figure 6-7**. Click Next.

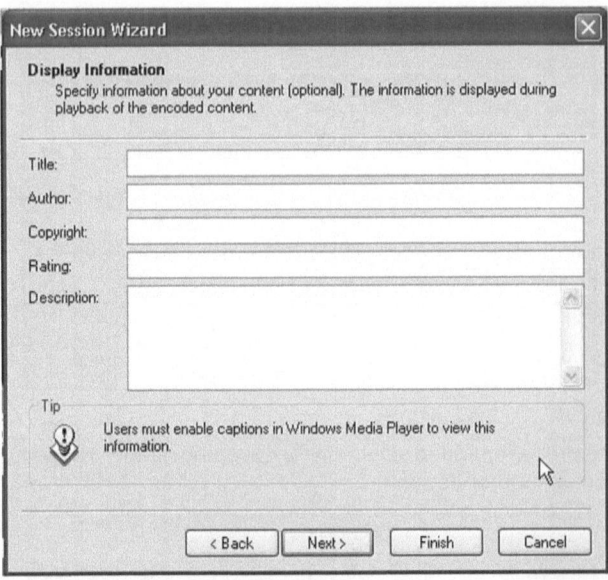

Figure 6-7
Don't forget to enter the title, author, and all-important copyright information.

8.   Review the settings, and click Finish to begin encoding, which may take several minutes, depending on the size of the file.

9.   Review the Encoding Results box, and click Close to end the session or New Session to encode another file, as shown in **Figure 6-8**.

10.   Optionally, save your session parameters into a session file. This is useful if you've customized your session for specific needs or if you want to use the settings again.

Your new Windows Media audio file will have the **.wma** extension. You should play the file in your Windows Media Player to make sure everything went well. Click Play Output File in the Encoding Results box to hear your work.

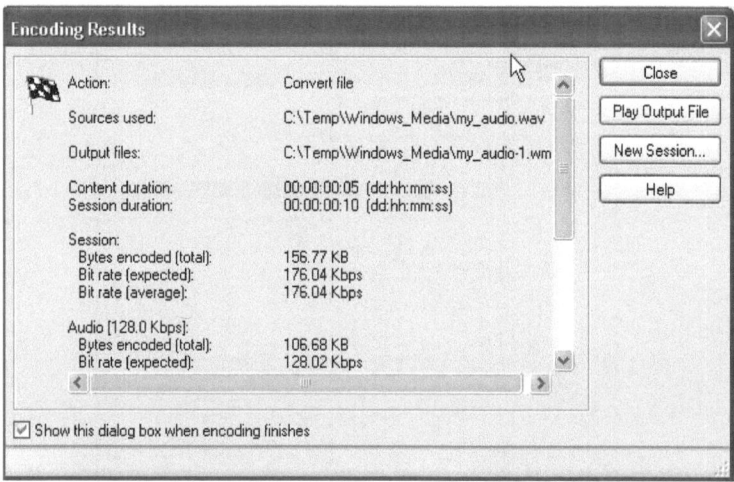

Figure 6-8
Review the results of your work by clicking "Play Output File," which will load the file in Windows Media Player.

Inside the Industry

The Platform for Internet Content Selection (PICS) specification enables labels (metadata) to be associated with Internet content. Originally designed to help parents control content accessed by their children, PICS also facilitates other code signing, privacy, and other types of content labeling.

Encoding Video Step-by-Step

Many of the steps for encoding video via the New Session "Convert a file" wizard are similar to audio, with added parameters for video.

1. Open the Windows Media Encoder and select "Convert a file" in the Wizards tab of the New Session dialog box. (If the dialog does not appear, click the "New Session" button in the upper left.) Click OK.

2. In the File Selection box, click "Browse" next to the "Source file" text box to locate the AVI file to be encoded.

3. The "Output file" location is automatically updated when you locate your source file. Note that the file extension is "**.wmv**". Click Next.

4. In the Content Distribution box, select "Windows Media Server (streaming)." Click Next.

5. In the Encoding Options box, select the video quality of the encoded file, as shown in **Figure 6-9**. Note the numerous types of video. If your video falls into one of these categories, try using them. If you're unsure, or your audience is broad, "multiple bit rates video (CBR)" is the best choice.

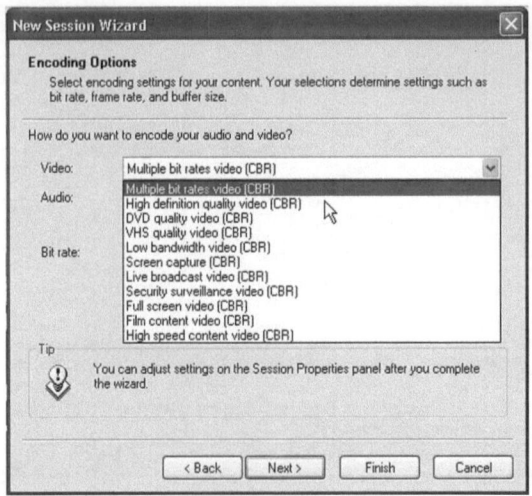

Figure 6-9
For on-demand video encoding, Windows Media Encoder offers several options. The safest is the default "multiple bit rates video (CBR)."

6.   Stay with the Encoding Options box, and select the audio quality of the encoded file. The options are similar to audio-only encoding.

7.   Stay with the Encoding Options box, and select the video bit rates for your encoded file, as shown in **Figure 6-10**. Note especially the frame rate and the output size. (See Frame Rate and Output Size in the Encoder below) Click Next.

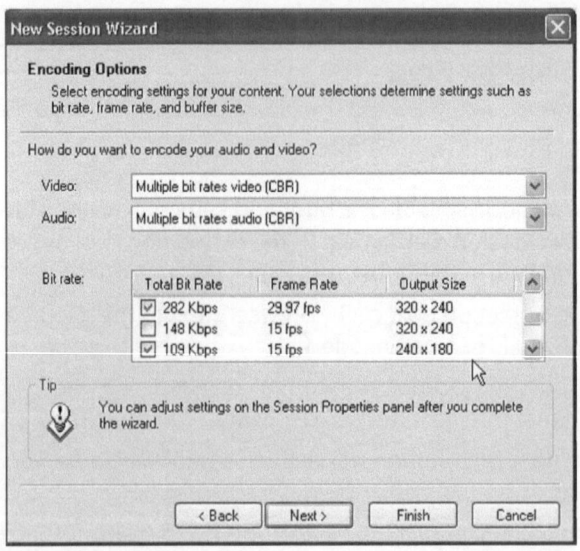

Figure 6-10
Select the bit rates for your encoded output file, taking note of the frame rate (frames per second) and the image size of the output file.

8. In the Display Information box, enter title, author, copyright, PICS rating, and description information for indexing purposes. Click Next

9. Review the settings, and click Finish to begin encoding, which may take several minutes, depending on the size of the file.

10. Review the Encoding Results box, and click Close to end the session or New Session to encode another file.

ALERT **Frame Rate and Output Size in the Encoder**

When you encode video via the New Session wizards, Windows Media Encoder will ask you to select a targeted bit rate with associated frame rates and image output size. If you look carefully, you'll notice the higher the bit rate (implying the targeted bandwidth of your user), the higher the frame rate. At the highest bandwidths, the frame rate, 29.97 frames per second, is the same as broadcast video. (The number is frequently rounded up to 30 fps.)

The pixel size of the video image, such as 320 × 240, is also larger as the bit rate increases. Smaller bit rates call for smaller image sizes, because there is less room in the bandwidth pipe to send the needed information.

Customize a Windows Media Encoder Session

At the end of each encoding session, Windows Media Encoder asked if you wanted to save your settings in a *session file*, which has the ".**wme**" extension. It's not necessary to save the session created through a wizard, because the settings are created automatically.

Author's Tip

Two-pass encoding is enabled by default for encoding on-demand or archived files.

However, if you modify settings created in a wizard to suit some specific needs, saving the session will save the headache of recreating the same parameters again and again. A customized session file can be used repeatedly in similar circumstances.

The following section looks at how to customize a session for specific needs and reuse over time.

If you have saved a session, open the session file by clicking File → Open and selecting the appropriate file with the **.wme** extension. Then click the Properties button, which opens the Properties panel.

If you have not saved a session, click the New Session button and select "Custom session" from the Wizards tab. The Properties panel opens automatically, as shown in **Figure 6-11**.

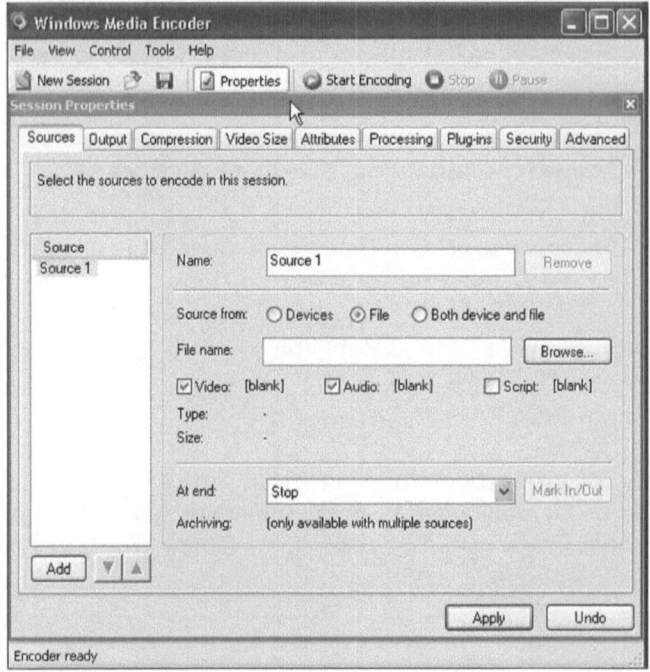

Figure 6-11
The Session Properties panel.

The following sections explain many of the options available for customizing an encoding session. Again, to keep things simple, the section assumes that you are encoding a source WAV or AVI for on-demand delivery via a streaming media server.

Sources — You can encode from one or more sources in a single encoding session. For example, if you want to apply the same encoding parameters to a number of files, list them as separate sources, and instruct the encoder in the "At end" drop-down to "Roll over to next source" when the previous source is complete.

The Sources tab also enables you to choose a device from which to capture audio or video, or gives you the option to choose from both devices and a file.

Output — The Output tab tells the encoder how you want to distribute the file. Overall, there are only two ways: live webcast or to a file, either for archiving or on-demand distribution. **Figure 6-12** shows selections for the on-demand option.

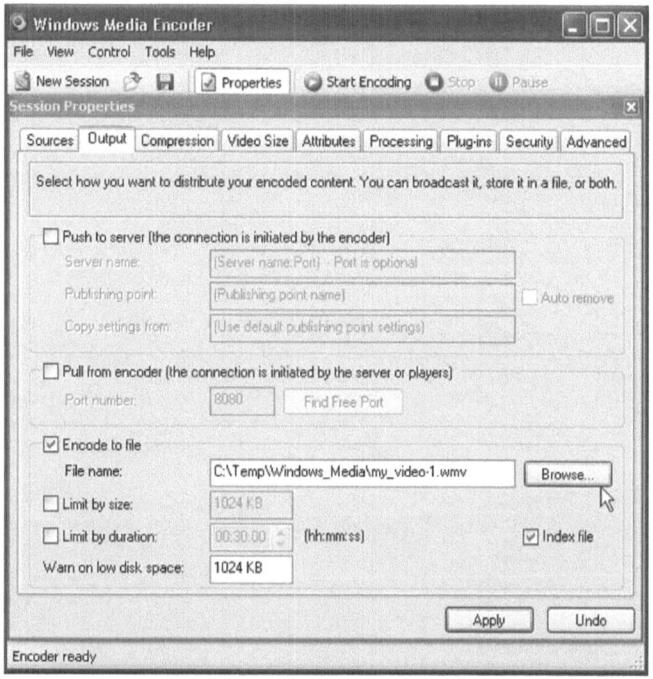

Figure 6-12
The Output tab of the Session Properties panel sets the output path of your encoded file. In this case, you're outputting to a file. The other options are related to live webcasting.

Note the indexing option, which is checked by default. By indexing the content, users can fast-forward or rewind through encoded files, making them easier to review.

Compression — The Compression tab is the heart of the encoder. It's also the place where you customize down to the smallest technical detail. As you'll see in **Figure 6-13**, many of the settings are familiar from the "Convert a file" wizard. Again, note the distribution method ("Destination") and quality choices (multiple bit rate, and so on) for audio and video. And note the target bit rates for multiple bit rate encoding. Because this section is focused on on-demand encoding, the figure shows "Two-pass encoding" checked, because it is not checked by default.

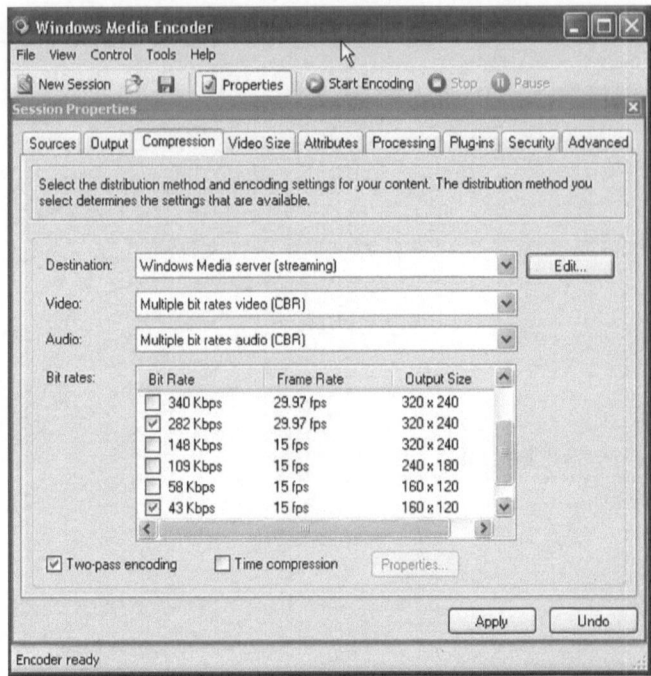

Figure 6-13
The Compression tab includes settings for codecs and bandwidth targets for encoded files.

Customizing Encoding Settings
Click the "Edit" button next to the Destination drop-down menu and a new box opens called *Custom Encoding Settings*, which enables you fine control of the codecs and their settings for each bandwidth target. You may select the mode, the specific codec, the source format of the video, and add custom bit rates.

For example, you may find yourself encoding a large number of video files for a customer who has very specific requirements for codec, image size, and bit rates. You can build a custom session for these requirements and export it in a Windows Media Encoder Profile. These profiles are stored in a file with the **.prx** extension. At a later session, you can import the profile in this dialog box with the import function.

In **Figures 6-14** and **6-15**, the operator is customizing settings for the output file targeted to 282 kbps. The "Audio format" drop-down contains numerous mono and stereo format selections of varying bandwidths. The operator can set a custom video size (remember to use a 4:3 ratio), frame rate (smaller rate means a smaller file, but jerkier motion), key frame interval (large for low action, small for high action), and the "smoothness" of the video, which adds or subtracts interpolated video information.

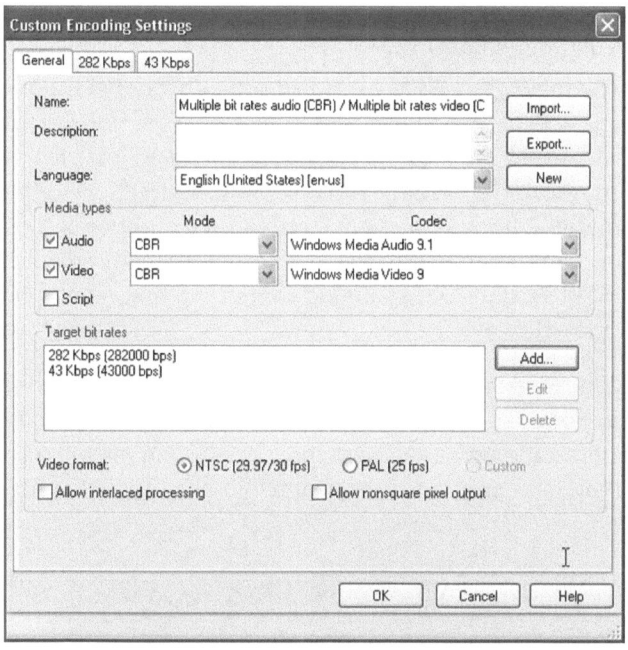

Figure 6-14
The Custom Encoding Settings dialog, accessed via the Compression tab in the Session Properties panel.

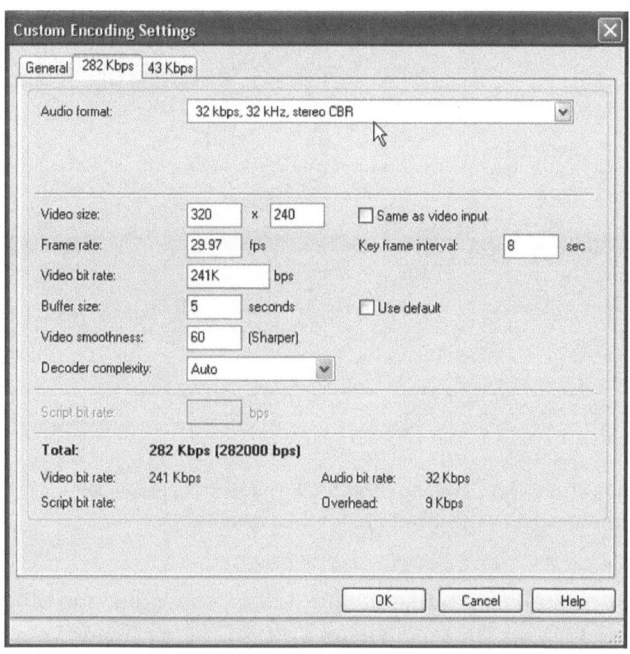

Figure 6-15
Customizing settings for an output file targeted to 282 kbps.

Video Size — The Video Size tab enables you to crop the video image to specific sizes, as shown in **Figure 6-16**. However, it's better to size the video to your final output size during the capturing and optimization process. Resizing video during the encoding process risks additional artifacts that may compromise final quality.

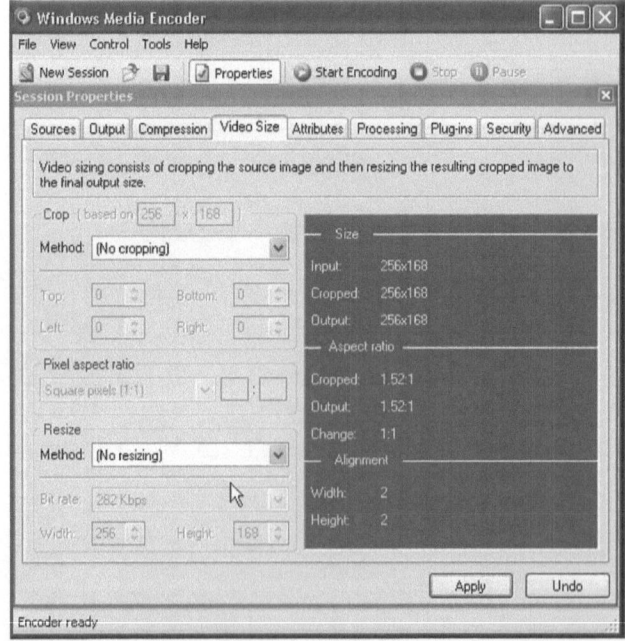

Figure 6-16
The Video Size settings allow you to change the final image size. However, it's recommended you encode to the same image size as the input file for best quality.

Attributes — In the Attributes tab, you edit title, author, copyright, and other information that describes the encoded file, as shown in **Figure 6-17**. You also can add your own attributes, perhaps for an internal catalog.

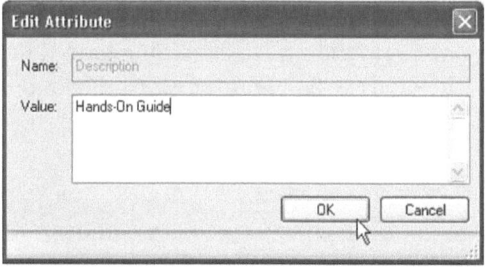

Figure 6-17
Set identifying attributes for your audio or video in the Attributes tab. You can add customized attributes as well.

Processing — The Processing tab, as shown in **Figure 6-18**, features settings that process video using some of the techniques discussed in Chapter 5, Optimizing Your Audio and Video. However, as with Video Size, its better to perform these procedures during the optimization process than in the encoding process. In other words, let the encoder encode, and let specialized audio and video processing tools do their jobs.

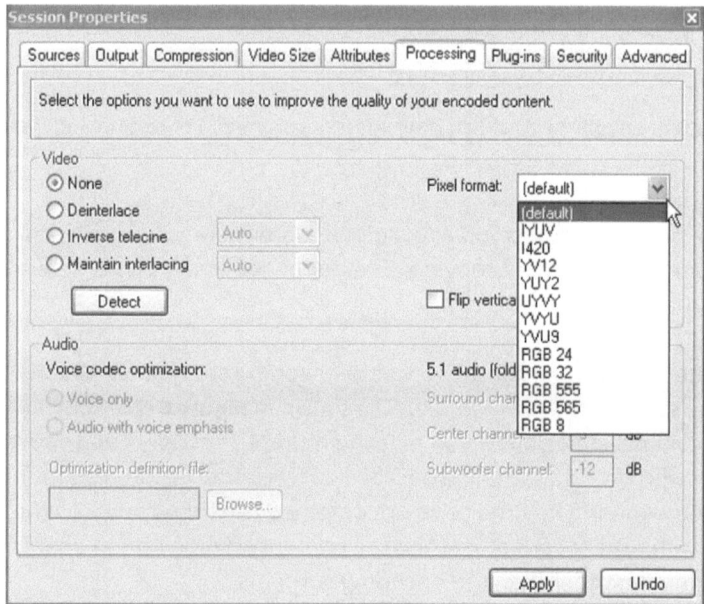

Figure 6-18
The Processing tab contains settings such as inverse telecine and deinterlacing, with the selection of pixel formats displayed. However, it's recommended that you process audio and video in the source file, rather than use the encoder for processing.

Plug-Ins — Plug-ins are specialized tools written by developers to accomplish specific tasks. They are generally used in highly specialized or unique situations. When you click the Register button, as shown in **Figure 6-19**, Windows Media Encoder shows you the available plug-ins, and lets you install them. Use plug-ins with caution.

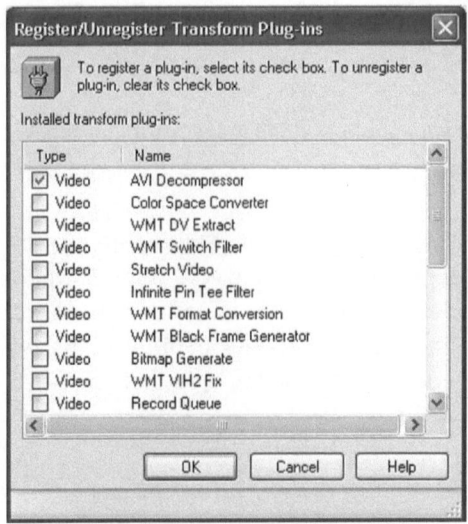

Figure 6-19
Developers can create highly specialized plug-ins for customized encoding and install them via the Plug-Ins tab.

Security — The Security tab lets you add a digital watermark to your streaming media content to prevent unauthorized copying. Security is discussed in more detail in Chapter 11, Going Beyond the Desktop.

Advanced — The Advanced properties for your encoding session refer really to several items that don't seem to fit anywhere else, as shown in **Figure 6-20**. You can give your encoder a specific name, especially if you're using multiple encoders and you need to identify a problem later with one of them. The packet size limitation is primarily for network and bandwidth management. The time code option embeds a time code into the file to allow easier seeking within an encoded file. And the content storage option enables you to archive content to a computer other than the encoding computer.

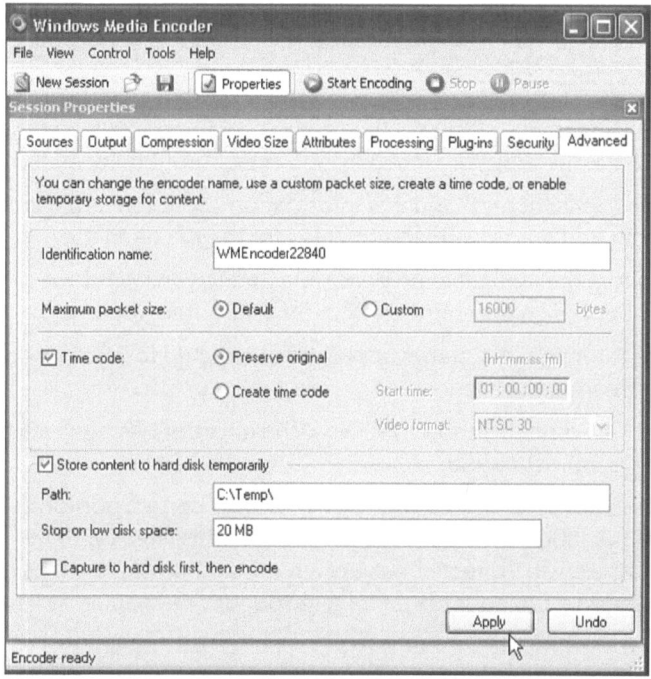

Figure 6-20
The Advanced tab in the Session Properties panel.

Author's Tip

Monitoring an Encoding Session

Windows Media Encoder includes a feature that enables you to monitor the progress of an encoding session and control outside devices. The feature is most useful during certain types of live encoding sessions, but you can also watch the progress of encodes for large files. The Monitor is divided into several panels, as shown in **Figure 6-21**.

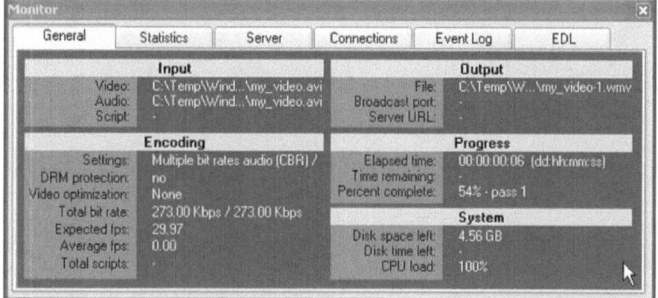

Figure 6-21
The Monitor panel lets you keep an eye on the encoder's activities.

(continued)

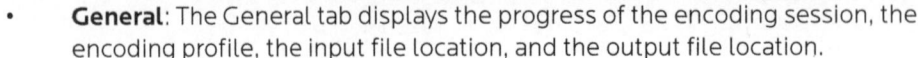
- **General**: The General tab displays the progress of the encoding session, the encoding profile, the input file location, and the output file location.

- **Statistics**: The Statistics tab updates information about the audio input and output, the video input and output, and the bit rates for the encoded file.

- **Server**: Monitors the status of servers connected to your Windows Media Encoder and the number of players connected to the distributed streams.

- **Connections**: Monitors the status of players connected to your encoder during certain live streaming scenarios.

- **Event Log**: The Event Log shows you what the encoder has been doing, which can be useful for troubleshooting.

- **EDL**: Edit Decision Lists enable you to encode only certain portions of a tape you mark via the tape's time stamp. The EDL features works with the encoder's device control, allowing direct control of a recording device, such as a VTR. Check the Windows Media Encoder Help File and your device manual for more specific information.

Windows Media Encoder Utilities

Windows Media Encoder comes with a number of utilities for working with encoded files. They allow simple editing, modification of attributes, and direct editing of encoder profiles (**.prx** files), and splitting or combining streams.

Windows Media File Editor

Windows Media File Editor enables you to edit a Windows Media file with a **.wmv**, **.wma**, or **.asf** extension, as shown in **Figure 6-22**. You can trim extraneous material from the beginning or end, change attributes, such as the title, and add markers and script commands. You also can import and export header files, which store information about the file, if you want to reuse edits in other encoded files.

Files edited with Windows Media File Editor are automatically indexed at each key frame. You cannot edit an encoded file protected with a digital rights management (DRM) watermark.

Author's Tip

Making Your Encoded Audio or Video More Dynamic

Script commands are specific actions associated with a designated time in an encoded file. These can make a simple audio or video file a more robust interactive and dynamic experience. Following are a few options:

- **Captions**: Captions added to video images and displayed in the player offer an opportunity to impart more information. Users must enable captions in their player for the text to be visible.

- **Closed captioning**: Most good capture cards support closed captioning, which is important for meeting regulations for serving disabled persons. You can encode the closed captioning directly into your Windows Media files.

- **URLs**: You can tell the Windows Media Player to open a user's browser and display a webpage at a specific point. This works best when using a standalone player, as opposed to a player embedded in a webpage.

- **Custom script commands**: These are useful for complex presentations, and require knowledge of scripting languages. They also work in tandem with Windows Media announcement (**.asx**) files, also called metafiles. Check the Windows Media Encoder Help file and the Windows Media 9 Series Software Development Kit (SDK) for more information.

Scripts are a source type you add when setting up your encoding session. It is done only in the Sources tab of the Properties panel.

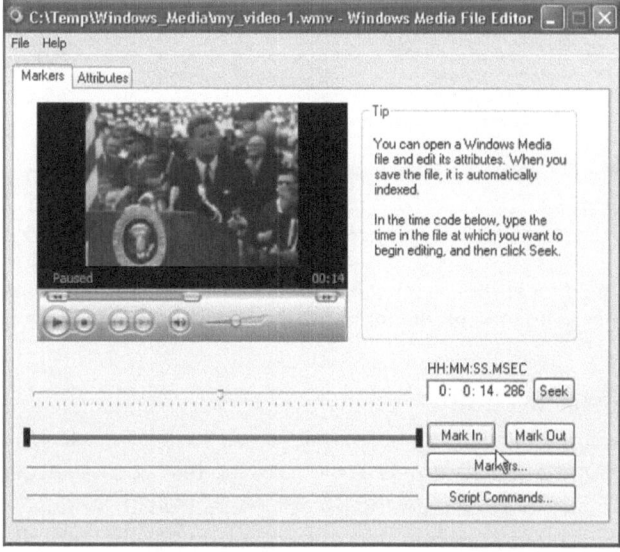

Figure 6-22

Windows Media File Editor enables simple editing of encoded files and modification of file attributes, such as title, author and copyright.

Windows Media Profile Editor

You may have created special Windows Media Profiles (**.prx** files) to store encoding information you use over and over. Windows Media Profile editor enables you to edit these profiles directly, instead of going through the encoder, as shown in **Figure 6-23**. You can change the codec, target bit rates, and bit rate modes, and save the changes to a new profile.

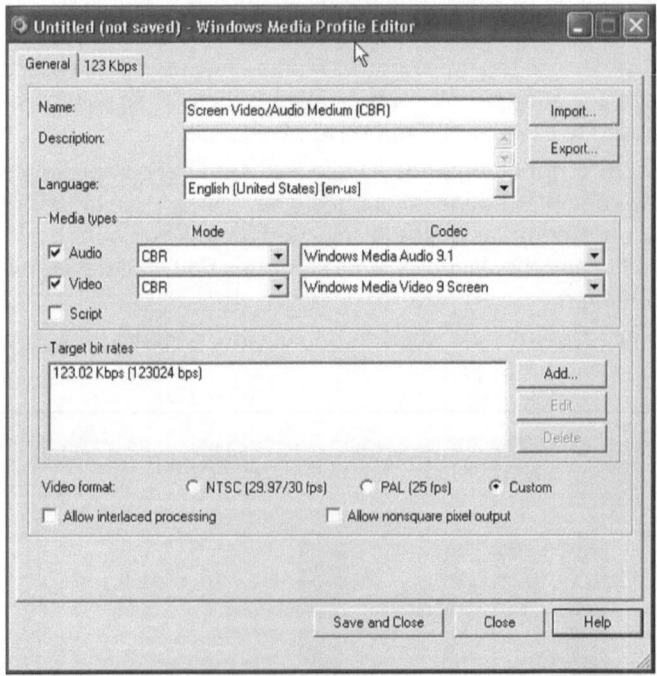

Figure 6-23
Windows Media Profile Editor allows direct editing of encoding profiles (**.prx** files). Note the tab next to the General tab. You can edit the profile for each bit rate in your profile as well.

Windows Media Stream Editor

Windows Media Stream Editor splits or combines streams in Windows Media files to create one or more output files for a new audience. One task you can accomplish is adding language support to a file, allowing users to select which language to listen to while watching a video. However, when you add a new or different language to a file, all the encoding parameters, such as codecs and bit rates, must be the same as the original encoded file.

Windows Media Encoder on the Command Line
Advanced users of Windows Media Encoder can set-up batch files or scripts to encode one or dozens of source files by using the encoder's command line functions. Scripts can also be written to start an encoding process at a specific time, such as in the wee hours when other resources are idle. Here are a few examples of command line calls and switches:

Simple AVI input to WMV output: cscript.exe wmcmd.vbs –input C:\my_video.avi –output C:\my_video.wmv

Encode all files in a folder: cscript.exe wmcmd.vbs –input C:\my_source_files –output C:\my_encoded_files

To use a custom profile: cscript.exe wmcmd.vbs –input C:\my_video.avi -output C:\my_video.wmv -loadprofile C:\my_profile.prx

For more information about using the encoder as a command line tool, view the Windows Media Encoding Script Help file installed with Windows Media Encoder 9 Series.

Other Utilities

The following Windows Media utilities are available for download from the Microsoft website at *http://www.microsoft.com/windows/windowsmedia/9series/encoder/utilities.aspx*.

Windows Media Audio 9 Lossless to PCM Converter — The Lossless to PCM Converter is a command line tool that converts files encoded using the Windows Media Audio 9 Lossless codec back to the original PCM WAV format.

Windows Media Mono to Multichannel Wave Combiner 9 Series — The Mono to Multichannel Wave Combiner command line tool combines 2, 6 or 8 mono WAV files into an audio-only AVI file that can be used as a source with the Windows Media Encoder 9 Series. This tool gets you around the size limitation of **.wav** files.

Windows Media Audio 9 Professional Channel Mask Mapping Tool — Another command line tool, the Channel Mask Mapping Tool remaps the channel mask of a multichannel Windows Media surround-sound file to support different channel configurations. The tool converts among traditional, home theater, and widescreen mapping in 4.0, 5.1 and 7.1 audio configurations.

Windows Media 9 Video Compression Manager (VCM) — A special version of the Windows Media 9 codec, the Video Compression Manager (VCM) enables earlier versions of encoding and editing applications to support the Windows Media Video 9 codec in AVI files. The VCM also allows .wmv files encoded with 9 Series codecs to be played in Windows Media Player 6.4.

Plug-in for Adobe Premiere 6.5 (Beta) — The Adobe Premiere 6.5 Plug-in adds import and export support for Windows Media 9 Series, including high resolution video up to 720p. Note that the latest version of Premiere is 7.0, later reconfigured to Premier Pro 1.5.

Conclusion

You have now prepared your material for distribution to your audience. In this chapter, you learned the fundamentals of codecs and how to select the right codec for your audience. You encoded audio and video source files into Windows Media Audio and Windows Media Video files. You learned how to customize an encoding and reviewed some of the utilities available for advanced Windows Media encoding and file management. In the next chapter, you'll begin exploring distribution strategies for your streaming media files.

CHAPTER 7

Getting Ready to Distribute Windows Media Streams

Now you're ready to take on the distribution of your newly encoded material over the Internet. Up to now, you've focused primarily on the client side of the equation, such as choosing the right codecs that will best reach your audience. In this chapter and the next, you'll learn about the server side. This chapter discusses:

- Whether or not you need to own/operate a streaming server
- How to get ready to serve your streams

Do You Need a Streaming Server?

In some ways, serving streaming media is the biggest challenge facing a streaming producer. You will have to work closely with the people who manage your organization's network resources, and they may have little or no experience with streaming media. Streaming media is a demanding technology, especially on *bandwidth*, which is the amount of data that can be transmitted over a network per second. Network and system administrators in organizations large and small have to balance all the demands made on a network, and streaming can throw their systems out of kilter. Hopefully, you've explained your plans to your IT department, so they can prepare for the day when you deliver your content. It's important to have them on your side throughout the process.

On the other hand, you may decide that your network can't handle streaming. Maybe the network expertise you need isn't available in-house. Perhaps you don't have enough bandwidth for the traffic you expect. You have another option: *outsourcing*.

Outsourcing to a Streaming Media Hosting Service

Most small to medium-sized businesses contract with a hosting company or their Internet service provider (ISP) to host their websites. The ISP handles all the files and processes that make a site work, such as HTML files, databases, programs that make the site dynamic, and so on.

Many hosting companies and ISPs offer streaming media services. Web hosting has evolved a standard set of options, such as web serving, e-mail accounts, and credit card order processing. However, streaming services vary wildly from one hosting company to another. Some offer none. Others offer everything. Furthermore, a few companies have sprung up that are devoted exclusively to streaming media hosting and delivery. The industry of streaming media hosting is something of a wilderness at the moment, but it has definite staying power, given the background trends.

Is outsourcing streaming media hosting a good option for you? Review your audience analysis and your assessment of internal resources. If the two seem out of balance, and it seems impractical in terms of time and/or money to bring them into balance by adding internal capacity, outsourcing streaming media hosting and delivery is a viable option.

What Hosting Companies Can Do For You

The most important benefit of a hosting contract is peace of mind. You'll rest easy because the hosting company is taking care of important variables that could make or break the success of your streaming project. This is especially true if you plan to stream audio or video to a consumer audience. All you have to do is supply the content.

Hosting companies offer another important advantage: Cost control. If you contract out hosting, you don't have to spend the money to upgrade your network and systems infrastructure. Your upgrade could be as simple as adding streaming services to your current web hosting arrangement. Your monthly or quarterly charge goes up by a few percentage points, and you get all the streaming capacity you need. Because you pay a set amount per month or quarter, your streaming costs are more predictable, and budgeting is easier.

If you prefer to go with a streaming media hosting specialist, expect to purchase an account based on key streaming variables, notably storage space for files and the amount of data transferred per month, which is another way of talking about bandwidth. The more you need, the higher the cost, though economies of scale play a role in lowering unit costs. In addition, streaming specialists may offer encoding services, priced on a per minute basis. The longer an audio or video program, the more you pay. However, the process becomes much easier and simpler for the customer. (Common pricing by streaming specialists is shown in **Table 7-1**.) You drop off a Beta SP or DV tape; they encode it, host it, and deliver it.

Other advantages of outsourcing include:

- **Security**: Hosting companies make security a top priority or they're out of business.
- **Dedicated infrastructure**: Streaming specialists and some web hosting companies optimize their networks for the unique demands of streaming. They design fault tolerant systems, that is, if one piece fails, another piece automatically jumps in to take over, meaning little if any interruption in service.
- **Advanced technology**: Hosting companies have to keep up with the latest technological developments or they risk falling behind competitors. This means you don't have to worry about buying the latest and greatest versions of everything every year or so.

Table 7-1 shows a pricing sample for selected streaming media encoding and hosting components offered by streaming media specialists. Caveat emptor: Use this table for your own rough guesswork only. Actual pricing formulas vary wildly among providers. You should also expect to pay setup charges for some or all of these services.

Encoding per format per bit rate	
Media length	Rate per minute
0 to 30 minutes	$5.00 – $10.00
30 to 60 minutes	$2.50 – $7.50
More than 60 minutes	$1.00 – $3.50
Media storage	
Total amount	Rate per megabyte
Up to 1 gigabyte	$.05 – $.10
Up to 500 gigabytes	$.03 – $.07
Up to 1,000 gigabytes	$.01 - $.07
Data transfer	
Total amount	Rate per gigabyte
Up to 1 gigabyte	$10.00 – $15.00
Up to 500 gigabytes	$4.50 – $7.50
Up to 1,000 gigabytes	$3.00 – $7.00

Table 7-1
Common monthly pricing for streaming media services.

Reasons to Avoid Outsourcing

The main thing you give up when you outsource is control. You are handing over an important part of your communications strategy, as well as tangible assets in the form of media files to others. Granted, a hosting company has a compelling interest in providing good service and in helping you succeed, but ultimately you have the responsibility to ensure they can deliver your streams to your audience in a way that meets your goals. It can be as simple as clicking your stream links once a day to make sure they work. Keep your hosting provider up-to-date on your needs and expectations, and monitor its performance.

How to Shop for Streaming Media Hosting

Shopping for streaming media hosting is just like anything else. Review your audience analysis and develop some criteria for deciding whether a hosting provider can meet your needs. Then call around. The following questions will get you started:

1. Do you support Windows Media?
2. What is the range of your services? End-to-end? Encoding only? Hosting only?
3. What is your streaming media infrastructure? Do you have redundant backup systems? Load balancing? What is your stream capacity?
4. Do you offer Digital Rights Management (DRM) services?
5. What Windows Media security features do you offer?
6. How often do you upgrade your streaming servers?
7. Do you offer any uptime (service availability) guarantees or service level agreements (SLA)?
8. What production facilities do you have? Do you offer live encoding at remote locations?
9. How much streaming experience do you have?
10. Can you show me a client list and references?
11. Can you report streaming media traffic?
12. Can you create customized webpages or embedded players?
13. Can you support advertising features, such as streaming ad insertion or banner ads?
14. What kind of customer support do you offer?

Get Ready to Serve Your Streams

Even if you decide not to host your own Windows Media streams, it's a good idea to familiarize yourself with some of the factors that affect stream distribution. This will help you speak intelligently about the process to your IT department or your streaming media hosting provider.

Hardware

It's important to remember that for servers, memory and disk input/output efficiency is more important than the power of the processor. Following are some suggested requirements for server hardware:

Minimum:

- 2.8 GHz HyperThread processor
- 1 GB RAM
- Fast disk I/O (e.g., SATA, ATA133, SCSI)
- 100 MB NIC

Recommended:

- 3.4 GHz HyperThread processor
- 2 GB double-data rate (DDR) RAM
- Multiple-disk configuration with the operating system on one drive, and streaming media content on the other.
- Fastest I/O disk available (10,000 RPM SATA or SCSI), with OS drive mirrored and data drive with RAID configuration.
- Dual-homed NIC with GigE connection.

The administrator should also disable all unneeded services on the server, such as virus scan and disk defragmentation. Because these services require disk access, they could cause input/output errors when serving large streaming files.

 ALERT   As you work with your network and server administrator, make sure you discuss issues such as load balancing and failover plans in case your streaming server fails. As always, it's best to have redundant systems.

Security

Computer viruses are among the biggest headaches of the Internet age. Most of us have experienced the malicious lines of code that invade our desktop computers, corrupt files, and erase hard drives. Criminal coders also attack servers, and streaming servers are no exception. However, security issues in the streaming world go far beyond self-protection. And they can even be a handicap to the delivery of your streams to the end user.

Firewalls — A computer firewall takes its name from a barrier that protects something valuable from something dangerous on the other side. In an automobile, the firewall protects people from a catastrophic failure in the engine compartment. Computer firewalls typically limit the kinds of Internet data that can pass into and out of an internal network. Most network administrators think of the Internet as a dangerous wilderness full of virtual beasts that could attack at any time. For them, a firewall is like a castle wall with limited access points, allowing only certain kinds of information in or out.

Firewalls cause the greatest heartache in the streaming world, because most firewalls are configured out of the box to reject streaming media. The nature of the back and forth communication between the media player and server, and the types of protocols and packets exchanged are usually problematic to firewalls. People behind a firewall at government organizations and large corporations are the most frequent victims of firewall issues; System administrators are correctly trying to limit access in an effort to thwart invaders. However, with a little bit of persuasion and elbow grease, firewalls and system administrators can be trained to safely allow streaming media data.

Here are some methods of coping with firewalls.

- **HTTP cloaking**: Most firewalls allow data packets that use the HTTP protocol, the protocol for webpages. If you are sending streams to others you think are behind a firewall, consider using *http cloaking*, which wraps data packets in a kind of HTTP envelope. The packets may get past the firewall, though the user experience may not be as good as it would be without cloaking. But at least they're getting the audio or video.

- **Special server location**: It's just unnatural for streaming media servers to live behind firewalls. They crave the freedom of the Internet because they need to communicate back and forth with media players. If you run a streaming server, ask your network administrator to put it in a *demilitarized zone*, or *DMZ*, as shown in **Figure 7-1**. In computer networking, a DMZ is a buffer zone just outside the firewall facing the stormy, unpredictable Internet "cloud." You have control of the streaming server, and it can talk freely to end users out in the wider world.

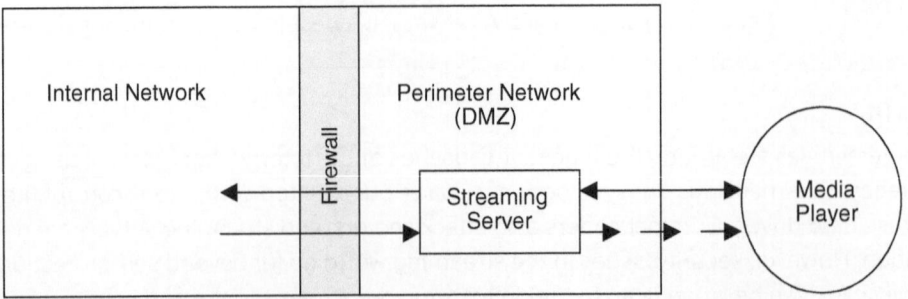

Figure 7-1
A typical network configuration with a "demilitarized zone," or DMZ. Administrators communicate with the streaming server from the internal network, while the streaming server communicates back and forth with one or more media players from the DMZ.

- **Education**: You should prepare yourself to educate end users, as well as network and system administrators, about configuring media players to work behind a firewall. Some networks may dedicate *ports*, a kind of virtual window through which streaming data travels. Or your network administrator may prefer to use a *proxy* server, which is a way to store Internet data for use by designated people. (Proxy servers are discussed in more detail in Chapter 8, Delivering Windows Media to Your Audience.) In each case, Windows Media Player settings need to be modified, as shown in **Table 7-2**.

Author's Tip

Letting Streams through Firewalls
Your network administrator may decide to allow streaming media data through your firewall. To do so, they must open specific *ports*, similar to a virtual window, in your firewall hardware and/or software. **Table 7-2** describes the protocol and the associated ports.

Protocol	Ports
MMS (TCP)	TCP port 1755
MMS (UDP)	UDP port 1755 and TCP port 1755
RTSP (TCP)	TCP port 554
RTSP (UDP)	UDP port 5005 and TCP port 554
HTTP	TCP port 80

Table 7-2
Protocols and associated firewall ports. If your network administrator decides to allow streaming media data, one or more of the above ports must be opened.

Streaming Protocols for Windows Media

Computer data has a kind of grammar, similar to human languages. When computers talk to each other across a network, they use a *communications protocol* or just *protocol*.

Computer programmers have come up with an alphabet soup of protocols. A few are directly related to streaming media. The protocols control the communications between the media player and the streaming server, and vice versa. **Figure 7-2** shows how one protocol works. During the data transfer, the player and server communicate with each other about network conditions and adjust the stream accordingly, especially if a file is encoded with multiple bit rates.

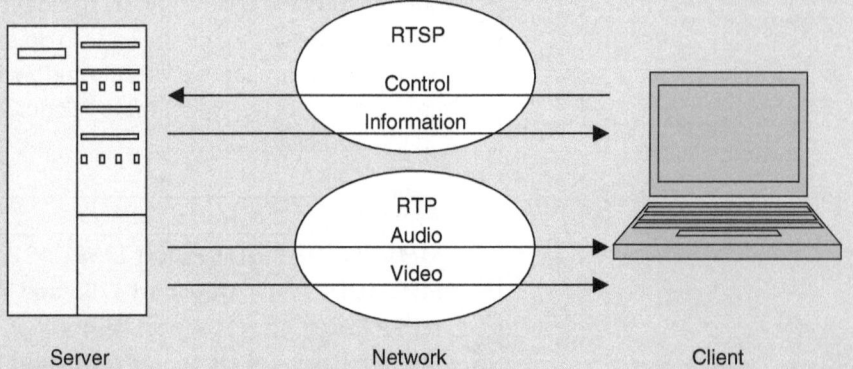

Figure 7-2
How the RTSP and RTP protocols work together. The client (Windows Media Player) requests data from the Windows Media Server, which sends audio and video.

Here's a list of protocols, plus a brief explanation:

- **User datagram protocol (UDP):** The UDP is one of the most common Internet protocols used for sending data in a continuous stream. It uses less error correction than another common Internet protocol, transmission control protocol (TCP), meaning fewer transmission delays.

- **Real-time streaming protocol (RTSP):** The RTSP is an open standard application-level protocol endorsed by the Internet Engineering Task Force (IETF), a body of prominent Internet engineers. Internet clients, in other words media players, use RTSP to talk to streaming servers, allowing features such as Play/Pause/Stop. You may see a URL starting with the letters "rtsp." That tells you the player will use RTSP to communicate with Windows Media Server.

- **Real-time transport protocol (RTP):** Streaming media servers build packets of data and send them off to the media player. The RTP (we're not sure what happened to the other "T") governs how the server constructs these packets. For example, RTP lays out rules for identifying the type of packet, how packets are numbered in sequence, and how they are stamped with the date and time. The architecture is similar to UDP and TCP, though RTP packets are meant to work specifically with the RTSP and RTCP protocols.

- **Real-time control protocol (RTCP):** The RTCP packets work with RTP packets to check the delivery of other packets. RTCP packets are often used to monitor the quality of service.

- **Microsoft Media Services (MMS):** Microsoft developed a proprietary streaming protocol, MMS, or Microsoft Media Services protocol. If you open a Windows Media announcement file, the first three letters of the streaming URL are usually "mms." Starting with Windows Media 9 Series, the server will stream to a Windows Media 9 Series player via RTSP, even if the declared protocol is MMS. Older players will still receive data via the MMS protocol.

- **Hypertext transfer protocol (HTTP):** Most kinds of data we see on the Internet, particularly webpages, use HTTP. Every time you see an "http" in a web address, you know it's using HTTP as the communications protocol. In streaming, HTTP is most often used for *progressive downloading*, sometimes called *pseudo-streaming*, because it doesn't have the control and data management features of "true" streaming protocols, such as RTSP. HTTP can also be used to stream in the more classic sense, if there are no web servers bound to port 80 in the server.

ALERT   Patching the Holes in Software

Most software has imperfections. Malicious programmers know this, and they relish the challenge of finding the problems and exploiting them. Microsoft releases code patches on a regular basis to plug holes hackers and others discover. Your server and network administrators are responsible for keeping your systems up-to-date. As a streaming producer, it's wise for you to keep an eye on Microsoft's website for news about its streaming products. When you see security warnings or patch announcements, notify your IT department.

Windows Media Player 10 Security

Streaming media is generally one of the most secure technologies on the Internet. That doesn't mean you shouldn't pay attention to security, and Windows Media Player 10 contains several advanced features for making sure malicious coders don't take advantage of your computer's vulnerabilities.

Network administrators may require special security settings in Windows Media Player to allow your users to view streaming content, especially if a proxy server is used. Before adjusting your player security settings, make sure you have downloaded and installed the latest Windows XP service pack from the Microsoft website. The service pack may contain updates specifically for Windows Media Player. And you should only play and download audio and video content, as well as install skins, visualizations, and plug-ins from websites you know and trust.

Here's an overview of the security features of Windows Media Player 10, as shown in **Figures 7-3 and 7-4**.

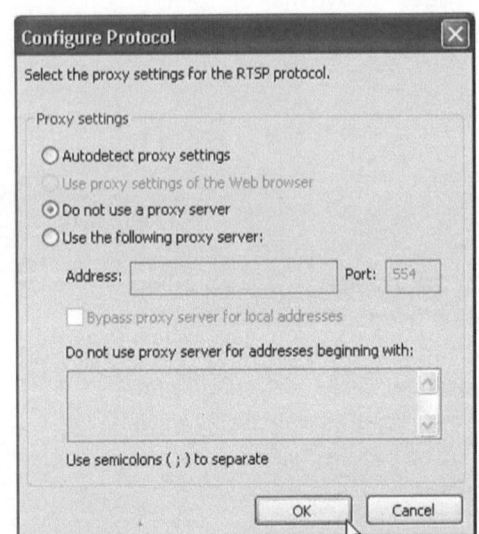

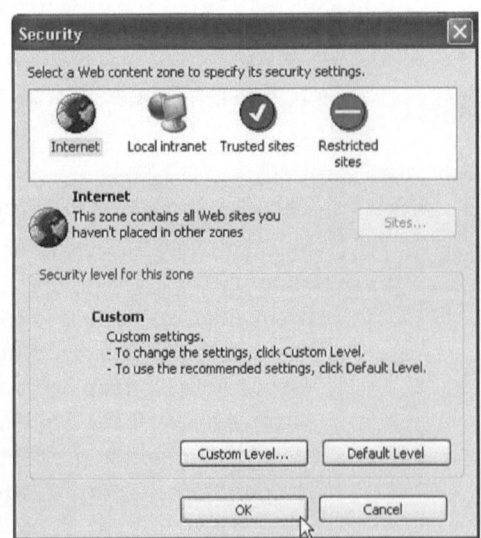

Figure 7-3
To change settings in Windows Media Player 10, go to Tools → Options and click the Network tab. To change proxy settings for a particular protocol, select the protocol and click the Configure... button. Your network administrator will supply the specific settings.

Figure 7-4
Some of the security features of Windows Media Player are similar to the features in Microsoft Internet Explorer.

To reach the settings, select Tools → Options and click the Security tab.

- **Run script commands when present**: This option tells the player whether to run *URL, FILENAME, or other* script commands when you play digital media content that contains them. For example, the media file may contain a command to open a certain webpage at a specified point. This option is turned off by default. Select this check box to enable script commands.

- **Do not run script commands and rich media streams if the player is running inside a webpage**: This option tells the player whether to run *URL, FILENAME, and other* script commands to run when you play digital media content embedded in a webpage via ActiveX controls. Embedded content may include HTML, Microsoft PowerPoint presentations, or streams. This option is turned off by default. Select this check box to prevent any script commands and rich-media streams from running in a webpage.

- **Do not prompt me before playing enhanced content that uses webpages**: This option tells the player to notify you when you are about to play digital media content enhanced with webpages. Because some webpages may contain malicious code, Windows Media Player will ask you to verify that you want to proceed. The prompt is enabled by default. To turn it off, select this box.

- **Zone Settings**: Clicking the "Zone Settings..." button in the Security tab opens the Internet Options Security dialog box, which closely resembles a similar box in Microsoft's Internet Explorer web browser. Internet Options Security lists zone settings that control which types of content can be displayed in the player, especially webpages. Changing these settings may affect the operation of the player or prevent information from being displayed. For more information about zones and zone settings, see the Help file in Internet Explorer.

- **Show local captions when present**: Synchronized Accessible Media Interchange (SAMI) is the Windows Media Player-supported method of captioning media content. Enabling local captions enables access to SAMI content in all of the content zones available to your computer, including CDs, DVDs and other distribution methods. Deselecting this option limits access to content delivered via the Internet. This option is cleared by default.

Other security features of Windows Media Player include:

- Support for "secure" webpages, primarily used for financial transactions or display of private data.

- Support for secure authentication protocols, such as Basic, NTLM, Digest, Kerberos, and Negotiate.

- Support for file format validation when files are renamed with different filename extensions in an attempt to trick you into downloading unwanted content. Windows Media Player verifies that the filename extension matches the format of the file. Formats that don't conform to naming conventions should be viewed with suspicion.

Authentication and Authorization in Windows Media Services

The Authentication and Authorization features of Windows Media Server control access to your content. These features are installed as plug-ins. You see these systems when producers want to limit access to special groups, such as subscribers. *Authentication* is the process of verifying who you say you are, while *authorization* is the process of giving you the right to view content based on that identity. More details on setup for these methods are available via the Windows Media Services Help files.

Authentication — Windows Media Services includes three methods of authenticating users—that is, ensuring that users are who they say they are.

1. **Anonymous User Authentication**: Anonymous authentication allows access without prompting users for a username and password. It means that you don't need a user to prove their identity. If you don't need to restrict access, use this authentication method. It's enabled by default.

2. **Negotiate Authentication**: If you plan to serve streams to users on your intranet only, and want to prompt for a username and password, use Negotiate Authentication.

3. **Digest Authentication**: If you want to prompt Internet users of your Windows Media Content for a username and password via Windows Media Services, use Digest Authentication. (This type of authentication is only available in enterprise and datacenter versions of Windows Server 2003.)

Authorization — The three authorization plug-ins in Windows Media Services allow you to restrict access to your content via access control lists or IP address. You enable these features at the server or the publishing point. (Publishing points are covered in more detail in Chapter 8.)

1. **NTFS ACL Authorization ACL (Access Control List)**: Authorization enforces access control via policies you set in your NTFS file system. Use this authorization when you want to limit access to some files or directories and not others. For example, once a user is authenticated, they may be authorized to view only certain files.

2. **Publishing Points ACL Authorization**: Publishing Points ACL Authorization is similar to the NTFS variety, although it limits access to content within one or more publishing points on a server.

3. **IP Address Authorization**: IP Authorization limits access via IP address. For example, you could limit access to a certain group of IP addresses on a company intranet.

It's important to note that most people password-protect their content via the web server rather than the streaming server. In other words, they protect access to the streaming URL, meaning you need special permission to click on the stream link. It's simpler than protecting the stream via the streaming server.

Digital Rights Management

We mentioned *digital rights management* or *DRM* in Chapter 6, Encoding for Windows Media, when we talked about encoding. Windows Media Services supports DRM on the server side as well. DRM is important to you if you want to prevent piracy of your media. Typical DRM features include:

- Strong encryption to prevent unauthorized use of content
- Producer-defined business rules for accessing content
- Content licensing verification (Are you authorized to view this file?)
- License auditing to allow tracking of royalty payments
- Support for nondesktop computer devices, such as handheld devices

See Chapter 11, Going Beyond the Desktop, for more information on DRM.

File Storage

Even though they're highly compressed, streaming media files take up more room than you might think, especially if you do a lot of encoding. If you plan to store and/or serve a large amount of video, you need very large hard drives, perhaps even whole networked systems devoted to file storage and retrieval. How much do you need? That depends on several factors, such as your encoding practices. Files encoded for dial-up delivery need less space than files delivered exclusively over a corporate LAN. See **Table 7-3** for some guidance.

Target Bandwidth	Audio	Video
56 Kbps modem	0.24 Megabytes/minute	0.25 Megabytes/minute
112 Kbps dual ISDN	0.47 Megabytes/minute	0.59 Megabytes/minute
Corporate LAN	0.70 Megabytes/minute	1.10 Megabytes/minute
256 Kbps DSL/cable modem	0.70 Megabytes/minute	1.65 Megabytes/minute
512 Kbps DSL/cable modem	0.70 Megabytes/minute	3.30 Megabytes/minute

Table 7-3
Use these per-minute figures to estimate the final sizes of encoded audio and video files. Multiply the length of the file in minutes by the number of megabytes per minute. If you use multiple bit rate encoding, add the figures for each type (audio or video) and bandwidth together. Always be conservative in your estimates.

Bandwidth

So far in this book, we've talked about bandwidth in the context of the end user. (Are they connecting with dial-up, DSL/cable, or by a corporate LAN?) The end user needs only enough bandwidth to view one audio or video stream. On the flip side of the coin, when you serve streams to your internal audience or the outside world, you think about bandwidth in terms of the aggregate number of simultaneous connections to your streaming server. In other words, if ten dial-up users connect to your streaming server, you'll need at least 600 kilobytes per second of outgoing bandwidth. (10 × 56 kbps = 560 kbps + 40 kbps [headroom] = 600 kbps.) You also have to take into account other activity on your network, such as e-mail and web browsing.

All this means is that you may have to add extra bandwidth capacity to your network, which can increase costs. Bandwidth is the single largest ongoing technical infrastructure expense in the streaming media delivery equation.

A quick review of how the client and the server work together will clarify things. Recall that the server sends continuous streams of data to the media player. Just like autos on an expressway need space to move smoothly and freely, data needs space in the form of bandwidth to travel. If too many autos try to get the freeway via the same on-ramp, you get a traffic jam. Data gets backed up or can't get through, and you get a frustrating user experience.

ALERT   A Stream's Overhead

A typical stream is more than just the audio and video data. Some of the data is control data or *overhead*, sometimes called *headroom*, exchanged by the player and server. For example, a 56K stream may reserve eight kilobytes per second for audio, 26 kbps for video, and 22 kbps for overhead.

How much bandwidth do you need? Go back to your audience analysis. Ask these questions:

- What's your best estimate of the peak number of connections you expect at a given moment? Ten? Hundreds? Thousands? This number is usually discussed using the term *simultaneous connections* or *simultaneous streams*.
- What streaming bit rates does your audience expect? Dial-up only? DSL/cable? Higher?

Use these two variables to calculate a rough estimate of the amount of bandwidth you need. For example, if you expect a peak of 100 simultaneous connections at 225 kbps (a common bit rate for DSL/cable connections), you'll need at least 2.25 megabytes of bandwidth—double the minimal figure for safety. Let your network administrator know you need at least 4.5 megabytes per second of outgoing bandwidth. Ask for as much bandwidth as you can get. You'll never have enough.

Unicasting and Multicasting

Most streaming media over the Internet follows a simple model: One stream for each client connection. This is called *unicasting*. It's the easiest model to grasp and implement, but it also uses the most bandwidth. What if you could get all your players to tap into a single stream? You'd need far less bandwidth. This is called *multicasting*, which requires a specially configured network, as shown in **Figure 7-5**. Ask your IT department if your network is multicast-enabled. If so, you may be able to add streaming capacity without drastically increasing your bandwidth consumption. It's unlikely, though, that you'll be able to multicast to audiences outside your internal network. The public Internet isn't set up for it.

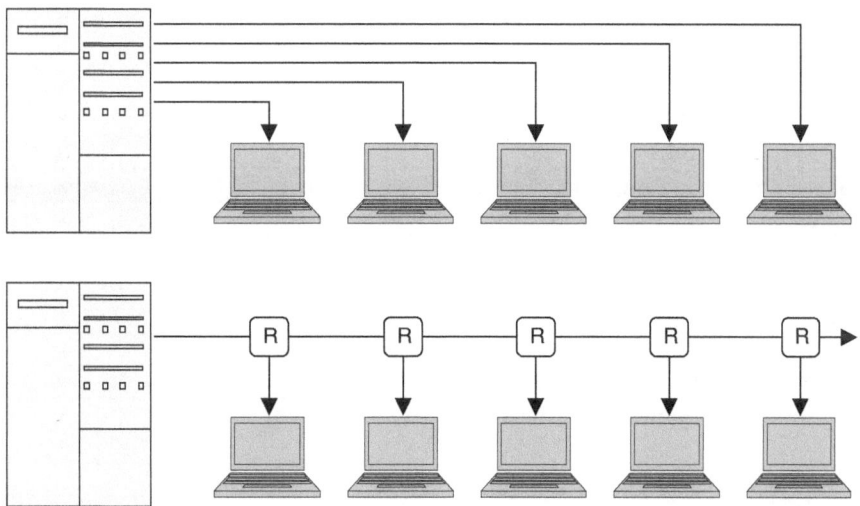

Figure 7-5
The unicasting and multicasting delivery models for streams. In unicasting, the server delivers as many streams as requested by as many clients as it can handle. In multicasting, the server delivers a single stream to multicast-enabled routers ("R" in the diagram), which allows clients to tap into the single stream.

Technical Support

Windows Media Services is bundled with Windows 2003 Server (and previous servers), which requires a license from Microsoft. Depending on your license, a certain level of Microsoft technical support is available to you. The level could range from an online archive of accumulated experience (*knowledgebase*) to a dedicated human being 24×7×365.

But what if you prefer not to call Microsoft or try to navigate their website? You have a few other options. There's a very good chance that someone else has experienced your problem. You might find a local user's group that has an online bulletin board where you can post questions. Several websites cater to technologists, and they include message board areas. Or, you can perform a global web search or a search of online newsgroups using the text of an error message. You'll be surprised by what turns up.

Inside the Industry

 Microsoft bundles Windows Media Services with Windows Server 2003 Standard, Enterprise and Datacenter editions. Some Windows Media features are only available with the Enterprise and Datacenter versions. **Table 7-4** shows the differences. For more information, visit Microsoft's website, *http://www.microsoft.com/server/*.

Feature	Standard	Enterprise, Datacenter
Absolute Playlist Time	X	X
Advanced Fast Start		X
Advanced FF/RW		X
Advertising Server Support	X	X
Broadcast Auto-Start	X	X
Cache/Proxy Server Support		X
Custom Plug-In Support		X
Event-Based Scripting Support		X
Fast Cache	X	X
Fast Reconnect	X	X
Fast Recovery		X
Fast Start	X	X
Fast Streaming	X	X
Internet Authentication Method (Digest)		X
Internet Group Management Protocol Version 3 (IGMPv3) support		X
Internet Protocol Version 6 Support	X	X
Intranet Authentication Methods (Negotiate Authentication, Anonymous Access)	X	X
Multicast Content Delivery		X
Multiple Authorization Methods (NTFS, ACL, IP Address)	X	X

Multiple Control Protocol Support (MMS, HTTP, RTSP)	X	X
Multiple Media Parser Support (Windows Media, MP3)	X	X
Multiple Playlist Parser Support	X	X
Play While Archiving		X
RTSP Streaming	X	X
Robust Event Notification	X	X
Server-Based Content Repacketization	X	X
Unicast Content Delivery	X	X

Table 7-4
Feature Sets for Windows Server 2003.

Conclusion

This chapter gave you the background to delve into the details of serving streaming media to your audience. You first learned whether the outsourcing of streaming media services might be a better choice for your needs. Then the book discussed some of the important considerations for choosing to serve content yourself, including security, file storage needs, and bandwidth needs. In the next chapter, you'll learn more details about actually publishing your streams.

CHAPTER 8

Delivering Windows Media to Your Audience

Chapter 7 offered some background about streaming media serving to help you understand some of the basics. This chapter goes into more step-by-step detail about publishing your work via a Windows Media Services. By the end of the chapter, you'll understand:

- The difference between HTTP streaming and "true" streaming
- How to install Windows Media Services
- More about publishing points
- How to use Windows Media Services Administrator
- The basics of testing and Windows Media Load Simulator

HTTP Streaming versus "True" Streaming

This book distinguishes between "true" streaming, which uses specialized streaming protocols, such as Microsoft Media Services (MMS), and a second type, called by various names, including *pseudo-streaming*, *progressive download*, or *HTTP streaming*. As the last name suggests, the second type of streaming uses the HTTP protocol. It's the same protocol web browsers use to communicate with web servers. The following discussion will use the term *HTTP streaming*.

How HTTP Streaming Works

With HTTP streaming, you treat your encoded file just like an HTML file or graphics file by putting it on your web server. You create a link to the encoded file in the same way you create a link to another webpage. The user clicks the link and the encoded media file starts to download. As it downloads, it starts the media player, which plays the file as it comes through. In many cases, the user experience with HTTP streaming is virtually the same as "true" streaming.

To make this work, ask your system administrator to configure your web server to understand the *MIME type* associated with Windows Media. (MIME [multipurpose Internet mail extensions] types are expressed as file extensions, which a software client, usually a web browser, uses to decide how to render an incoming file.) All they have to do is add the following listing to the web server's MIME area in its configuration file:

```
video/x-ms-asf
```

(Even though it says "asf," it will work for files with the extensions **.wma** and **.wmv**.)

Your system administrator may need to make other changes. One advantage to HTTP streaming is that you can put your Windows Media files on the same machine as your web server, eliminating the need for a second, dedicated streaming server. But for HTTP streaming to work properly, your administrator should install a separate network interface card (NIC) with its own IP address and port for use by Windows Media Services. Otherwise they'll both try to use port 80 on the same card, which will create a bottleneck.

Alternatively, the administrator can assign a different port to Windows Media Services, or they can assign multiple IP addresses to the same NIC. Check your server Help files for specific instructions on assigning IP address and ports to server applications.

The Problems with HTTP Streaming

Problems may crop up for your users if you choose HTTP streaming. First, they may notice poorer performance, such as dropped frames or unexpected stops after a certain amount of playback time.

Second, if large numbers of people request the stream all at once, your network could be easily swamped. Web servers, unlike streaming servers, typically don't know how to manage the bandwidth allocated to them. You also miss out on such features as multiple bit rate encoding, because web servers can't detect network connection speed. Therefore, they don't know when to serve a high-bandwidth or low-bandwidth version of your stream. In addition, the server can't adjust the stream quality based on changes in network conditions, and users also lose the options of fast-forward and rewinding streams.

HTTP streaming is a good option under these circumstances:

- Your audio/video files are less than 60 seconds in length
- You expect a minimal number of simultaneous requests
- You encode with only one bit rate
- You need on-demand access only (web servers can't serve live streams)

The Advantages of "True" Streaming

As discussed, "true" streaming relies on specialized network transport protocols, which are supported by streaming servers, not web servers. The protocols enable the client and server to speak to each other and adjust to *net weather*, the dynamic network conditions that pervade the Internet and even some internal networks. The final result is better network performance, more efficient use of resources, and a higher-quality user experience. Use a streaming server under these circumstances:

- Your encoded files are more than 60 seconds long
- You expect more than a minimal amount of simultaneous connections
- You plan multiple bit rate encoding
- You may stream live events some time in the future.
- You want consistent performance for long files
- You need intelligent management of your outgoing bandwidth

Install Windows Media Services

Before you can install Windows Media Services, including Windows Media Server, you need access to a Windows Server, preferably Windows Server 2003 or later. You also need administrator privileges to install new software. Make sure the system is fully updated with all Microsoft patches, including security patches, before installing the media server.

Here's the procedure for installing Windows Media Services:

1. Click Start → Control Panel → Add/Remove Programs.
2. Click Add/Remove Windows Components.
3. In the "Windows Components" dialog box, highlight the Windows Media Services checkbox, as shown in Figure 8-1.
4. In the "Windows Components" dialog box, click the "Details..." button, as shown in **Figure 8-1**.

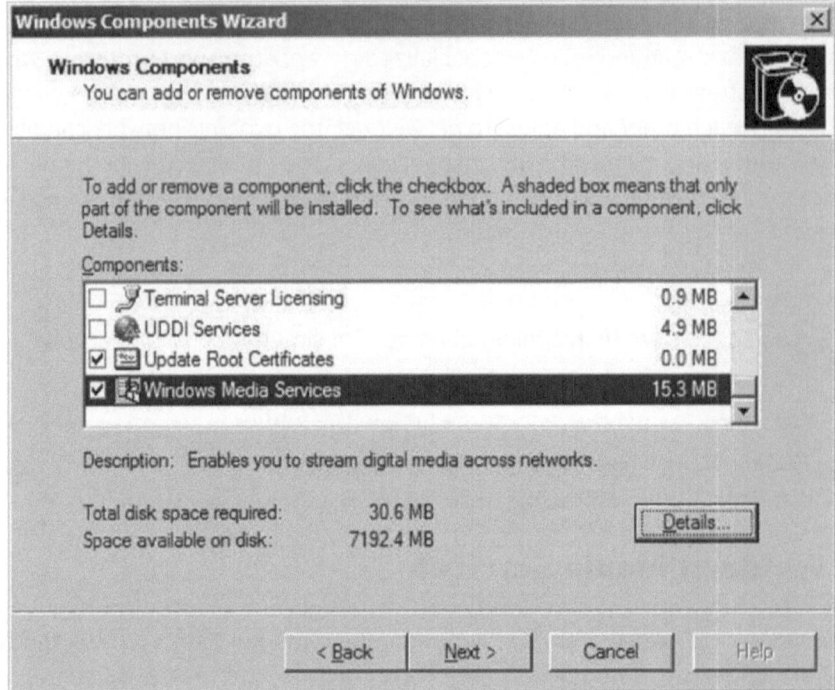

Figure 8-1
In the "Windows Components" dialog, highlight "Windows Media Services" and click Details to install all components.

5. In the new dialog box, check all four boxes. If a warning message appears, such as the message in **Figure 8-2**, click OK. (You may be prompted at some point in install Internet Information Services 6.0)

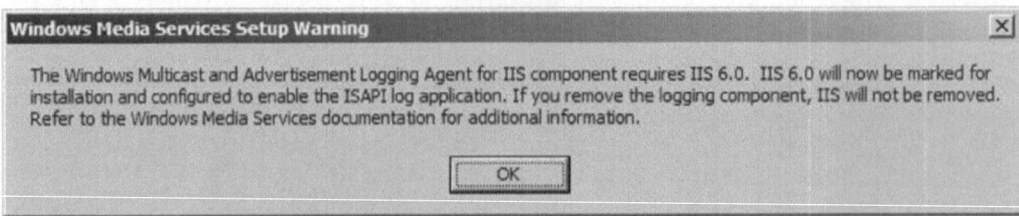

Figure 8-2
This warning may appear when you check options in the Windows Media Services Details box. You can safely click OK, though you may be asked to install other components.

6. Click OK in the Details box.
7. When prompted, insert the Windows Server CD-ROM into your CD-ROM drive, and click OK.

8.   In the "Completing Windows Components Wizard" box, click Finish.

To access the media services administrative tools, click Start → Programs →
Administrative Tools → Windows Media Services.

Publishing Points

Chapter 1, Windows Media Series Quick Start, contained a quick tutorial about how to create
a publishing point via the Publishing Point wizard in Windows Media Services. As you'll
recall, a publishing point is a virtual directory in Windows Media Server that refers to the
real directory where your encoded files reside, usually *c:\WMPub*. If you haven't created
a publishing point, review the Chapter 1 tutorial to create and configure a new publishing
point. Once created, the listing will look similar to the listing in **Figure 8-3**.

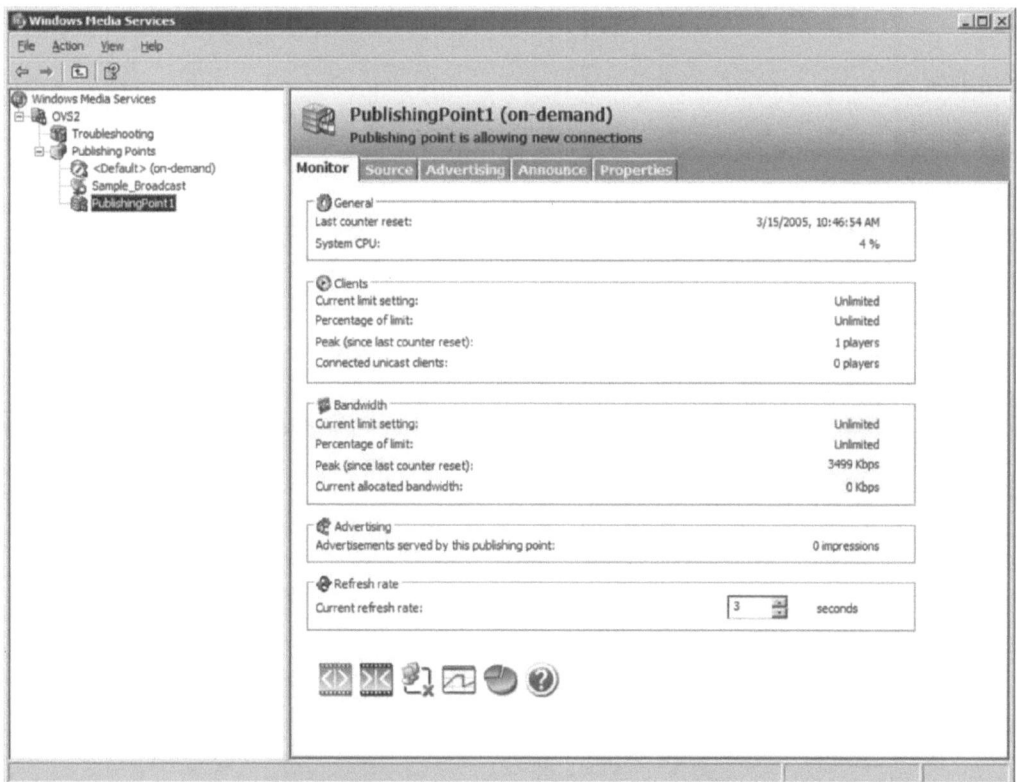

Figure 8-3
Your publishing point, called PublishingPoint1 in this example, is a virtual directory pointing to the
location of your Windows Media files, usually c:\WMPub.

Using Windows Media Services Administrator

Now that you've set-up your publishing point, you'll examine the Windows Media Services Administrator in more detail. It is the console in Windows Server 2003 for controlling the configuration of Windows Media Server and accompanying features.

To open the Administrator, click Start → Programs → Windows Media Services. Open the directory trees in the left panel until you find "PublishingPoint1" (or the name you gave your publishing point) to display the console. Click each tab (Monitor, Source, Advertising, Announce, and Properties) to display the data and features.

Monitor

The Monitor in Windows Media Services Administrator gives you a snapshot of your publishing point status, as shown in **Figure 8-4**. The values are based in part on configuration settings in other tabs, which are discussed in the following pages. The Monitor tells you if you need to change these values. For example, you may find that the percentage of bandwidth used by streams is very near the bandwidth you allocated. You may need to increase the allocated bandwidth to ensure you don't exclude people who want to see your streams and ensure that you haven't created an audio and/or video data transfer bottleneck.

The refresh rate refers to the frequency statistics that are updated in the Monitor. The icons at the bottom perform the following functions: Allow new unicast connections, Deny new unicast connections, Disconnect all clients, Reset all counters, View performance monitor, and Windows Media Services Help.

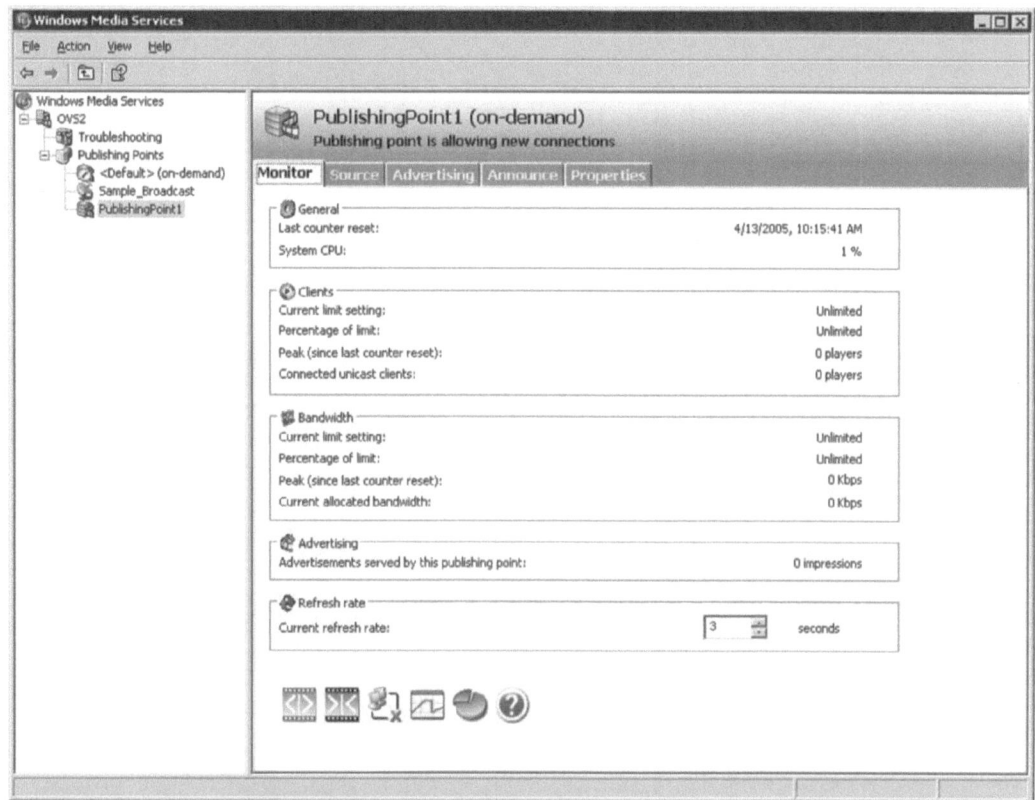

Figure 8-4
The Monitor tab in the Windows Media Services offers a snapshot of activity on your publishing point.

Source

The Source tab enables you to select the content to be published via your publishing point, as shown in **Figure 8-5**. The content is usually an encoded media file. But it can also be a playlist, which is essentially a list of media files played one after the other. (Playlists are discussed in more detail in the following pages.)

To select your content, click the "Change…" button and find your file in your server directory structure, usually under *c:\WMPub*.

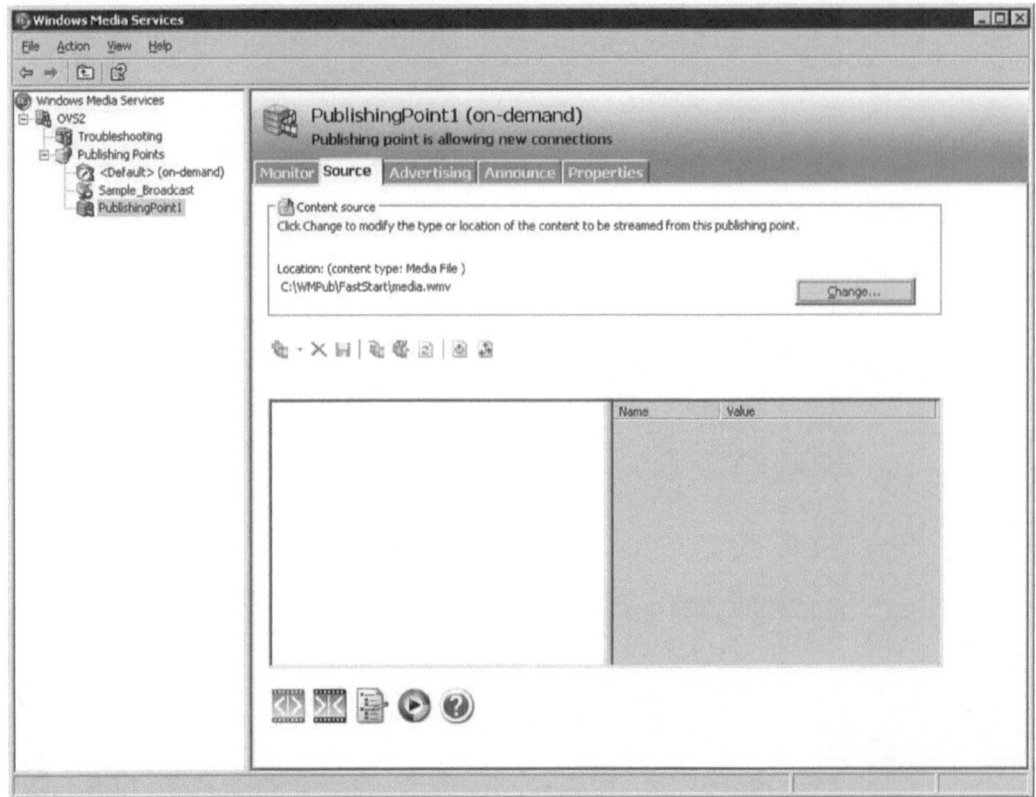

Figure 8-5
The Source tab sets the media file you wish to deliver via your publishing point. The Source tab also
lets you build a server-side playlist.

Author's Tip

Creating Server-Side Playlists

You may be familiar with music playlists created for Windows Media Player or on portable
media devices. These let you customize your listening experience. You can create sophisticated
versions of these playlists on Windows Media Server to perform several tasks, including:

- Displaying a welcome message
- Showing a sponsorship message or advertisement
- Playing related media files in sequence
- Playing a live webcast after an on-demand file
- Showing a thank you message at the end of a file

A server-side playlist also gives you more control over the user experience if you're unsure about the bandwidths your listeners connect at. For this, you use a *switch* statement, which tells the server to deliver a low-bandwidth or high-bandwidth file to the player based on the player's bandwidth settings.

To create a playlist, click the View Playlist Editor icon at the bottom of the Source tab, as shown in **Figure 8-6**. You also can write a playlist using a text editor, such as Notepad. The playlist structure and values are based on SMIL, or synchronized multimedia integration language, an extensible markup language (XML)-compliant, World Wide Web Consortium (W3C)-approved standard for creating multimedia experiences via streaming media. To learn more about SMIL, visit the W3C SMIL page at *http://www.w3.org/AudioVideo/*. The Windows Media Service Help files also offer more details on creating server-side playlists.

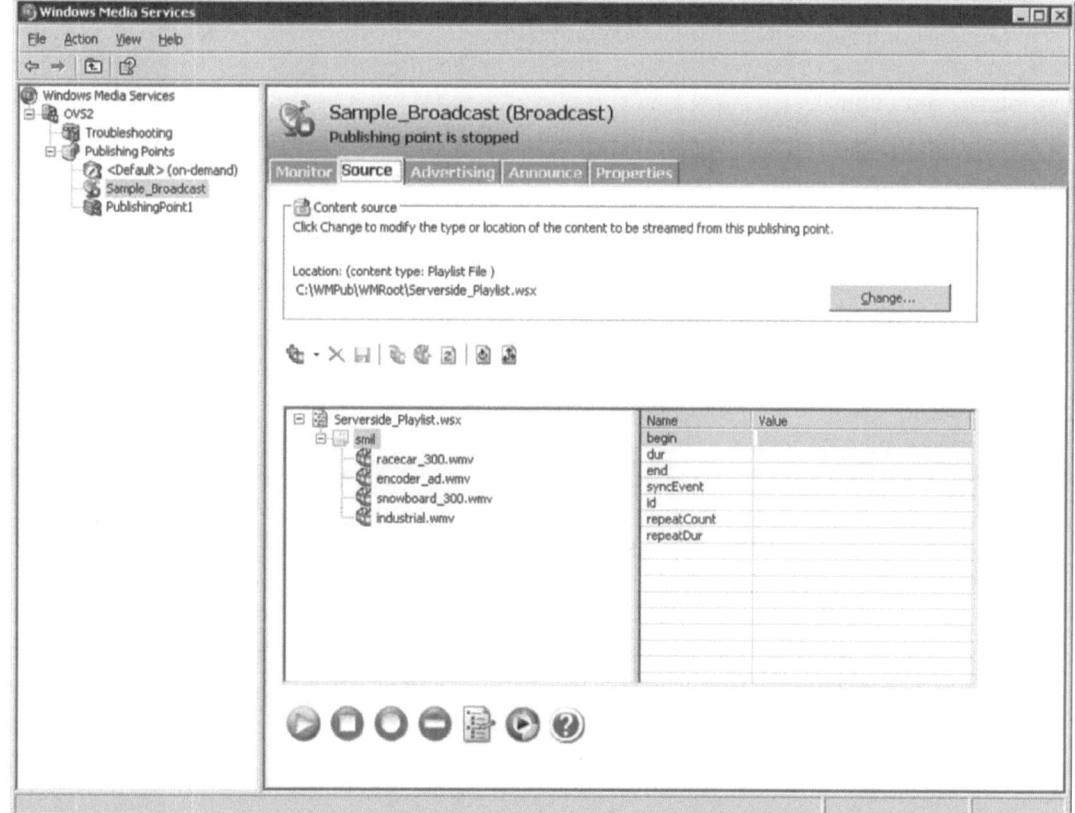

Figure 8-6
You can build server-side playlists with the Windows Media Playlist Editor, a snap-in for Windows Media Services.

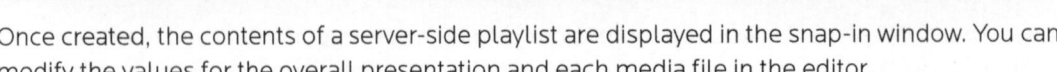

Once created, the contents of a server-side playlist are displayed in the snap-in window. You can modify the values for the overall presentation and each media file in the editor.

> **ALERT**
>
> !
>
> Microsoft's Windows Media supports only a portion of the SMIL standard, not the entire standard.

Once you've created a playlist you can make it the media source for your publishing point. To do so, click the "Change…" button in the Source tab of your Windows Media Service Administrator. Locate the playlist file, which has a **.wsx** extension.

Server-side playlists are easily confused with a type of client-side playlist written inside Windows Media announcement files, also called *metafiles*. Client-side playlists have the extension **.asx**, and they are placed on web servers. (Announcement files are discussed in more detail in the following sections.)

Advertising

Technologies such as playlists mean new opportunities to earn revenue from your streaming media. Windows Media Services offers a special kind of playlist via the Advertising tab, as shown in **Figure 8-7**. Called a *wrapper*, this playlist lets you quickly add a streaming media advertisement before and/or after the encoded media or playlist in your publishing point. (Ads at the beginning are called *gateway* ads; ads after content are called *bumpers*.) Wrappers can also be used for other messages, such copyright notices, and they can be built dynamically with scripts.

To create a wrapper playlist, click the Advertising tab in Windows Media Services Administrator. Then click the Wrapper Editor icon next to the Help icon at the bottom. The wizard will walk you through the process.

You also can write a wrapper playlist with a text editor, such as Notepad. Following is simple code for a wrapper playlist. The special variable *%requestedURL%* tells the server to insert the source media file or server-side playlist between the two ads.

Note also the attributes "Advertisement" and "noSkip." The first value places an entry in your server logs so that you can track how many times the ad was viewed, which is important to report to advertisers. It also trips a counter in the Monitor to show "impressions," that is, how many times the ad was viewed. The "noSkip" attribute prevents the user from skipping the ad via Windows Media Player's playback controls.

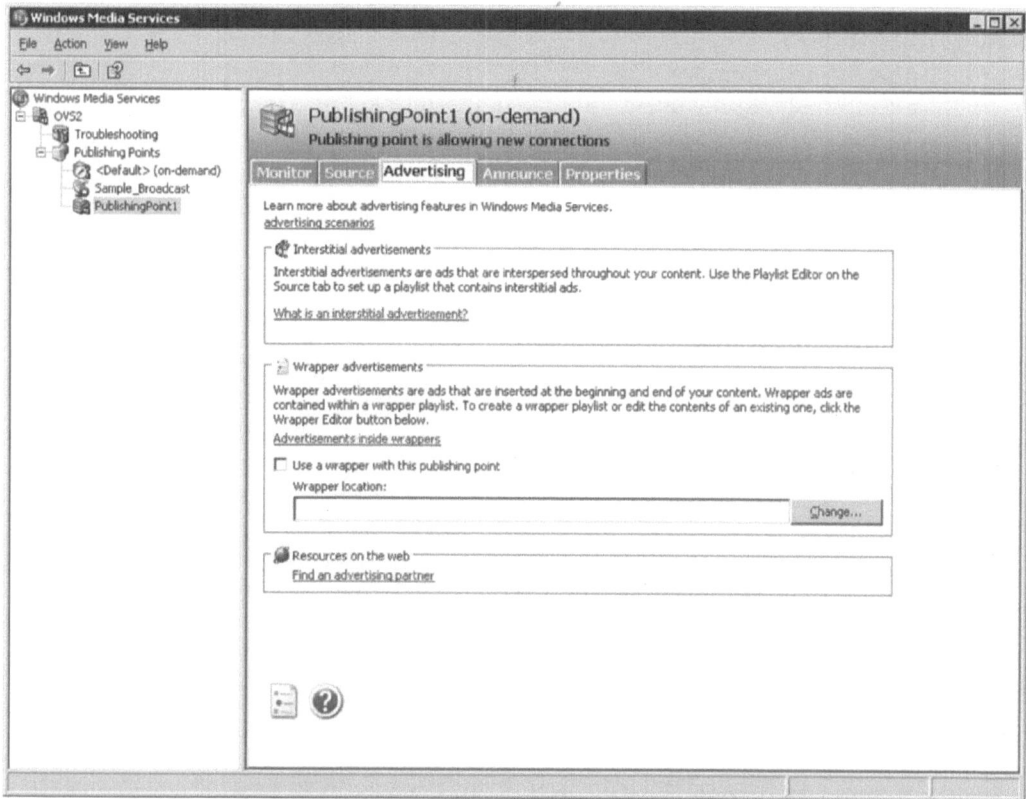

Figure 8-7
The Advertising tab lets you put a wrapper playlist around your source media file or server-side playlist. Click the Wrapper Editor icon at the bottom of the panel to create the wrapper playlist.

```
<?wsx version="1.0"?>

<smil>

    <media src="gateway_ad.wmv"

        role="Advertisement" noSkip="true" />

    <media src="%requestedUrl%"/>

    <media src="bumper_ad.wmv"

        role="Advertisement" noSkip="true" />

</smil>
```

Inside the Industry

Use Advertising Carefully

Historically, Internet users have hated advertising. They generally see techniques such as banner ads and pop-ups as intrusive and wasteful of their time and their limited bandwidth, especially for dial-up users. However, there's some evidence that streaming media users are more tolerant of ads, perhaps because the ads resemble television and radio advertising.

If you decide to include advertising in your streaming experiences, think carefully about your users and their expectations. Here's the most important question to ask as a streaming media producer: Does the advertisement integrate as seamlessly as possible within the overall user experience? For example, is the quality of the encoding significantly worse (or better) than the quality of the content that the user believes they will receive when they click the Play button or a web link? The answer may make the difference between an angry user who tells their friends how bad your site is versus a user who accepts the ad as part of the content package.

Inside the Industry

Interstitials and Banners

Advertisements scattered among several clips are called *interstitials*, because they appear between the clips. Use the Playlist Editor in the Source tab to place ads among two or more media clips. Use the Wrapper Editor in the Advertising tab to place ads before and/or after media clips references via a playlist created via the Playlist Editor.

You also can include traditional *banner* ads, such as static images, within a server-side playlist. You use the "bannerURL" attribute with a "clientData" element in the Playlist Editor to insert a banner ad. Or you can add the code by hand to a playlist file via a text editor, such as Notepad.

Banner ads can also be added to client-side playlists via the "Banner" element. See the Microsoft website for more information about banner ads in announcement (**.asx**) files.

Announce

The Announce tab in Windows Media Services Administrator helps you create and manage announcement files for your encoded media or server-side playlists. You place the URL to your publishing point here, as shown in **Figure 8-8**. Note the reference to the Unicast Announcement Wizard, which you used in Chapter 1 to create an announcement file. An option in the wizard enables you to create a simple webpage with an embedded Windows Media Player, as discussed in the following section.

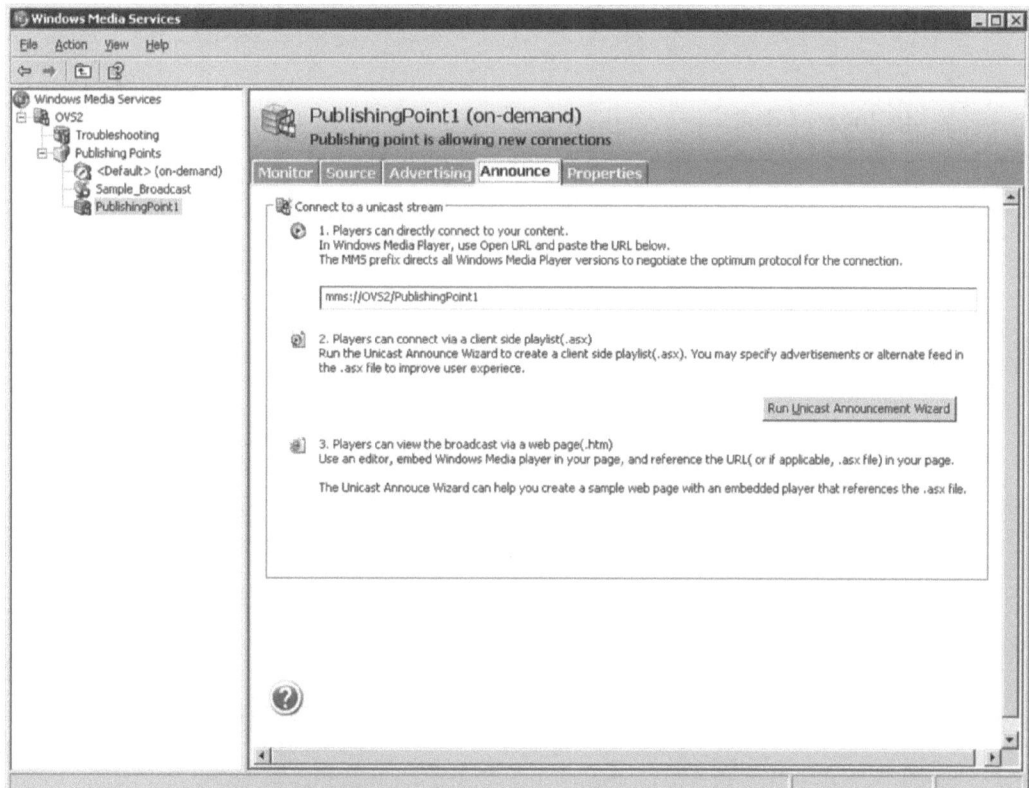

Figure 8-8
The Announce tab gives you the streaming media URL for your encoded media file or server-side playlist. You'll also find a wizard for building an announcement file or a simple webpage with an embedded player pointing to your media file.

The Role of Metafiles — As discussed in Chapter 1 and elsewhere, an announcement file is also known as a *metafile*, meaning that it contains *metadata* that describes or refers to another file. In streaming media technology, metafiles are small text files residing on a web server that refer to at least one encoded media file or playlist. The reference to the media file usually starts with an "*mms://*" or "*rtsp://*", which signals the required streaming media protocol. The balance of this URL includes a domain, likely a dedicated streaming media server, and a file name.

On a website, a link in a webpage points to this file and when the user clicks the link, the browser downloads the metafile and hands it off to Windows Media Player. The player opens the file, locates the streaming media URL, requests the stream, and begins playing the file.

Figure 8-9 shows the role of the metafile. Here are the steps:

1.   A user clicks a link in a webpage to a metafile. The browser asks the web server for the metafile.
2.   The web server delivers the metafile to the browser.
3.   The browser sends the metafile to Windows Media Player.
4.   The player opens the metafile, locates the streaming media URL, and requests the audio and/or video file from the streaming media server.
5.   The streaming server streams the media file contents to the player.

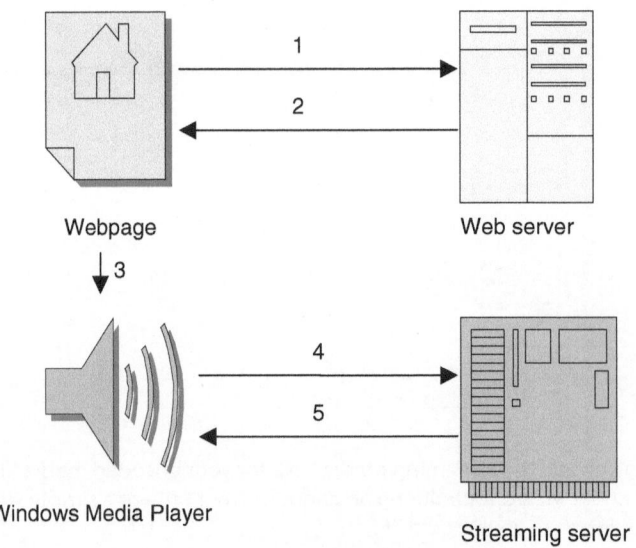

Figure 8-9
How metafiles work.

Linking a webpage to a metafile is as simple as writing an anchor tag. Here's an example:

<a href="…/metafiles/mymetafile.asx">My Video</a>

Note that the anchor tag uses a relative reference to the metafile in a directory called "metafiles." If you plan to present a lot of streams, it's best to put all your metafiles in a single directory.

Metafile Contents — A metafile always contains at least one reference to a media file. It also may contain several parameters controlling playback. For example, the metafile may tell the player to seek inside a large encoded file and play only a minute's worth of content. The following code example shows the contents of a typical announcement file:

```
<asx version="3.0">

        <entry>

                <ref href="mms://myserver.com/myfile.wmv" />

                <starttime value="2:30" />

                <duration value="1:00" />

                <title>My Streaming Video</title>

                <banner href="http://www.myads.com/myBanner.gif">

                </banner>

        </entry>

</asx>
```

Here's a detailed description of the code:

- The ASX element defines the file as a metafile. It commonly includes at least one attribute defining the version.
- The ENTRY element specifies a Windows Media file to render. The ENTRY element contains at least one child element (the REF element) and may contain several more.
- The REF element includes the HREF attribute that points the player to the media file on the streaming server.
- In this example, the STARTTIME element tells the player to begin playback at 2 minutes, 30 seconds from the beginning of the file.
- In this example, the DURATION element tells the player to play the file for 1 minute and then stop.
- The TITLE element displays the title of the media file. (Using this in a metafile will override title information embedded in the encoded file.)
- The BANNER element tells the player to find and display a banner advertisement in the player.

Dynamic Metafiles

The preceding ASX example assumes the file will live on a web server more or less unchanged over time. However, you can create metafiles dynamically with Active Server Pages code, either in "classic" ASP or ASP.Net. For example, imagine a set of 50 training videos residing on your streaming server. Instead of writing 50 **.asx** files, you can put the URLs plus any other information into a Microsoft Access or SQL Server database. You then write ASP or ASP. Net code that generates the **.asx** file "on the fly." As you add training videos, you simply enter the data in the database, and the ASP code automatically writes the metafile whenever the video is requested.

Note carefully the structure of the ASX file. The structure is *XML-compliant*, meaning there are strict rules about how you open and close the various elements. For more details, review the Windows Media Metafile Elements Reference on the Microsoft website.

Embedding Playback in a Webpage — The Unicast Announcement Wizard in the Announce tab of the Windows Media Services Administrator can also create a sample webpage that plays a media file within the page, instead of the standalone player. *Embedding* the streaming experience directly in a webpage gives you extra control over the look and feel of your streaming presentation. Next to player skins, embedded players allow for maximum customization.

Using an embedded player requires a fairly sophisticated understanding of HTML and Microsoft ActiveX. But if you feel comfortable coding in HTML, you should have no problem with embedded players.

Here's an example of code that will embed Windows Media Player into a webpage.

```
<OBJECT ID="MMPlayer1" WIDTH="320" HEIGHT="350" CLASSID="clsid:6BF52A52-394A-11D3-
B153-00C04F79FAA6" TYPE="application/x-oleobject">

        <PARAM NAME="FileName" VALUE="my_video.asx">

        <PARAM NAME="ShowControls" VALUE="1">

        <PARAM NAME="AutoStart" VALUE="1">

        <EMBED NAME="MMPlayer1" TYPE="application/x-mplayer2" SRC="my_video.asx"
AUTOSTART="1" SHOWCONTROLS="1" WIDTH="320" HEIGHT="350"></EMBED>

</OBJECT>
```

The following is a detailed description of the embedding code.

- The opening OBJECT tag includes the ID attribute, which is a name in memory for the player object. WIDTH and HEIGHT attributes correspond to the video image size plus the height of the player controls. (In this example, the height of the image is 240 pixels, and the height of the player controls is 110 pixels, for a total of 350 pixels.) CLASSID identifies the ActiveX control. The MIME TYPE is also included in the opening OBJECT tag.

- The FileName parameter tells the plug-in where to find the metafile on the web server.

- The ShowControls parameter tells the browser to show the Play/Pause/Stop controls.

- The Autostart parameter tells the browser whether or not to start the video when the page loads. A value of "1" means "Yes." A value of "0" means "No."

- The opening and closing EMBED tag is required for cross-compatibility with older versions of the Netscape Navigator browser. The attributes perform the same functions as the parameters in Internet Explorer's OBJECT tag. Note how the EMBED tag is contained with the OBJECT tag.

For more details on the OBJECT and EMBED tags, visit the Microsoft website.

ALERT The code above is tested and known to work, but that doesn't mean it will work for you. Be prepared to experiment with the settings to get it functioning the way you want.

Properties

The Properties tab in Windows Media Services Administrator controls a number of configuration settings related to security, networking, and logging, as shown in **Figure 8-10**. The box displays each property and its settings when clicked. The box may also include a number of plug-ins, depending on your publishing point. This section gives an overview of each default property. For more detail, review the Windows Media Services Help files or the Microsoft website.

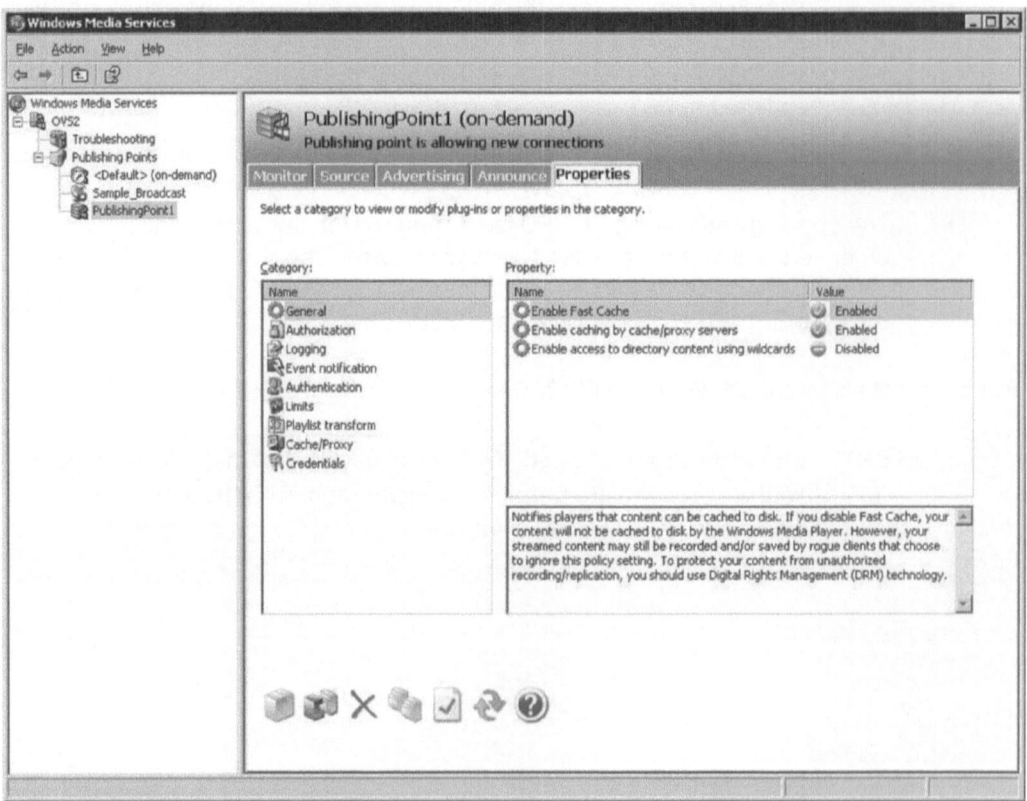

Figure 8-10
The Properties tab of Windows Media Service Administrator includes configuration settings related to security, networking, and logging.

General — The General property contains three settings: "Enable Fast Cache," "Enable caching by cache/proxy servers," and "Enable access to directory content using wildcards."

Enable Fast Cache — *Fast Cache* is a Windows Media Player feature that lets the player *cache* or temporarily store media files it has streamed on the user's computer. If the user wants to view the content again, the player calls it from the user's hard drive, saving time and bandwidth by avoiding a new connection to the streaming server.

Enable Caching by Cache/Proxy Servers — Many large companies and virtually all content delivery networks (CDNs) use *cache servers* and/or *proxy servers*. Imagine a large company based in Seattle with offices in Singapore and London. Instead of having the workers in Singapore and London contact a streaming server in Seattle for a video, the media is cached at a streaming server at each city, and the workers access the file locally. This saves bandwidth and eliminates potential Internet bottlenecks and other problems that may worsen the user experience.

Proxy servers act as a kind of gateway to the main network infrastructure of an organization. Governments and corporations use proxy servers to hide information about themselves from folks who aren't supposed to know, such as hackers. Proxies can also filter incoming information, hiding it from people behind the proxy.

Enable Access to Directory Content Using Wildcards — This allows users and producers to play all content in a directory at once. It is disabled by default.

Authorization — The Authorization property lets you enable or disable each of the three authorization methods: NTFS ACL, Publishing Points ACL, and IP Address. See the Security section of Chapter 7 for more information on each.

Logging — The Logging property contains a single setting, Client Logging. This lets Windows Media Services log certain kinds of activity data generated by Windows Media Player. Logging is disabled by default as an extra measure to protect the privacy of users. However, without logging, you will not be able to track information about your streams, such as how many times a specific stream was played. The logs are stored to the folder *%systemroot%\System32\LogFiles\WMS*. They follow a defined W3C format. And they can be viewed with Notepad, Microsoft Excel, or imported into a database application, such as Microsoft Access, for analysis.

Event Notification — The Event Notification property contains a single setting, WMI Event Handler. Enabling this setting lets you capture events through Windows Management Instrumentation (WMI). WMI is the Microsoft implementation of a method for accessing management information in large networks.

Windows Media Performance Monitor

You can check the performance of your Windows Media Server over time by viewing the Performance Monitor, available by clicking the Performance Monitor button in the Monitor tab. The Performance Monitor uses a set of counters to keep track of certain server parameters in each publishing point or the whole server. It may help you diagnose certain problems. Some of the data is similar to the client activity logs. Here's a description of some of the fields:

- **Total Connected Players**: Reports how many players connected to the server or publishing point.
- **Total UDP Resend Requests**: Reports the number of times players asked the server to resend data packets. A high number may indicate a networking problem.
- **Total UDP Resends Sent**: Compare this value to Total UDP Resend Requests. If the number is significantly lower, the server load is probably too high.
- **Total Stream Errors**: Reports certain networking parameters, such as dropped packets. A high number indicates a networking problem.
- **Total Stream Denials**: Reports the number of packets discarded by the server. A high number may indicate the server can't handle all the stream requests it receives.
- **%Processor Time**: A value of 85% or greater suggests the need for a faster CPU.
- **Current Late Read Rate**: A value greater than zero may indicate the disk drive can't keep up with data read requests.

Authentication — The Authentication property lets you enable or disable the authentication methods Anonymous User Authentication and Network Authentication. See the Security section of Chapter 7 for more information on each method.

Limits — The Limits property allows you to set limits on a number of parameters related to player connections. The default value for most is "unlimited." You may want to limit connections to your content if you have limited bandwidth or you know that your audience will be no larger than a certain size. The available values include:

- Limit player connections
- Limit outgoing player distribution connections

- Limit outgoing player bandwidth
- Limit aggregate outgoing distribution bandwidth
- Limit bandwidth per stream, per player
- Limit bandwidth per outgoing distribution stream
- Limit Fast Start bandwidth per player
- Limit Fast Cache content delivery rate

ALERT *Fast Start* is a feature in Windows Media Player that lets it buffer a media file at a rate faster than the encoded bandwidth. For example, a stream may be encoded for delivery at 300 kilobytes per second (kbps). But when the stream is requested, the available bandwidth is 1.5 megabytes per second. The player fills the buffer at the higher rate, which means it can start playback faster. After playback begins, the player returns to its normal buffering rate of 300 kbps.

Playlist Transform — The single entry in the Playlist Transform property, also called *playlist transform*, lets you change the order of playback of contents in a directory or playlist when the WMS_EVENT_INITIALIZE_PLAYLIST event is sent by the server. You may need this if you want to exclude media files in a playlist for certain individuals or groups of audience members.

Cache/Proxy — The "cache expiration" value in the Cache/Proxy property allows you to limit the length of time in seconds that stream data is held in cache or at a proxy server. After the time limit is reached, Windows Media Player or the proxy server requests the file again. (See the General property above.)

Credentials — The Credentials property is related to the Authentication and Authorization properties, especially when custom plug-ins are involved.

Testing and Windows Media Load Simulator

Once you have created and configured your publishing point, written your announcement file, and placed your announcement file on your web server, you should test your streams. Testing may be as simple as opening the webpage and clicking the link to make sure everything works. (See the Troubleshooting section of Chapter 1 for a description of common problems.) You might send the webpage link to co-workers or friends, have them click the link, and report errors to you.

However, if you are in a large enterprise or you are uncertain about just how much capacity your network has for serving Windows Media, you should set-up a detailed testing regimen, starting with a test plan. Network configuration and testing is beyond the scope of this book, but you should know about a free tool that can help you understand your Windows Media environment better and troubleshoot problems. The tool is Windows Media Load Simulator (WMLS), as shown in **Figure 8-11**. You can download WMLS from the Windows Media download pages on the Microsoft website.

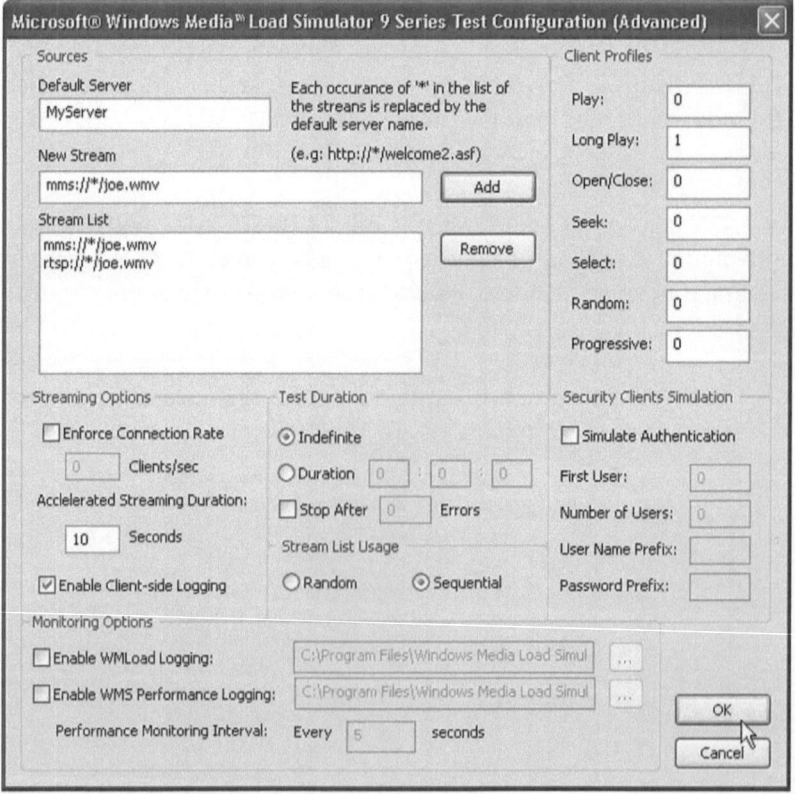

Figure 8-11
Windows Media Load Simulator (WMLS) This application is designed to mimic the traffic of dozens or hundreds of Windows Media Players as they contact a single media server or a cluster of servers.

Essentially, WMLS resides on a client computer somewhere on the Internet or your intranet and mimics the behavior of one or more Windows Media Players contacting your media server over a period of time. WMLS does not actually render the streams, but the server responds to the simulator's requests for data in the same way it would to dozens of individual players.

WMLS is most effectively used in conjunction with the Windows Media Services Performance Monitor. You also need to enable the client-side logging plug-in via the Properties panel in Windows Media Services Administrator. To see test results, review the logs in *%systemroot%\System32\LogFiles\WMS*. Because the log files may be very large, it's best to import them into a spreadsheet or a database application for easier analysis. Based on the results of the test, you may want to reset certain server parameters, such as the number of player connections you allow at any one time. After some experimenting, you'll find just the right balance between delivering a good user experience and maximizing the use of your hardware, software, and networking resources.

Conclusion

You are now ready to deliver on-demand streaming media to your audience. The chapter described in detail how to deliver streaming media, starting with a discussion of HTTP streaming. The chapter showed how to install Windows Media Services on Windows Server 2003. The chapter briefly reviewed publishing points, and then took you through the Windows Media Service Administrator, explaining each of the features. The chapter closed with a discussion of testing and Windows Media Load Simulator. In the next chapter, you'll learn the basics of live webcasting with Windows Media.

CHAPTER 9

Get Ready to Webcast Live with Windows Media

Up to this point, you've learned about streaming with Windows Media from the on-demand perspective. The encoded files you created were archived for viewing at the user's convenience. In the next two chapters, you'll apply what you've learned to live webcasts, that is, sending the audio and video signals to an audience as they are produced. By the end of this chapter, you'll understand:

- Whether or not a live webcast is appropriate for your project
- The difference between live and on-demand webcasting
- Preparing a studio for live webcasting
- Preparing for a live webcast at a remote location

Live versus On-Demand

Until the twentieth century, all types of time-based productions, such as plays or music performances, were only available "live." The advent of recording technology did little to stem the demand for live entertainment or action. In fact, producers often tout a live experience as a selling point to get you interested. Have you ever wondered why television news departments go "live to the scene" whenever possible? Because a "live" storyteller (the reporter) adds an extra emotional edge, even drama, to a story when they tell it as it happens. That feeling is very hard to capture in a recording.

Theoretically, all audio and video can be webcast live. But that doesn't mean live is an appropriate choice in all circumstances. Setting aside the added expense of a live broadcast, some content just isn't well suited to a live situation.

When Should I Produce Live?

You should consider producing a live broadcast when you can capture and deliver action as it happens. And you need to judge whether the action, or the information delivered as part of the action, would have the most impact if delivered immediately, rather than at some later point. Here are some good candidates for a live streaming media broadcast:

- An annual address by a CEO or prominent political leader
- A new product rollout at an important industry conference
- An event where the outcome is uncertain, such as a game or debate

When Should I Produce for On-Demand Delivery?

Consider producing your content for on-demand delivery when the content stays relatively fresh over time. Some people call this kind of content *evergreen*, because it reminds them of the pine and fir trees that retain their green color over the darkest winter, unlike their deciduous cousins. Another factor that argues for on-demand is audience interest. Will the potential audience want to watch this content long after it was first produced? If the answer is yes, you should produce and store an on-demand streaming media file.

Some good candidates for on-demand production and/or archiving include:

- A training presentation on sexual harassment (this could be delivered live and archived for later access)
- An early audio recording of the community's first radio station
- Almost any kind of music production

One major advantage of on-demand delivery over live delivery is your ability to enhance the stream with interactive elements. For example, you can apply some advanced techniques to add a navigation menu to a stream, allowing users to go to specific sections of a recording. This isn't possible in a live broadcast.

Some streams may fall into both live and on-demand categories. A live broadcast of a presidential speech is usually archived, because his words carry interest both at the time they were delivered and for many days, perhaps years afterward.

To help you make a decision on live versus on-demand (or both), see the suggested decision matrix in **Figure 9-1**. To use the matrix, follow these steps:

1. Give each criterion a weighting from 1 (not important) to 10 (very important).
2. Rate how well each criterion meets the criteria.
3. Multiply the weighting by the rating for a score.
4. Add the score for each platform. The highest score suggests the right decision.

| | | Broadcast Choices | | | | | |
| | | Live | | On-Demand | | Both | |
Criteria	Weight	Rating	Score	Rating	Score	Rating	Score
Uncertain outcome							
Dramatic tension							
Info stays same over time							
Potential for inter-activity							
Budget							
Potential to promote stream							
Prep time							
	Totals						

Figure 9-1
A decision matrix for live versus on-demand.

Fundamental Differences between Live and On-Demand

From a purely streaming media perspective, there are only a few significant differences between live and on-demand webcasting. In on-demand encoding, the encoding computer can take its time encoding the file, thus you have options such as two-pass encoding. Live encoding happens in real time, and the processor in the encoding computer has to be powerful enough to keep up with the audio and video signal. In addition, there are differences in set-up and configuration of the encoder and server, which the book discusses later.

Author's Tip

A hybrid form of on-demand is called *live-to-tape*, or *roll tape live*. Essentially, you produce a program as if it were live, but record it, instead of webcasting it live. Then you encode it to an archive file for on-demand access.

However, the most important differences between live and on-demand exist in the pre-production phase. In short, your motto is preparation, preparation, preparation. In on-demand production, you can start over if you make a mistake. Not so with live webcasting. You have one chance and one chance only. That means spending the bulk of your resources, both time and money, preparing for every contingency.

Think of yourself as an engineer designing a spacecraft carrying a human. If something breaks, the pilot can't run down to the hardware store to get a part. To overcome this limitation, the engineer builds "redundancy" into his systems, so that if one part fails, another part takes over. The engineer often builds three, four, or more layers of redundancy. Furthermore, the engineer tests every part and system several times before launch to ensure everything works well together in every imaginable contingency.

In a live webcast, you may find yourself at a remote location with little access to new parts or even expertise. Allow yourself a little paranoia in the time leading up the webcast, and try to imagine every contingency that could prevent your stream from reaching your intended audience. And expect the unexpected. Good planning will see you through most problems.

Preparing a Studio for Live Webcasting

You may be fortunate enough to work for an organization that produces its own internal videos for distribution to employees, investors, or customers. Perhaps your company has a small studio designed for *live-to-tape* production, that is, producing a video in real time as if it were live, but placed on tape or DVD for distribution. Given these capabilities, it's relatively easy to add live webcasting capabilities to your studio.

Adding Encoding Capacity to Your Studio

Most studios contain basic pieces of equipment, such as a broadcast-quality camera, microphones, studio lighting, and so forth. They also feature a control room that contains an audio pre-processor and mixer, video switcher, audio tape or CD player, and one or more video tape recorders. Most of this equipment is wired together with access for operators via a *patch bay*. To reroute signals, operators use *patch cords*.

With the help of a wiring technician, you can add new inputs or reconfigure old inputs to send audio and/or video signals to an encoding computer. For example, if you have two audio outputs, originating in your studio microphones and routed through your audio mixer, you can *normal* or hardwire these outputs to the input for an encoding computer. **Figure 9-2** shows a simplified control room layout that includes two encoders.

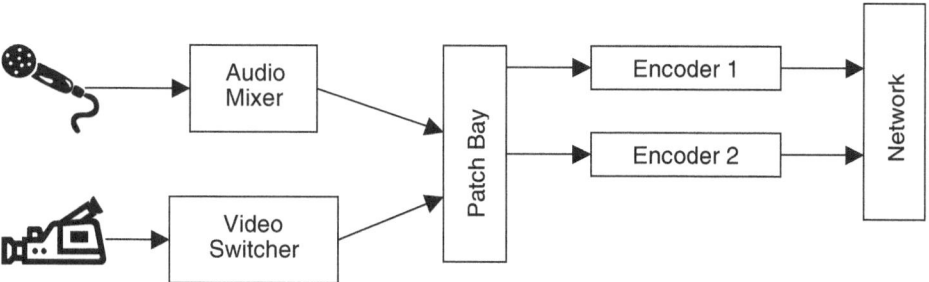

Figure 9-2
A simplified diagram showing placement of two redundant streaming encoders.

The Encoding Computers

To get started with in-studio encoding, you can bring in two desktop computers that are dedicated to encoding and can take the audio feed from the patch bay. However, it's likely that most of your other equipment in the control room is mounted in a *rack*. Instead of relying on desktop computers, you should purchase two *rack-mounted* computers, which can be placed in your rack along with the tape decks and other equipment. This saves space and prevents someone from accidentally bumping the desktop CPUs. Be sure to leave room somewhere nearby for a keyboard, mouse and monitor.

As for the computers themselves, buy the fastest, most powerful you can with a minimum of 512 megabytes of RAM and Microsoft Windows XP Professional. Install the latest version of Windows Media Encoder. A smallish-hard drive is fine, because you should not plan to store any files on these machines. If you need to archive material, talk to your IT guru about storage on the streaming media server or elsewhere on the regular company network.

Notice the use of the plural "computers." This is part of your plan for redundancy, or back-ups. During a live broadcast, you'll run both encoders at the same time. In case one of them fails, the other can pick up the slack (hopefully) without anyone noticing. (Failover configuration is discussed in more detail in Chapter 10, Encoding and Distributing Live Webcasts.)

Of course, you'll also need to discuss connectivity of your encoders to your company network, which might be as easy as running network cable from the computer to the wall socket. However, your networking professional may want to dedicate a network address to your encoders or otherwise isolate them from the rest of the network, given their special duties.

Inside the Industry

Buying a Rack-Mounted Computer

Internet service providers and large enterprises typically collect their server computers in a dedicated room called a *server room* or *machine room*. The rooms are air-conditioned with special equipment for collecting and distributing information under the client/server model of networking. Physical space is at a premium in these rooms, especially in a fast-growing organization, so computer makers designed thin versions of desktop computers that can slide into racks.

The space in a rack is measured in units of 1.75 inches. For example, a 1U rack-mounted computer is 1.75 inches tall. A 2U computer is twice the height of a 1U machine. The taller the computer, the easier it is to fix, should something go wrong. In other words, replacing a NIC in a 1U computer could be difficult, especially during a live broadcast. Thinner units tend to be more expensive as well, partly because they are harder to make, and partly because they are in greater demand by organizations with little space.

When planning your purchase, don't forget that you need space for a mouse, keyboard, and monitor. You can purchase special mounts for these peripherals so that they are in the rack and out of the way. You'll also need a *KVM switch*, which allows you to use one mouse, keyboard, and monitor for both encoding computers.

Building Standard Session Profiles

Chances are you'll webcast similar kinds of programming from webcast to webcast. Over time, you'll figure out which encoder settings work best in your particular circumstance. These settings will include image sizes, codecs, and most importantly, bit rates. Ideally, you should work with your IT department to understand how much capacity your network has to deliver your streams.

Back in Chapter 6, Encoding for Windows Media, you learned about building reusable, custom encoder profiles and loaded them when you needed them. Now is the time to use this feature. And you can create a session profile on one encoder computer and copy it to the other. This keeps you from reinventing the wheel for every webcast and ensures a certain amount of predictability from webcast to webcast. It also saves a lot of time.

Session profiles are stored with the extension **.wme**. To access a session profile, click File → Open and select a profile, as shown in **Figure 9-3**.

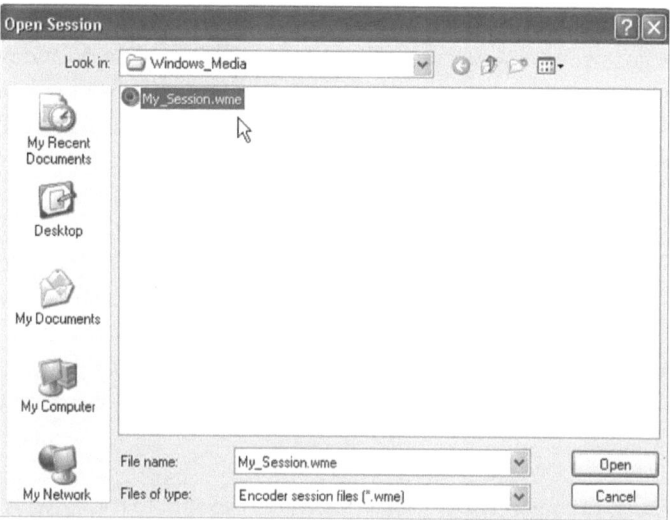

Figure 9-3
Accessing a session profile.

Preparing for Remote Live Webcasting

Webcasting at a remote location can be one of the most thrilling jobs for a streaming media producer. Unlike other information technology specialists, you're out in the field mixing it up, so to speak, where the action takes place. You're literally part of the show.

On the other hand, live remote webcasting is a streaming media job fraught with danger. You may find yourself in an environment with few assets but your own resourcefulness. As the nineteenth century chemist Louis Pasteur once said, "Fortune favors the prepared mind." That means you have to prepare for every contingency ahead of time. If you spend five hours planning for every one hour on location, you have a better chance of coming out of the experience with a successful webcast and a nice feather in your cap.

A Remote Webcasting Checklist

Here's a checklist of all the main items you'll need to get ready for a remote webcast. The following sections explain each item in detail. You can follow these in order, or move items around, depending on your situation.

- Connectivity and bandwidth
- Permissions
- Project management and budgeting
- Location scouting
- Authoring
- Road kit
- Setup
- Testing

Connectivity and Bandwidth — Almost from the moment you get the first call asking for a remote webcast, your first question should concern connectivity and bandwidth at the venue. Connections to the Internet are nearly ubiquitous at major venues such as convention centers and large hotel complexes, but it still varies at smaller facilities. Double-check the available bandwidth; you need at least DSL/Cable. And remember that at some facilities, such as hotels, you may be sharing bandwidth with other users.

On the other hand, if you are called on to produce a live webcast outdoors or at someone's sprawling estate, connectivity may be minimal or not exist at all. If the latter is the case, investigate whether a minimum DSL/Cable connection can be run to the site in the time you have before the webcast. Depending on the telephone company and availability, installations can take up to six weeks. And get two lines installed, if possible, so one can be used as a backup.

Once you confirm your connectivity, check the upload speed. In most types of DSL and cable, the upload speed is different, and usually smaller, than the download speed. Buy the highest upload speed you can afford.

By the way, NEVER rely on wireless connectivity for remote webcasts.

ALERT When you set up your encoder to work with your network, ask your network manager to give your network packets priority over other network traffic. This can improve the quality of delivery to the end user.

Author's Tip

If you find yourself in an extremely remote location, and/or you have deep pockets, consider contracting with a *video switching service* such as Globix or FisherPathways. In this scenario, you would send your encoded stream to a remote truck with a satellite uplink. The signal is pulled down from the satellite to the service's home facility and then routed to your media servers for distribution.

Video switching services are great, but don't forget the principal of redundancy. Even if you can afford these services, get a land line installed as a backup.

Permissions — If you are preparing a remote webcast for public consumption, and the webcast will include copyrighted works, such as songs, you need to get permission from the artist to webcast your material. Other organizations, such as ASCAP or BMI, may demand a fee. If you're lucky, the person or organization asking you to produce the webcast can take care of these for you. If you're very unlucky, you may have to contact each artist and possibly the publisher of their work, for permission. But the upfront headache is better than a lawsuit down the road.

Project Management and Budgeting — Successful streaming media requires careful planning. With on-demand webcasting, you can get away with a certain informality when it comes to planning, but with live remote webcasts, you need to take planning seriously. That means assembling a team with you in charge as the producer. The team may only be two people, but someone has to take the reins, map out each step, and make decisions. There are several tools out there to help; Microsoft Project is fast becoming a standard project management application. After you get through your first live remote webcast, you can use your Project file as a template for later webcasts.

Once you establish that connectivity is available and permissions won't be an issue, it's time to set a budget. Every webcast is unique, but here's a list of typical items you should include:

- Connectivity (may be zero if connectivity and sufficient bandwidth already available)
- Fees to venue or rights holders
- Your labor costs (don't forget yourself!)
- Contract labor, i.e., extra help on-site
- Travel
- Air freight or ground shipping for equipment
- Webpage authoring (see following section)

Location Scouting — The first rule of live webcasts: No surprises. That means you should scout the location of the webcast, even if it's at a major venue. Scouting could be just a phone call to a facility manager. Ideally, it means a site visit, especially if the webcast is at an unusual location. Here are a few questions to ask:

- Where can I set up my equipment?
- Are there network jacks available? If not, where do I run cable?
- Are there enough power outlets, especially if I have to share space with other technicians?
- Is there a place nearby to park my van or the satellite remote truck?
- Is there enough room for all my equipment?
- How will I take the audio/video feed? From the house feed? From some other place?

During your site visit, take photographs of the area and copious notes. You may need this information in later planning. If you end up doing a lot of remote webcasts from the same place, a single site visit may be enough, although you may want to check with the facilities manager occasionally to see if there are any changes in floor plan, access, or connectivity. Also, check if the facility has an IT manager. They could be valuable for setup and troubleshooting.

Authoring — Live remote webcasts are by definition "special" events deserving special treatment. Since your viewers will access the webcast from a webpage, you may need to create a new webpage that's devoted to the event. It may be no more than a dedicated page with a single link to the webcast. Or it may be more elaborate, especially if you want to embed Windows Media Player in the page. You can even go so far as to build an application that tests the visitor's bandwidth and player version to indicate whether the visitor has the right tools for a good experience.

You may have the right expertise to create the new page. However, if you have a complex webcast on your hands, consider handing off the page authoring to a specialist.

Road Kit — Going on location entails bringing everything you might need with you, including encoding computers and all the support equipment. Most professional streaming media specialists build a road kit that puts everything in place for easy setup. In many cases, it's a studio on wheels.

Road kits start with a heavy-duty shipping case, as shown in **Figure 9-4**. More elaborate cases have a rack for rack-mounted computers and signal processing equipment. Both types are packed with thick foam and the wiring, in the latter type, bound securely. Many of these cases have built-in wheels, or you can put the case on a furniture dolly. When the shipper delivers the kit to the venue, you roll the case to the work area, take off the covers, plug it in to both the network jack and the power outlet, and you're ready to boot up.

Here are some typical components for a road kit:

- Two rack-mounted encoding computers, one primary and one backup, each loaded with appropriate software, including Windows XP Professional and Windows Media 9 Series encoders. Ideally, you've already created encoder session (**.wme** or **.prx**) files for the event.
- Keyboard, flat-screen monitor, mouse, one or more KVM switches
- Four-port switch
- Audio and video signal processing equipment
- CD player (for fill music before and after the show)
- Distribution amplifiers for both the audio and video signal. DAs allow you send a single audio or video signal over shielded cables to multiple outputs over long distances.
- Power panel with a master switch
- Surge protector
- Connection panel for audio/video inputs and outputs. The panel will take the audio and video inputs from your sources and distribute them to your equipment.
- Spares, spares, and more spares

Figure 9-4
A simple type of case for shipping electronic equipment, such as computers.

- – Extra shielded cables
- – Extra extension cords
- – Various cable adapters, such as BNC to RCA
- – Extra mouse and keyboard
- – Gaffer's tape and duct tape
- – Extra NICs
- – CD-ROMs for reinstalling software
- – Software and hardware manuals (maybe even this book)
- • Credit card for buying whatever you don't have on hand

It can't be stressed enough that Murphy's Law prevails on live remotes: Whatever can go wrong, will go wrong. But thinking ahead will prevent most problems, or at least allow you cope with them easily.

Set Up — As you plan your live remote webcast, build in a pad of several hours, perhaps a full day, for setting up and testing your equipment. Coordinate this with the show producers or the audio/video technicians at the venue. They may be unfamiliar with your technology, so take the time to explain what you're doing; they can be valuable helpers in an emergency. Get everything working *exactly* the way it's meant to work when the show begins. Take advantage of rehearsals before the event to test your whole system, from inputs to encode to serve. Everything should work before the event begins.

While you should remain flexible, there's nothing more frustrating than a last minute change that requires a reconfiguration of your equipment. Try as hard as you can to work out all the kinks before the show starts.

Testing — Testing was mentioned in the previous sub-section on setup. But it's worth discussing again. You cannot test enough. And don't wait until the last minute to test. As soon as you walk in the door, test your connectivity and bandwidth. Without these two elements, nothing else matters.

Once you have an audio or video feed to play with, test whether you can get an encoded stream to your servers, then test whether your servers are delivering streams to users. Make your live remote webcast webpage available to colleagues and even friends and relatives, so they can view the test stream. If problems crop up, solve them immediately; don't put them on a to-do list. When everything seems to be working, take a break, and then test everything again. You'd be surprised at how many times during a previous "perfect" test, you missed something.

Conclusion

Live webcasting is becoming more and more common as bandwidth grows and companies discover the power of sending a streaming media signal live over the Internet. After first deciding that an event is appropriate for a live webcast, you need to prepare your in-house studio, if you have one, for live webcasting. If you're called on to produce a live webcast at a remote location, you'll need to prepare even more carefully and purchase special equipment to ensure the remote webcast goes smoothly. In the next chapter, you'll learn more about using the Windows Media Encoder and Windows Media Services during a live event.

CHAPTER 10

Encoding and Distributing Live Webcasts

Chapter 9 focused on planning and preparing for a live webcast, whether you're webcasting from a studio or on location. No matter the source of your live signal, you need to encode that signal for distribution over the Internet or your company intranet. This chapter discusses the streaming media technology both types of webcasting have in common, which is the Windows Media Encoder. You'll learn:

- The two types of live stream distribution
- How to configure Windows Media Encoder for live streaming
- How to configure Windows Media Services for live streaming
- An elegant way to keep your viewers with you while you cope with a disaster

Live Stream Distribution

Before you learn the details of setting up an encoder and server for live streaming, you need to know about the two options for connecting an encoded stream with a server. The two options are *pull distribution* and *push distribution*, as illustrated in **Figure 10-1**.

Pull Distribution

The most common method of connecting an encoder with a server is *pull*, because it works fine with most network situations. With this method, the server establishes the connection with the encoder and distributes the streams to players. You configure pull distribution in the Windows Media Server Administrator, as discussed in following sections. (All examples in this chapter use the pull method.)

Here are a few scenarios in which pull is the preferred distribution method:

- **Standby for connections**: If you don't know how many streams are needed, or don't know when players might request a stream, putting the encoder in a

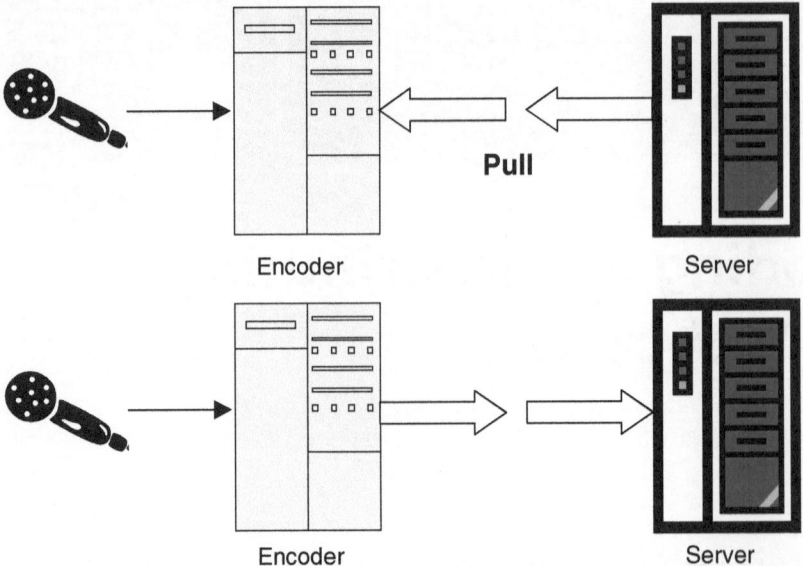

Figure 10-1
In pull distribution, the server makes the connection to the encoder. In push distribution, the encoder initiates the connection to the server.

kind of "standby mode" allows the server to connect to the encoder only when necessary. This saves valuable bandwidth and processing resources. To do this, you simply start the encoder and wait for the server to request or "pull" the encoded stream distribute it.

- **Encoder outside firewall**: If you are at a remote location and are webcasting a company meeting or a speech by your CEO, your encoder will most likely be outside the corporate firewall. Once you start the encoder, you can configure your Windows Media Server to pull the encoded stream from your encoder through the firewall.

- **Bypassing the server**: The Windows Media Series 9 Encoder can deliver up to five streams to Windows Media Players without the need for a server. In this case, the player pulls the stream from the encoder directly. To ensure that your encoder isn't accidentally (or deliberately) overloaded, you can limit access to the stream by IP address or groups of IP addresses.

Push Distribution

Push distribution is your choice if you face a situation where you may not know when you must distribute a stream, or you're unsure if a server administrator is available to help. Here's an example. You've been asked to set up a live stream at a remote location. You're expecting an important announcement from your CEO, but you don't know when the announcement will start.

Before you left the office, you persuaded the IT department to give you administrator rights in the Windows Media Services Administrator. This is done via the Publishing Points ACL Authorization plug-in and the HTTP Server Control Protocol plug-in. They enable you to set up a broadcast point on the server and start the webcast from the Windows Media Encoder. Instead of the server initiating the session, the encoder gets the ball rolling. When the CEO shows up for their announcement, you start the encoder, which sends the stream to the waiting server. Don't forget to tell the audience that the show has started and how to access it!

ALERT Unlike streaming servers, which may use one of several protocols to distribute a stream, such as MMS, RTSP, and HTTP, Windows Media Encoder uses only the HTTP protocol to deliver its stream to the server. This gives the encoder more flexibility under certain network configurations, especially when coping with firewalls.

Using Windows Media Encoder for Live Streaming

The following section takes you step-by-step through the Windows Media Encoder live broadcast wizard. To simplify things a bit, the book assumes that you're webcasting an audio-only event.

1. Open Windows Media Encoder, and select the "Broadcast a live event" wizard, as shown in **Figure 10-2**. Click OK.

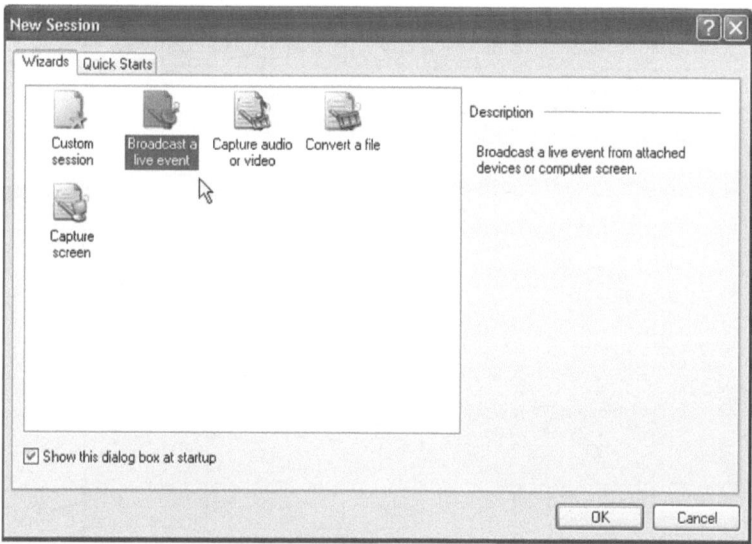

Figure 10-2
Select the "Broadcast a live event" wizard to begin a live encoding session.

2. Check the "Audio Only" box, and select the audio device, usually your sound card, as shown in **Figure 10-3**. Click Next.

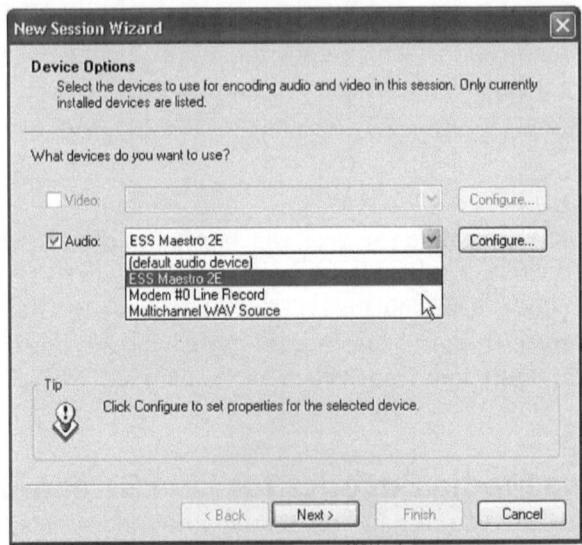

Figure 10-3
Select an audio device. For video, select a video and audio device.

3. Select "Pull from the encoder" as your distribution method, as shown in **Figure 10-4**. Click Next.

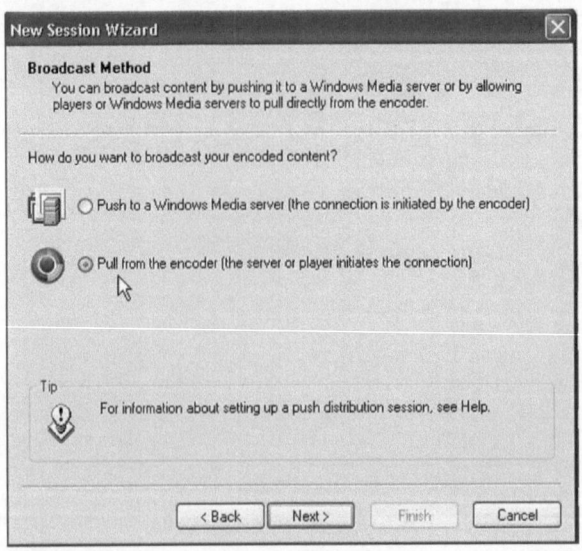

Figure 10-4
Select Pull as your method of connecting to the media server.

4.   Check the port number through which the encoder will communicate with the server, as shown in **Figure 10-5**. The default is the HTTP port of 8080. (Your network administrator may designate another port, especially if security is an issue.) Write down the URL for Internet connections and LAN connections; you'll need these when configuring the server. (Again, your server administrator may designate a special IP address for your encoding computer to get the encoded stream through a firewall.) Click Next.

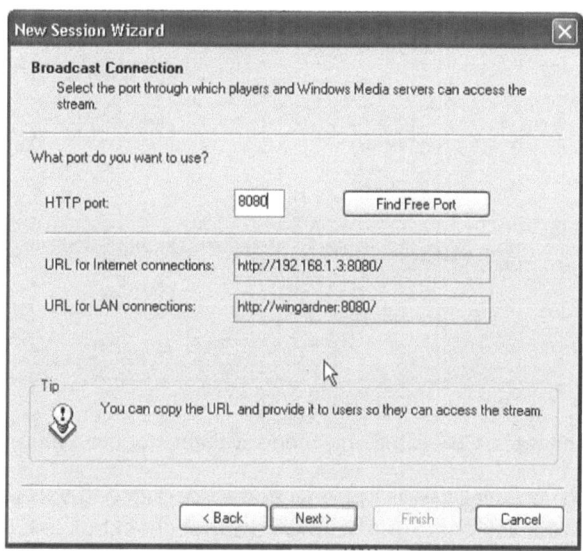

Figure 10-5
The port number for communicating with the server is usually 8080.

5. In the Encoding Options box, select the mode and bit rates for your webcast, as shown in **Figure 10-6**. (Only Constant Bit Rate is allowed for live streams.) Click Next.

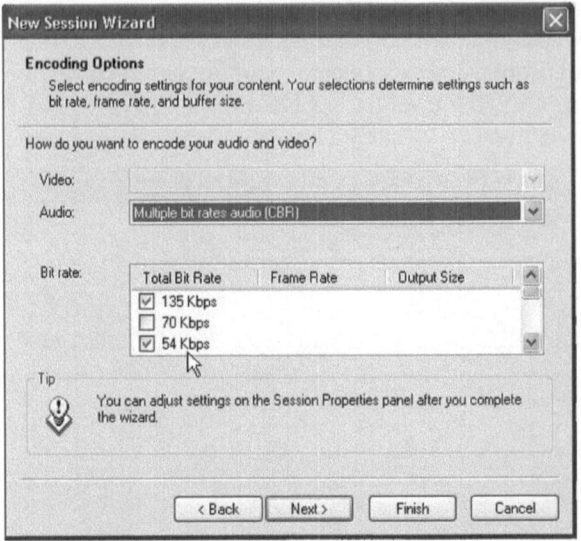

Figure 10-6
Select the mode and bit rates. CBR is the only mode available for live webcasts.

6. Archiving your webcast is optional and a good idea. If you want to save a copy of the live webcast, check the "Archive a copy" checkbox and click Browse to locate a directory on your server or network hard drive and assign a filename, as shown in **Figure 10-7**. Click Next.

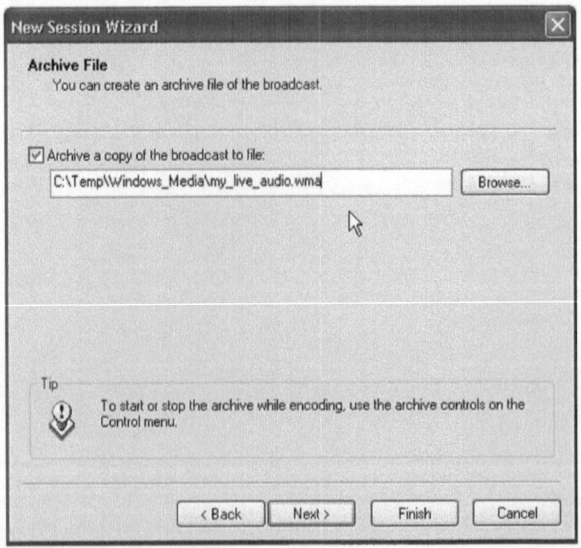

Figure 10-7
Archiving a webcast to a file is optional and a good idea.

10. Encoding and Distributing Live Webcasts

7. In the "Display Information" box, enter information that will appear in Windows Media Player identifying your stream. This information is also used for indexing, especially if you do a lot of encoding. Click Next.

8. Review your settings, and click the Back button to modify as necessary. Click Finish.

9. Windows Media Encoder reminds you that you can restrict the number of connections to the encoder. Click OK.

10. Click the green "Start Encoding" button at the top of the encoder user interface. Encoding begins, as shown in **Figure 10-8**.

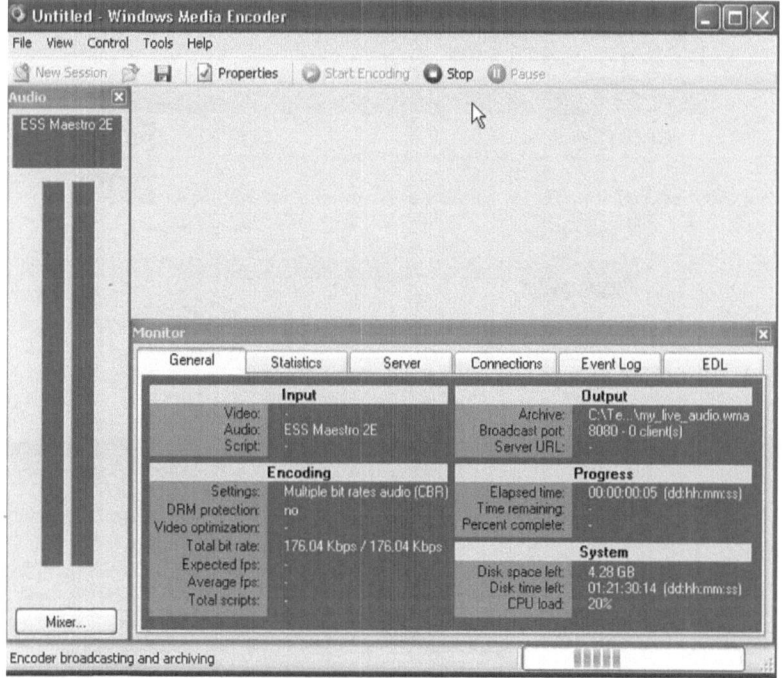

Figure 10-8
To start the encoding session, click the green "Start Encoding" button.

11. To stop the encoder, click the red "Stop" button at the top of the encoder user interface. Review the results of the encode, and click the Close button.

Using Windows Media Server for Live Streaming

The next section walks you through the set-up for a live broadcast publishing point in Windows Media Services Administrator. This section assumes that Windows Media Services have been installed on a computer with Windows Server 2003.

1. At your Windows Server 2003 computer, open the Windows Media Services Administration Tool by clicking Start → Programs → Administrative Tools → Windows Media Services.

2. With your mouse, highlight "Publishing Point" in the left panel.

3. Right-click, select Add Publishing Point Wizard, and click Next. This starts the wizard.

4. Enter a name for your live broadcast, as shown in **Figure 10-9**. Click Next.

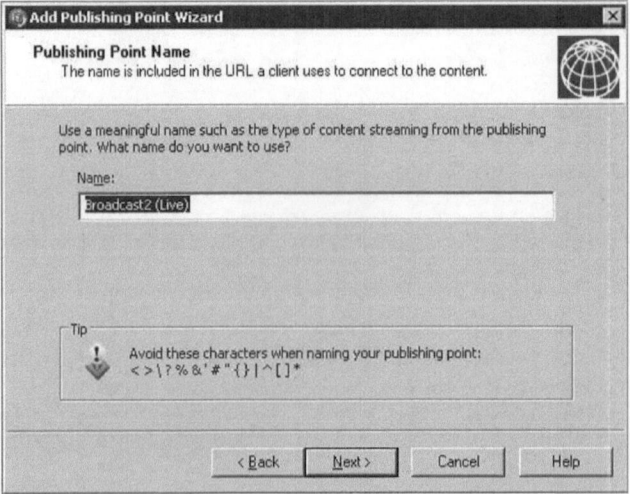

Figure 10-9
Enter a name for the live broadcast publishing point.

5. In the "Content Type" box, select "Encoder (A live stream)," as shown in **Figure 10-10**. Click Next.

6. In the "Publishing Point Type" box, select "Broadcast Publishing Point," as shown in **Figure 10-11**. Click Next.

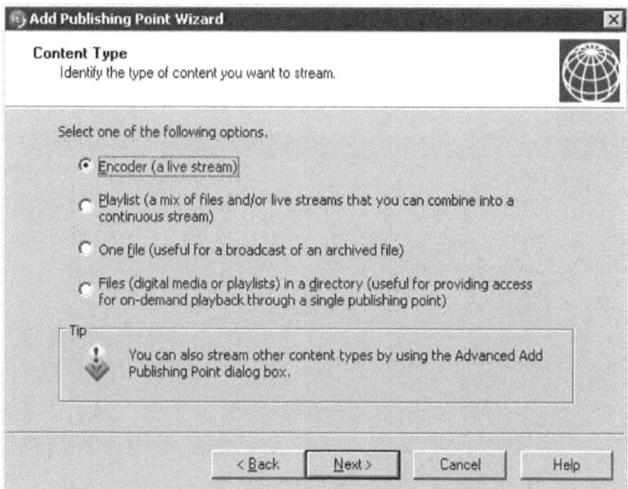

Figure 10-10
Select "Encoder (A live stream)."

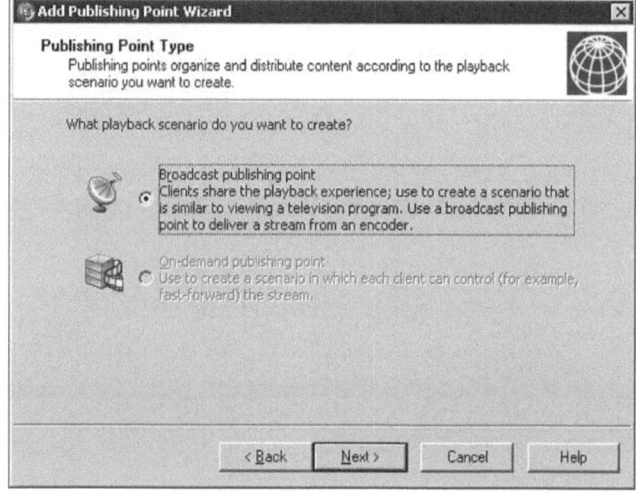

Figure 10-11
Select "Broadcast Publishing Point" as your publishing point type.

7. In the "Encoder URL" box, type the Internet URL or LAN URL for the encoding machine, as shown in **Figure 10-12**. (You wrote this address down in Step 4 of the preceding encoder section.) Click Next.

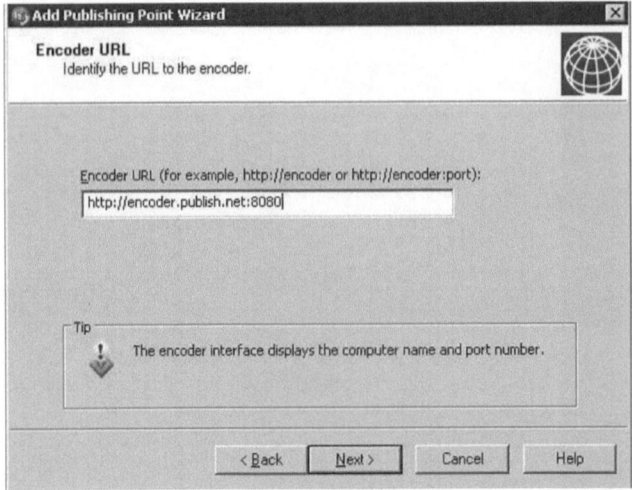

Figure 10-12
Enter the URL of your encoder, as you noted when setting up Windows Media Encoder for the live webcast.

8. If you want to log activity of Windows Media Players for this stream, check the "Yes" box in the "Unicast Logging" dialog, as shown in **Figure 10-13**. Click Next.

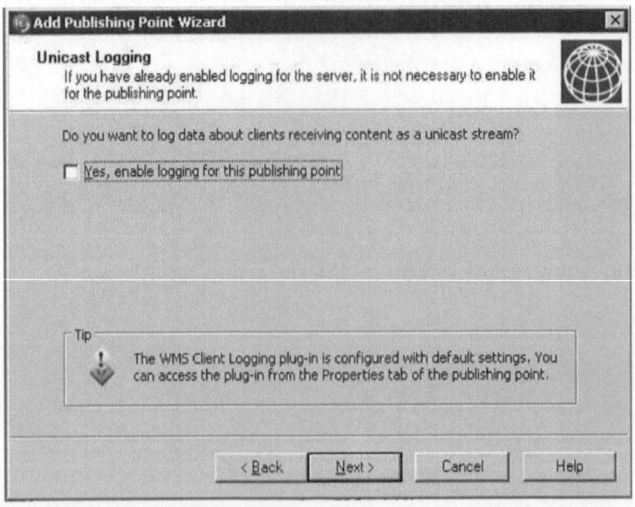

Figure 10-13
Check "Yes" if you want to log activity by connecting Windows Media players.

9. Review the publishing point settings, as shown in **Figure 10-14**, and modify as needed. Leave the options under the review panel in their default configuration.

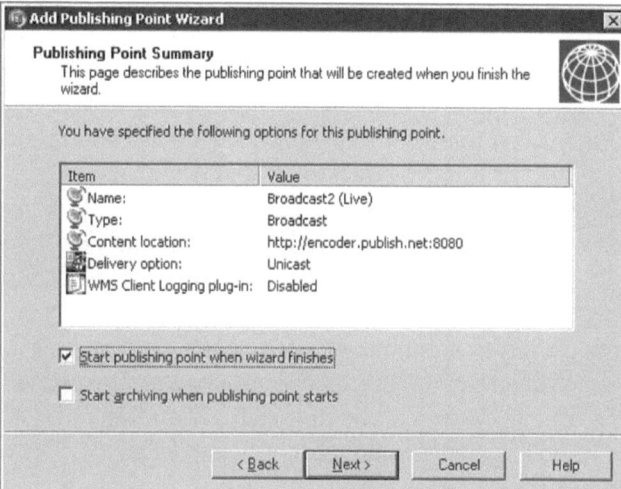

Figure 10-14
Review the publishing point settings and modify as needed.

10. Click Finish in the final box, as shown in **Figure 10-15**. To review the steps for creating an announcement file, go to the section "Create an Announcement File" in Chapter 1.

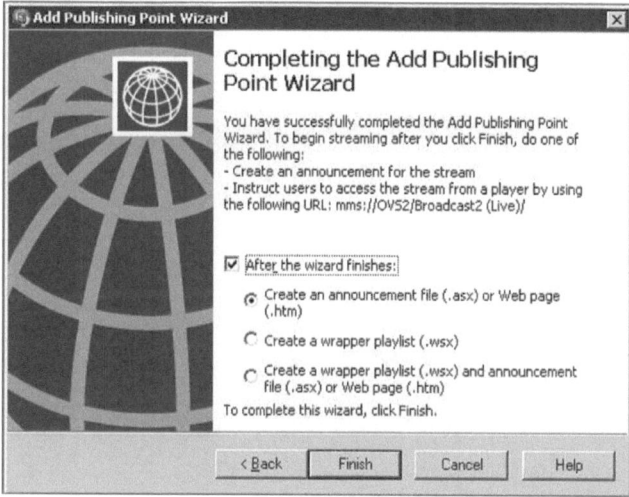

Figure 10-15
Click Finish to start the announcement wizard.

Similar to on-demand webcasts, you can monitor the number of live connections, bandwidth usage, and other metrics in real time via the Monitor tab of the Windows Media Services Administrator. You can modify the URL to the encoder via the Source tab. And you can also generate a new announcement file via the Announce tab.

Creating Rollover Playlists

In live webcasting, anything can happen, including the loss of the webcast stream at a critical moment. Inevitably, something will break. A camera will fail, a wire comes loose in a cable connector, or the power goes out. In a near worst-case scenario, an encoder fails.

However, if you've planned ahead and followed the principle of redundancy, in most cases the viewer may not ever know something went wrong. They may experience a brief interruption in the stream. At worst, they may see a "Please stand by" message for a short time.

Windows Media Services offers a technique called a rollover or *failover* playlist. Essentially, it's a server-side playlist of stream URLs that are played when the primary stream disappears for some reason. When a player senses that a stream has gone away, it first tries to reconnect, and if it can't, it moves to the next URL in the list.

For example, imagine you are at a live event at a remote location. You have both encoders going, and everything is running smoothly. Suddenly, the NIC in your primary encoder, which you've named Encoder1, fails, and the stream goes away. It's annoying, but you're not worried, because Encoder2, the backup encoder, takes over. Then, a few seconds later, the power in the building disappears. Encoder2 shuts down. Ten seconds later, the power comes back, everything in your road kit restarts, nothing is damaged, and you're able to get a stream out of Encoder2 within a minute or so.

Your viewers experienced nothing except a short interruption in service and a brief notice to "Please stand by." It happened automatically. You did it by creating a **.wsx** file in the Windows Media Services Administrator. Use the Add Publishing Point Wizard to create a playlist and remember to check the "loop" checkbox.

The contents of the playlist are:

```
<?wsx version="1.0" encoding="utf-8"?>
<smil>
    <media src="http://www.Encoder1.com:8080"/>
    <media src="http://www.Encoder2.com:8080"/>
    <media src="C:\trouble\standby.jpg" dur="10s"/>
</smil>
```

Here's what happened on the client side when disaster struck:

- When Encoder1 failed, the player tried to reconnect, and when it couldn't, it successfully connected to Encoder2.
- When Encoder2 failed, the player tried to reconnect, and when it couldn't, it successfully requested a JPEG image called "standby.jpg" and played it for 10 seconds.
- After 10 seconds, the player tried Encoder1, then Encoder2.
- Failing again, the player displayed standby.jpg (which never went away from the player window).
- This loop continued until Encoder2 restarted, and the live stream continued.

The viewer may have noticed the loss of audio and the player trying to reconnect by showing the message "Connecting to media..." But the player window displays "Please stand by." If the interruption of signal doesn't last too long, the viewer will wait patiently for its return.

 ALERT For rollover server-side playlists to work properly, you must set Windows Media Server to loop the playlist. Otherwise, the player will display only the "Please stand by" message, even if the streams return.

Conclusion

Encoding for a live webcast is similar to encoding for on-demand distribution, with the exception that the live stream is delivered immediately in real time. Serving a live stream is similar to on-demand, except that you set-up a live publishing point, as opposed to an on-demand publishing point. Live streaming is one step further advanced that on-demand streaming. In the next chapter, you'll learn about encoding techniques for the newest generation of content and devices.

CHAPTER 11

Going Beyond the Desktop

Streaming media is primarily an application for the desktop or laptop computer. Most people at present access and view streams from these devices. But the technology isn't limited to the desktop. Microsoft, among other companies, is moving streaming technology to other platforms, namely *high-definition television* (HDTV) and portable devices, such as cell phones. And the proliferation of these devices, as well as continued growth in desktop use, has made copyright protections ever more important. This chapter surveys some of the most important technological developments in these areas. You'll learn about:

- Advances in streaming high-definition video
- The potential for streaming on portable devices
- Protecting your intellectual property with encryption

Windows Media High-Definition Video

The greatest advance in television technology for almost half a century occurred with the advent of high-definition television (HDTV) in the 1980s. Though adoption by broadcasters and producers was relatively slow, more and more consumers are enjoying video with larger images and sharper pictures produced and broadcast in HDTV format.

Inevitably, streaming media developers, particularly Microsoft, jumped on the HDTV bandwagon, creating tools and technologies for taking advantage of high-definition video on computer displays. The Windows Media Series 9 Encoder features codecs specifically designed for encoding high-definition video into Windows Media files.

Windows Media High Definition and Streaming

Typical high-definition (HD) video differs from standard video in three main ways, insofar as streaming is concerned.

- 16:9 aspect ratio (standard video has a 4:3 aspect ratio)
- 720p and 1,080i resolutions (standard video is 480p)

- Multichannel or surround sound audio (standard audio for video is mono or stereo)

The result is an extremely sharp image that's been compared to 35 millimeter film, the standard film size for movies and professional photography. The audio has more depth and detail as well.

Inside the Industry

High-def video comes in two resolutions, 720p and 1,080i, which refer to the number of horizontal pixels in the image. High-def resolution is at least two-thirds greater than standard video, which means a sharper, more realistic image.

The "p" in "720p" refers to "progressive scan," the method for painting an image on a computer screen. Television monitors use another method called "interlacing."

For the streaming media specialist, working with high-def video poses a number of problems:

- **File size**: Because high-def video contains much more information than standard video, the sizes of source files and encoded files are much larger. A full-length movie can take up a minimum of 300 gigabytes of storage.
- **Processing power**: Both encoding and playback of high-def files requires much more processing power than standard video. In fact, high-def pushes even the most advanced personal computer hardware, including processors, hard drives, and other peripherals, to its limits.
- **Bandwidth**: The bit rates for Windows Media High-Definition (WMHD) start at the 1 megabyte range, which is near the limit of the fattest DSL lines. In fact, most material encoded into WMHD today is either downloaded for playback from a hard drive or burned onto a DVD.

As you can see, the problems are similar to the ones you face working with standard video, just magnified.

Building a WMHD Encoding Machine

An encoding computer for WMHD needs much more power and storage than any encoding computer to date. The sheer amount of information in a high-definition AVI file would overwhelm most off-the-shelf boxes. Here's a few requirements:

- **Multiple, high-speed processors**: Windows Media Encoder can take advantage of dual-processor machines, encoding audio with two processors and video with four. Pick a machine with a pair of high-speed Pentium 4 or Athlon 3000 processors.

- **Multiple, high-speed SCSI hard drives and other high-performance hardware**: SCSI drives running at 15,000 rpm in a redundant array of independent disks (RAID) level 0 are about the only drives that can handle the work needed to store and access high-def files. You'll need a minimum of 300 gigabytes of storage for one full-length movie. It's also a good idea to get a dual PCI bus motherboard. This allows you to separate the capture card from the SCSI card, reducing the chances for dropped frames. Finally, install a multichannel audio card.

- **Microsoft Windows XP Professional x64**: The newest Microsoft operating system for professionals has multithreading technology that maximizes the use of dual-processor boxes. While you're at it, upgrade to the latest service pack and the most recent version of DirectX, Microsoft's system for managing graphics of all types.

Capturing for WMHD

Although a discussion of high-definition video production is outside the scope of this book, the basic steps for capturing and encoding are similar to standard video.

You can capture video from a high-def tape or a high-def camera using specialized capture cards that create AVI files the encoder recognizes. If you already have high-def computer files, you need to convert them to AVIs using the features of a high-def nonlinear editing system (NLE). High-def MPEG2 files can also be encoded using a special plug-in for Windows Media Player installed on the encoding computer.

Put Punch into Your Playback Computer

Playback computers for high-def require nearly the same power as encoding computers. Microsoft recommends the following configurations for playing Windows Media High Definition files without too many hiccups.

Minimum Configuration for 720p high-def video:

- Windows XP
- Windows Media Player 9 Series
- 2.4 GHz processor or equivalent
- 384 MB of RAM
- 64 MB AGP4s video card
- DVD drive
- 1024 × 768 screen resolution
- 16-bit sound card
- Speakers

Optimum Configuration for 1080p with Dolby 5.1 surround sound:

- Windows XP
- Windows Media Player 9 Series
- DirectX 9.0
- 3.0 GHz processor or equivalent
- 512 MB of RAM
- 128 MB AGP4x video card
- DVD drive
- 1920 × 1440 screen resolution
- 24-bit 96 kHz multichannel sound card
- 5.1 surround sound speaker system

The monitor is key to a good high-def experience. You can get good results with the latest flat-panel displays, provided you get a big one. You can also hook up your playback computer to flat panel TVs that hang on the wall. Visit the Microsoft website for more information. Lastly, make sure your computer supports DxVA (DirectX Video Acceleration). This helps the decompression of your video for playback.

When capturing high-def video, keep these practices in mind:

- Capture content at the original frame rate, especially if it's from a motion picture shot on film. Movies are shot at 24 frames per second.
- Capture to a YUY2 format to maintain good colors.
- Capture at the video's original pixel size.
- If you capture audio separately, synchronize the audio with the video in a high-def video editing suite.

Once you've captured your video, use a high-quality high-def editing suite to add effects, titles and other enhancements, and render the files to an AVI file the encoder can read.

Encoding for WMHD

Encoding for Windows Media High Definition video is similar to standard video. The main difference is distribution. Although WMHD can be streamed, most WMHD files are either downloaded for playback on a hard drive or burned onto a DVD. Streaming HD is about ten years behind standard video streaming, mostly due to limited bandwidth.

To encode a high-def file for download or DVD distribution, use the "Convert a file" wizard in Windows Media Series 9 Encoder. In the "Content Distribution" box, select the appropriate method, as shown in **Figure 11-1**.

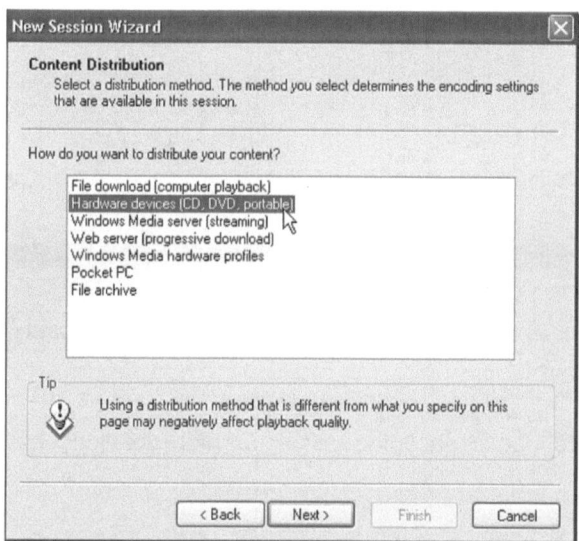

Figure 11-1
Choose the appropriate method for distributing your Windows Media High Definition video.

After selecting the method, choose the audio and video codecs, as shown in **Figure 11-2**. The main difference between the download and device (CD, DVD, portable) options are the bit rates, which reflect the differing capabilities of hard disk drives and other storage devices. You also have more codec options with distribution by download.

Inside the Industry

 Encoding professionals are taking a close look at an update to Windows Media Video 9 called *Windows Media Video 9 Advanced Profile*. Included with Windows Media Player 10, the Windows Media Format 9.5 SDK, and the latest codec installation packages, Advanced Profile offers better interlaced support and transport format independence. It works best with Windows Media Player 10, but it can be used with older players. To use this codec with Windows Media Encoder 9 Series, Windows Media Player 10 must be installed.

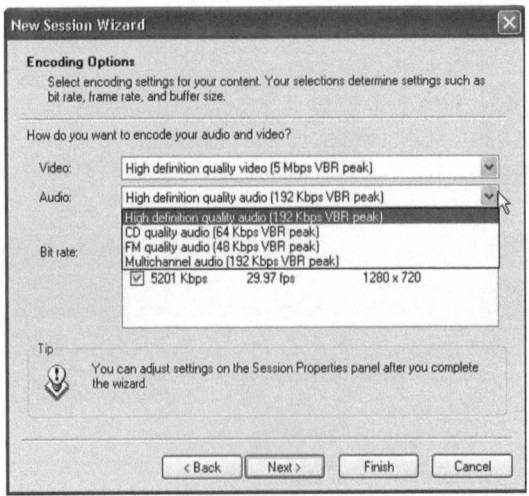

Figure 11-2
Select the audio and video codecs. Options for distribution via CD, DVD and portable devices are shown.

If you choose to customize an encoding session for high-def video, keep these principles in mind:

*   Preserve the aspect ratio of the source video, usually 16:9.
*   Higher bit rates mean better image and sound quality.
*   Match the encoded frame rate to the frame rate of the source video.

- Keep your target playback device in mind. Unlike standard streaming video files, WMHD files may be played back on a television, which uses interlacing instead of progressive scan. For example, if you're targeting a TV as the playback device, you may want to skip de-interlacing during the editing process.

- Maintain the pixel aspect ratio if your source has nonsquare pixels.

- Choose a key frame rate that suits the content. If your content is talking heads, fewer key frames mean a smaller file size without sacrificing quality. An action movie needs more key frames, because the image changes so much during the timeline.

Author's Tip

Because Windows Media High Definition files are rarely streamed, you'll find yourself using variable bit rate (VBR) encoding. VBR codecs maintain quality of the video image no matter the type of shot or scene, whether it's high action or talking heads. VBR is used exclusively for encoding files meant for playback from a hard drive or other storage device.

If you have enough bandwidth to stream high-def video, use constant bit rate (CBR) codecs, which you'll access when you select streaming as your distribution method in the encoder.

ALERT Before encoding the entire video file, encode a minute's worth and play it back to check quality. Encoding high-def video is in its infancy, so don't be surprised if you have to make further adjustments and do some troubleshooting before encoding the whole file.

Windows Media on Portable Devices

Two related types of communications technologies promise a revolution comparable to the emergence of the Internet in the early 1990s. Multifunctional cellular telephones and the growing capabilities of wireless communications are combining to form a mobile communications network that puts a planet-full of information at your fingertips, whether you're at a mall, on the freeway, or on top of Mount Everest.

Streaming video on wireless networks is taking the first baby steps toward reality, at least in the United States, where wireless technology and deployment is several years behind the rest of the world. Even so, a revolution is happening all around. Just look at picture phones. It's fun to send a picture of your daughter playing softball on a muddy field to grandma's cell phone 500 miles away. Some observers predict camera phones will outsell standard still cameras over time, as shown in **Figure 11-3**.

Wireless streaming isn't limited to the cellular network. People are using 802.11b networks at their local coffee shop with laptops and *personal digital assistants*, or PDAs, such as Pocket PCs. But the real buzz is about streaming to cell phones. And the key to the success

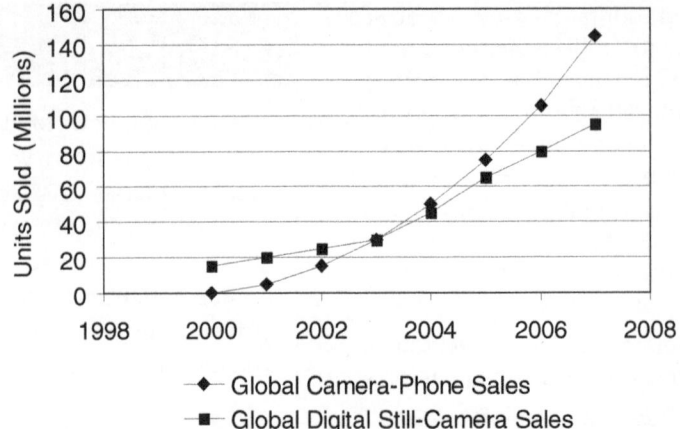

Figure 11-3
Sales of cell phones that can take and send photos is expected to outsell sales of still cameras.
Source: Strategy Analytics, www.strategyanalytics.com

of streaming media over the cell phone network is the deployment of *3G wireless networks*, which feature as much as 2 megabytes per second of bandwidth when the viewer is standing still. (The amount of available bandwidth falls as the viewer moves, such as walking or driving.) Japan and other Asian countries, as well as Europe, have enjoyed 3G for years. American companies are just now deploying 3G networks.

Differences between Mobile Streaming and Wired Streaming

The basic client/server model of streaming media as described in this book applies to mobile streaming. Source files are encoded, placed on a server, and made available through the wireless telephone network. But mobile streaming, especially with Windows Media, faces some important challenges.

- **Inconsistent hardware**: Streaming media professionals can safely assume that the hardware player streaming media over a wired connection or even certain kinds of wireless connections, such as 802.11b, are using an IBM-compatible personal computer or an Apple Computer product.

  Wireless phones, however, are built with proprietary technologies often incompatible with one another. Mobile devices vary widely in terms of processor power, memory, operating system, protocol support, client software, screen size, and color depth. Furthermore, new devices are introduced every day, it seems, and the new features in new phones are sometimes incompatible with similar features in older cousins.

- **Video formats**: The only common video format supported by all 3G phones is MPEG-4. Support for MPEG-4 is mandated by the 3rd Generation Partnership Project (3GPP), the leading industry standards body for 3G devices and networks. In addition to designating MPEG-4 as the standard video format, the 3G industry has set media format standards regarding audio, graphics, and

MIDI support. As a rule, most mobile phones with streaming capabilities do not support Windows Media.

- **Mobility**: The cell phone's greatest strength, its mobility, is the major technological drawback from a streaming perspective. Whereas the bandwidth for a wired connection can remain fairly consistent over time, the amount of bandwidth on a mobile network can change dramatically from one city block to the next.

  Two other factors affect bandwidth: 1) The number of devices operating simultaneously within a cell, and 2) the speed at which the device is traveling through the cell. (You have less bandwidth when talking while driving than talking while walking.) Lastly, high bandwidth coverage remains spotty within the emerging 3G networks and seamless roaming between 3G networks is problematic.

Solutions and Windows Media

Several mobile streaming media companies are working on the problems. Packet Video has focused on porting their software client to a wide selection of handsets and operating systems. Vidiator Technology is enabling its server to *transcode* and *transform* streams to match the capabilities of the target device. Transcoding involves a format change, such as delivering a Windows Media video file as a 3GPP-compliant MPEG-4 file. Transforming involves changing display characteristics of a file such as dimensions, aspect ratio, pixel density and color depth.

For its part, Microsoft has built Windows Media Player 10 Mobile, specially designed for cell phones that run Microsoft Windows Mobile 2003 SE operating system. The software runs on these cell phones in the United States:

- Audiovox SMT 5600
- i-mate SP3
- Motorola MPx220
- Samsung SCH-i600
- Voq Professional Phone

Check with your cellular provider for details on availability of 3G-capable cell phones and services in your area.

Encoding and Serving Windows Media for Mobile Devices

Preparing your video content for streaming over mobile devices such as cell phones isn't that much different than for other streaming. The most obvious difference is the image size. For example, Microsoft recommends an image size of 208 × 160 pixels with a frame rate of 20 frames per second for Pocket PC. Not exactly high-def, but it's a beginning.

The "Convert a file" wizard in Windows Media Series 9 Encoder contains an option for Pocket PC encoding, as shown in **Figure 11-4**. The video and audio codecs are limited to "standard" and "widescreen" for video, and "CD quality" or "voice quality" for audio.

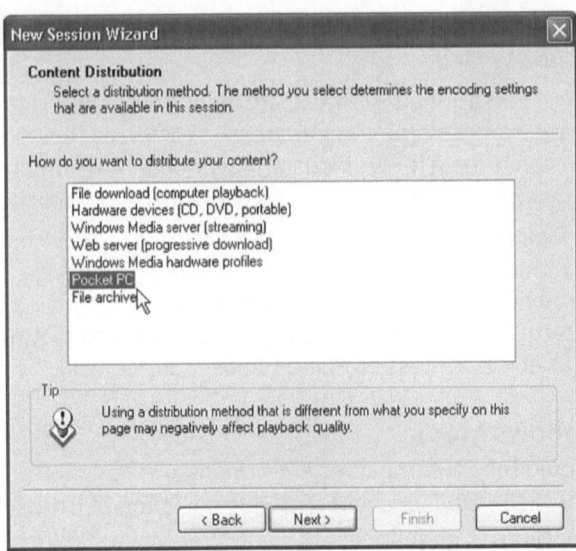

Figure 11-4
The "Convert a file" wizard in Windows Media Encoder offers a Pocket PC option.

You also can customize an encoding session for mobile streaming and save the session as a session profile.

On the server side, ask your network administrator to enable forward error correction on your publishing points. This helps maintain the integrity of data transmitted over unreliable cellular networks with spotty coverage. With forward error correction, the server sends out extra packets of data on the assumption that some will be lost on the way to the client. The client then has an easier time reconstructing a stream. It's another variation on the theme of redundancy.

Windows Media Digital Rights Management

One of most heated debates of the last years of the dot-com boom concerned file sharing. Music lovers, particularly college students, found they could convert music files on CDs to mp3 format and send them to friends over networks or burn custom CDs. Thus began the controversy over copyright protections for digital media. Although file-sharing continues, copyright protection and media distribution technologies have advanced significantly, allowing companies and individuals to enjoy income from their work while distributing their creations to fans over the Internet and recently over cellular telephone networks.

The most sophisticated protection technologies come under the heading of *digital rights management* or *DRM*. In simplest terms, the 1s and 0s of a digital media file, whether audio or video, are scrambled or *encrypted*. The file (live or on-demand) is said to be *protected*. To hear or see the file, the user must purchase a license, often via a website with a credit card. Windows Media Player applies the license key to the file and unscrambles the data.

DRM can be applied to a variety of business scenarios:

- Individual songs
- Sets of songs or whole albums
- Pay-per-view movies or TV programs
- Movie rentals (license limited by time or number of playbacks)
- Subscriptions (license applied to range of services for limited periods of time)

A prerequisite for a successful application of DRM is a business model. How do you want to limit access? For example, do you want to allow a limited number of playbacks for promotional purposes before requiring a fee for unlimited use? What value do you want to place on the exclusivity of your encrypted content? In other words, can a user get the same content for free or lower price somewhere else?

Although business models are still evolving, it seems that users are willing to pay for access if the content is compelling. The best historical precedent is cable television. Before the advent of modern cable channels, people could access virtually all television programming free over the air. In the late 1970s, cable companies began offering full-length movies without commercials to subscribers. But you had to pay a fee to get the movies. Consumers liked the convenience and availability of movies in their homes, and the businesses thrived. The Internet age added a new twist: customization. Downloading individual songs for a fee allowed users to build their own lists of songs and play them back whenever it pleased them.

How DRM Works

Digital rights management starts with one or more *rights* sold to a media user allowing him or her to play an encrypted file. The rights are available only to that user on that device. If a file is copied to another device, it can't be played unless another license is acquired.

From a technological point of view, it's relatively easy to apply a set of rules to a file and match a right to the file allowing playback. The hard part is managing those rights to thousands, perhaps millions, of individual files or sets of files. The rights themselves can be very complex. Variables include time, number of plays, fee or no fee, artist, publisher, country, anything that a company or individual (or lawyer) can come up with. Different rights could be applied to the same content at different times. And you may even need to revoke all licenses if the copyright comes into dispute or you detect tampering. In short, DRM rules can be designed to meet just about every need.

Here's one scenario from the user's perspective:

1. User visits a website and registers
2. User downloads a protected music file
3. The license allows the user to play the file three times

4. At the fourth playback attempt, the user is prompted to re-visit the website and purchase a license to play the file again
5. The user purchases the license with a credit card
6. At the next playback attempt, the file plays normally

Most of the background stuff is invisible to the user. At each playback attempt, Windows Media Player checks whether the user has the correct rights, first by looking on the hard drive, then by checking a database at a remote computer with license information. The database may be run by a third-party license provider. Throughout the process, the player reacts accordingly to the rules you have written.

Figure 11-5 shows a simplified DRM process.

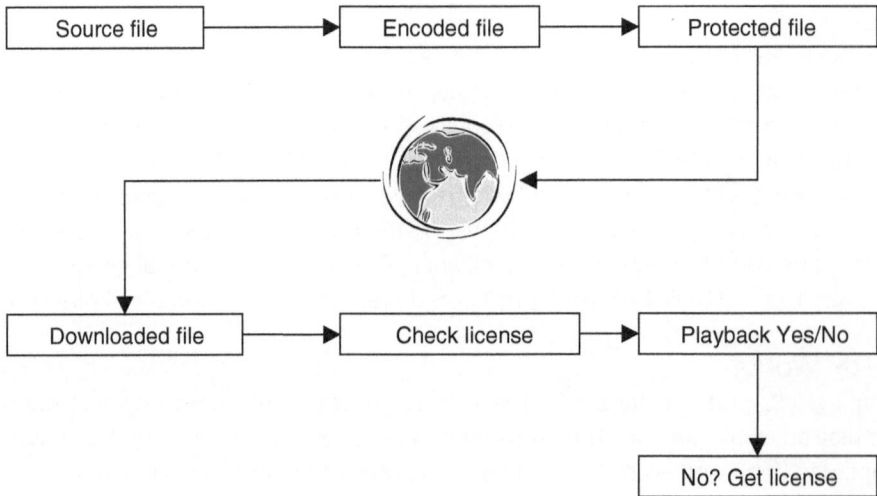

Figure 11-5
A simplified process for digital rights management.

Inside the Industry

Until recently, most digital rights management focused on desktop or laptop computers. With the release of Microsoft's latest DRM system, version 10, rights holders can apply licensing strategies to portable devices, such as cell phones, and to home entertainment devices networked to a personal computer.

Protecting Files with Windows Media Encoder

Before you can protect an encoded Windows Media file, you need an account with a *license provider*. (Check the Microsoft Windows Media website for a list.) The provider creates a *DRM profile* for you and gives you information for generating encryption keys. The provider will ask how you want users to pay for the licenses, the rights you want to provide, and information about your content. The provider may send you a file that you'll use with the encoder. Everybody does things a little differently, which is good, because it sows confusion among prospective copyright criminals. Note that DRM does not require a Windows Media Encoder; you can apply DRM rules with other applications after encoding.

Here's a typical scenario that assumes a license provider has e-mailed you a Windows Media Digital Rights Management (**.drm**) file. The provider will also send you a *key ID*, which is stored in the encrypted file.

1. Open Windows Media Encoder and start a custom session.
2. Load the source **.avi** file, designate an output file, and set the other parameters, such as codecs.
3. Click the Security tab.
4. Click the "Import..." button.
5. Enter the password for the **.drm** file given to you by the license provider.
6. After the DRM profile loads, check the box labeled "Use DRM to protect content from unauthorized use."
7. Copy and paste the key ID into the "Key ID" text box, as shown in **Figure 11-6**.
8. When you are ready to encode, click the green "Start Encoding" button.

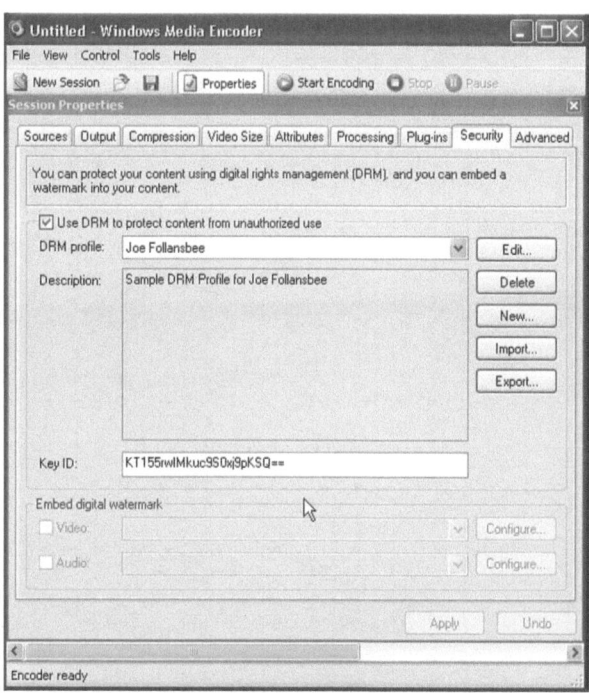

Figure 11-6
The Security tab in Windows Media Encoder with a sample DRM file loaded and key ID entered.

Conclusion

Streaming media is steadily moving into the still murky territory of high-definition television and wireless communications. But the potential, especially in wireless, for new types of streaming content and applications is enormous. The new channels of distribution call for more vigilance in the fields of copyright protections, which digital rights management attempts to provide. In the next chapter, you'll learn more advanced techniques related to customizing Windows Media Player and measuring the success of your streaming programs.

CHAPTER 12

Advanced Topics

As you gain experience with Windows Media Series 9, you'll discover a wealth of features that let you create and manage a cutting-edge streaming media communications system. You can customize the user experience by adding webpages embedded within the player interface or manage the entire interface with skins and borders. As your streaming media delivery system becomes more complex, you can test their ability to deliver streams reliably with advanced testing techniques. And you can analyze your traffic patterns via logs generated by Windows Media Server. By the end of this chapter, you will:

- Understand the principles behind player customization
- Know the options for testing performance with the Windows Media Load Simulator
- Learn how to evaluate streaming traffic with server logs

Customizing Windows Media Player

In Chapter 8, Delivering Windows Media to Your Audience, you learned that you don't have to limit the end user experience of your audio or video to the standalone Windows Media Player. The section "Embedding Playback in a Webpage" described how to place player objects, such as the video window and Play/Pause/Stop controls, in an HTML page. In this section, you'll explore three other methods for customizing the user experience: HTMLview, skins, and borders.

HTMLView

Just as you embed player objects in an HTML page using the OBJECT tag, you embed HTML pages within the Windows Media Player interface with the HTMLView parameter of the Windows Media announcement or metafile, which has the .asx extension. See **Figure 12-1** for an example.

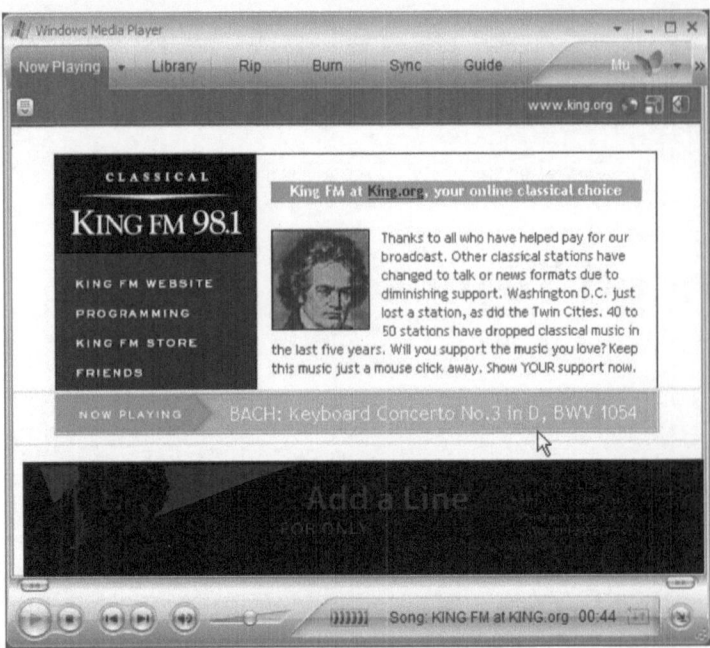

Figure 12-1
HTMLView lets you embed an HTML page inside the Now Playing pane of Windows Media Player.

First, create an HTML page with a DIV element containing the images and text you want to display.

Next, add an embedded player using the OBJECT tag, similar to a page with an embedded player that would be displayed in a web browser. (To review the use of the OBJECT tag, see Chapter 8.) The OBJECT tag includes additional PARAM key/value pairs, for example:

```
<PARAM name="uiMode" value="invisible">
```

The "uiMode" parameter tells Windows Media Player not to display the player controls, such as Play/Pause/Stop, in the HTML, because they're not needed.

Then add scripting that pulls data from either the HTML page or the ASX file and displays it in the player. Caveat: You need to use Jscript, Microsoft's answer to JavaScript, to build the functions needed to display the data. For example, a Jscript function may contain the line:

```
d.innerHTML=WMP.currentMedia.getItemInfo('Abstract')
```

This tells the player to extract information from the ABSTRACT parameter of the ASX file (see below) and display it in the HTML element with the ID "d".

Finally, create an ASX file with the HTMLView parameter. Here's a sample:

```
<ASX version="3.0" >

<PARAM name="HTMLView" value="http://www.myserver.com/info.htm" />

<Entry>

    <Abstract>A description of the file now playing. </Abstract>

    <ref href="mms://www.mediaserver.com/file.wmv" />

</Entry>

</ASX>
```

When the user clicks the ASX file, the player contacts the web server for the HTML file as well as the Windows Media Server for the media file. It also grabs the ABSTRACT data and displays it in the proper place in the HTML file.

As you can guess, this type of coding isn't for the faint of heart. It's worth getting the help of an experienced web developer to make this work.

Skins and Borders

One of the main problems with Windows Media Player and most other kinds of desktop software is that they are boring to look at. Early twenty-first century user interface design is usually a compromise between a contemporary look and a fear of terrorizing the user. It's a little like oatmeal—nutritious, but dull.

You can mitigate this problem with skins, which the book discussed briefly in Chapter 2, Streaming Media Basics. Although skin design is beyond the scope of this book, you don't need to be an expert programmer or designer to play around with them. If you have some experience with HTML and especially XML, which is like HTML only more flexible, basic scripting, and you have a graphics program, you can build a skin.

Before doing anything, plan your skin. What do you want it to look like? Do you want the Play button to look a certain way? For example, you may be designing

Author's Tip

Why build a skin at all? Other than giving users something new to look at, there are some solid business reasons to offer a skin. Perhaps you work at a media company that has a very strong identity among consumers. Perhaps that identity is tied to a widely-known character or logo. Building a skin around that identity reinforces an association between your media product and that identity, while differentiating your product from competitors.

You may also want to remove features or functions of the player you don't like or need, perhaps for security reasons.

a skin for your Formula 1 racing videos. The Play/Pause/Stop buttons could represent a stoplight. Green means "Play"; yellow means "Pause"; red means "Stop."

Graphic Elements — Next, create the graphic elements for your skin, including the background graphics, the buttons, a logo, text, and so on. The art files for skins fall into three types:

1. **Primary**: These images are the default images the user sees when they first load the skinned player.
2. **Mapping**: When a user puts their mouse over a mapped image, the mouse indicates that the area is clickable. The player does something when the area is clicked.
3. **Alternate**: These images offer feedback about what's happening or could happen. For example, using the Formula 1 racing example, rolling a mouse over the green button makes it turn a slightly brighter shade of green, indicating the potential for some action. When the button is clicked, the button remains bright green until the pause or stop button is clicked.

Save these elements in a commonly used graphics file format, such as GIF or JPEG.

Skin Definition File — After you've created the skin elements, you'll write a *skin definition file*, which is a script that tells Windows Media Player what to do with the graphic elements and how to behave when users click on elements. A skin definition file is a plain text file that follows a defined format using XML. The code below gives you a sense of what a definition file looks like.

```
<theme id="main" title="MyTheme">

  <view id="topView">

    <subview id="sub1">

      <button id="play" />

    </subview>

  </view>

</theme>
```

The above code doesn't actually do anything. To see a real skin definition file, look for files on your hard drive with the **.wmz** extension, typically located in "*C:\Program Files\Windows Media Player\Skins*". Use your favorite archiving application, such as WinZip, to open the file. Now locate and open a file with the **.wms** extension. This is the skin definition file for the skin you selected.

As you'll see, a highly functional skin is fairly complex, making use of Jscript and a variety of actions and attributes available to the skin programmer. For a full explanation of skin programming possibilities, visit the Windows Media section of the Microsoft Developer Network, *http://msdn.microsoft.com/*.

When you're finished writing your skin definition file, save it with a **.wms** extension.

Testing and Distribution — Once you have created your graphics files and your skin definition files, test your new skin as extensively as you can. Archive all the graphics and the definition file into a single **.zip** file and change the extension to **.wmz**. Send it around to a few friends and ask them to test it out. Once all the bugs are fixed, post it on your website for download.

The skin will be installed in the Skins directory of your Windows Media Player. To load the skin, click the View menu and select Skin Chooser. The player will offer a selection of skins, as shown in **Figure 12-2**.

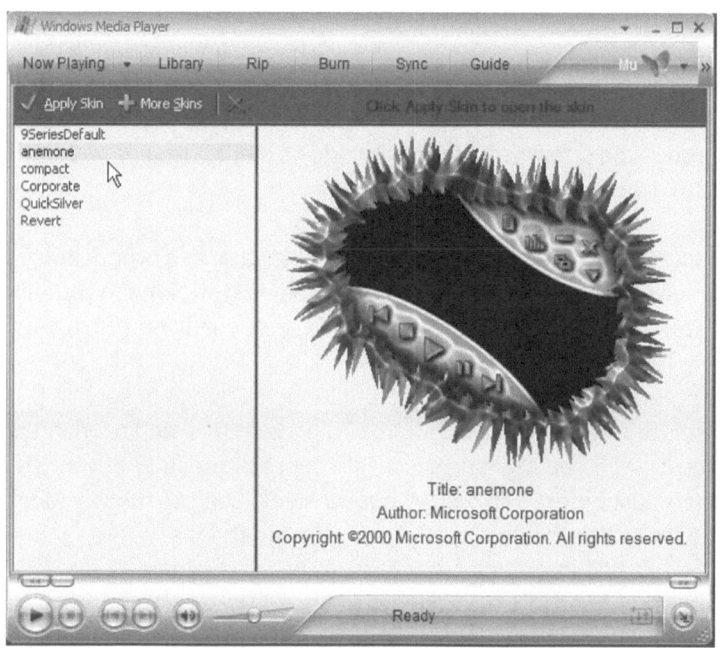

Figure 12-2
Skin Chooser in Windows Media Player showing skin options and a preview.

Borders — Borders are a toned-down version of skins that display within the Windows Media Player "Now Playing" panel. (Despite the name, it actually appears within the player window.) To create a border, build a skin as described above. Then write a normal ASX file, adding this line:

```
<skin href="myskin.wmz">
```

Archive the **.asx** and **.wmz** files into a single **.zip** file and changed the **.zip** extension to **.wmd**. You've just built a Windows Media Download Package file. Post it on your website, and when your users download it, the border will install and the stream will play.

Advanced Testing Techniques

A plan to distribute streaming media that anticipates any more than a few hits a day requires extensive testing before deployment. You don't want to be caught unaware of a problem because you didn't anticipate the effects of a heavy load on your servers from a popular stream. It's not practical to recruit hundreds of folks to hit your streaming boxes. Besides, it's best to test in an environment where you can eliminate as many unrelated variables as possible and run as many scenarios as time and resources permit.

Fortunately, Microsoft offers a free tool that lets you simulate the kind of traffic you expect. Called the *Windows Media Load Simulator,* it pretends to be one or hundreds of Windows Media Players requesting streams from your Windows Media servers, without actually getting any stream data.

A couple of warnings: First, you should not use the simulator in a production setting, that is, don't send simulated requests to servers already serving streams to your audience. That could negatively affect the delivery of other streams, potentially hurting the user experience.

Second, programmers with bad intentions could launch a denial of service (DoS) attack on your streaming servers with the load simulator. To prevent this, find a small Windows Media video file, rename it "WMLoad.asf," and place it in the root directory of your steaming server, *\WMPub\WMRoot*, just before you test. Windows Media Load Simulator looks for this file before beginning the test. When you're finished, remove the file.

Using the Windows Media Load Simulator

Here's a typical scenario with the Windows Media Load Simulator (WMLS):

1. Download and install Windows Media Load Simulator from the Microsoft website.
2. Once installed, open WMLS.
3. Click Tools → Configurations Wizard. Click Next.
4. Enter your Windows Media Server name, for example, *www.myserver.com*. Click Next.

5.	In the "Streaming Content Sources" box, enter the name of the file you want to test, as shown in **Figure 12-3**. Note that the check boxes "MMST," "MMSU," "RTSP," and "RTSU" are checked. Click Next.

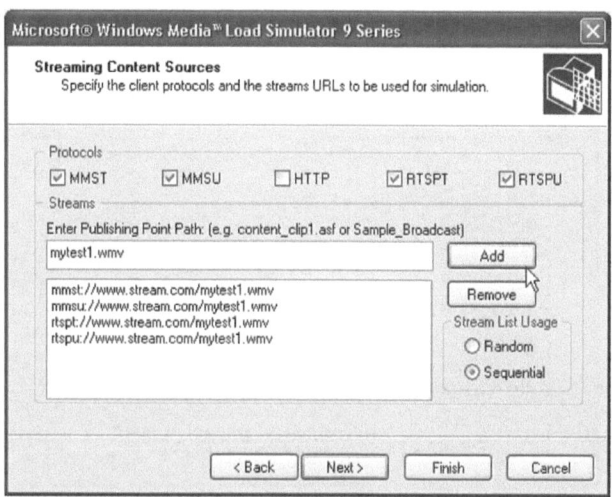

Figure 12-3
Enter the name of the streamed file to be tested in Windows Media Load Simulator.

6.	In the "Client Profiles" box, enter a set of numbers you think accurately represents a reasonable amount of traffic to your streaming server, as shown in **Figure 12-4**. There's a bit of guesswork at this point. However, you can run a number of tests across a spectrum of scenarios to see where the breaking points of your server might be. Click Next.

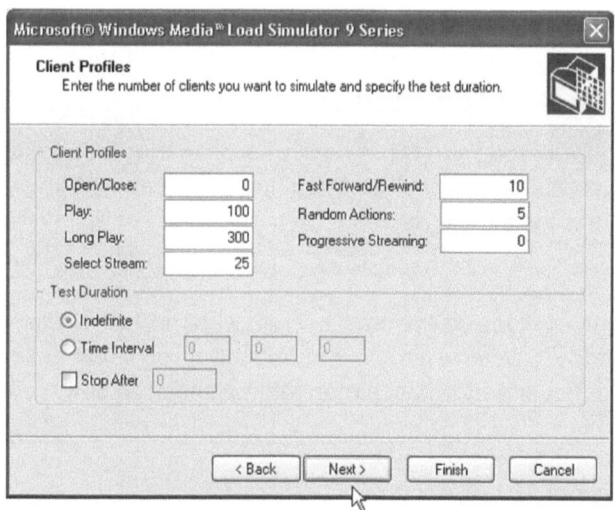

Figure 12-4
Enter some numbers you think would represent traffic to your server.

7. In the "Advanced Test Options" box, click Next.

8. In the "Simulate Authentication Clients" box, click Next.

9. In the "Load Simulation Monitoring Options" box, check the box labeled "Enable Log Simulator Logging," as shown in **Figure 12-5**. This creates a log storing the experience of each simulated client. Click Next.

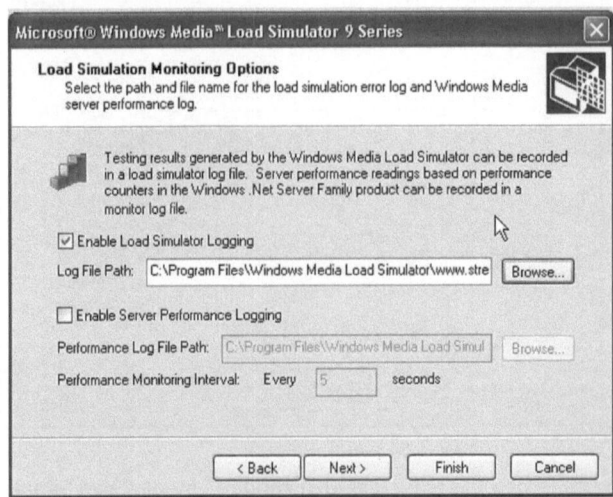

Figure 12-5
Enable the logging feature of WMLS.

10. Click Finish.

11. Review the simulation you've created by clicking on the Properties button at the top of WMLS, as shown in **Figure 12-6**. You can also get a thumbnail of the test properties by clicking the "Test Configuration Details" tab.

12. When you're ready to begin the test, click the Start Test button.

ALERT If you find yourself using similar scenarios for a lot of tests, save the scenarios in a configuration file, known as a "WMLoad Projects" file. It has the extension **.bts**.

While the test is running, keep an eye on the server with the Task Manager and the Performance Monitor. You'll know almost immediately if you're overloading it. Also, watch the Windows Media Server performance monitor as a check on how the WMLS is working with the server.

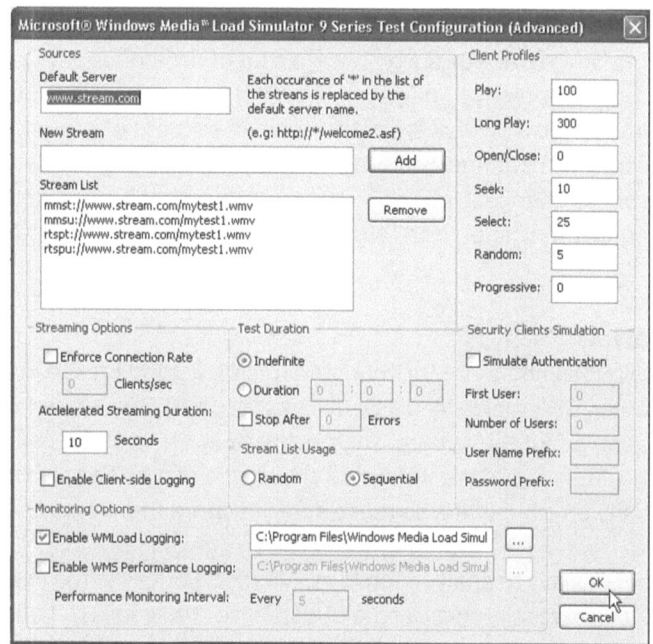

Figure 12-6
Review the properties of your test in the Properties box of WMLS.

Reviewing the WMLS Log

When your test is complete, look for a **.csv** file in the root directory of Windows Media Load Simulator. This is the log of the test. Open the file in a Microsoft Excel spreadsheet or load it into a Microsoft Access table for analysis.

Interpreting the results takes some understanding of networking and experience with log files. If you get a lot of connection failures, there's obviously a problem with your network. Or if you notice more failures as the number of connections rises, you may not have enough bandwidth to handle the load you expect. Run several tests in order to narrow down a particularly mysterious problem.

Author's Tip

For best results, perform load tests with two or more computers running WMLS clients.

ALERT Remember that a simulation is just a very fancy game of pretend. If you run a sophisticated model, you can predict with some accuracy the results of certain loads on your streaming servers. But there always seems to be one variable that you forgot, so keep a skeptical eye on your testing.

Measuring Success

All the fancy technology in the world won't make a bit of difference if it's not successful in the marketplace. Furthermore, you need to prove that it's successful, and generating some sort of positive return. Media owners typically measure success of properties, such as radio shows and TV sitcoms, with ratings. Streaming media also requires measurement of stream quality and the user experience. Online technology provides the most detailed types of data for gauging by storing information from each click in a log that can be analyzed in near real-time.

Client Log Analysis

When you create a publishing point for your streams, it's a good idea to enable unicast logging. (See Chapter 1, Windows Media Series Quick Start.) These *client logs* are text files that store information about the stream, such as the IP address of the computer that viewed it, the codec for the stream, and the version of the media player. The text files can often be enormous, especially on a busy site, so make sure you store them appropriately.

There are a number of ways to analyze log files. Microsoft offers a free log analysis tool called *LogParser*. It treats your log as a type of database. You can also build your own tools that insert your logs into a database table, letting you run specialized queries.

An analysis of your client logs can answer several questions:

- How many unique IP addresses requested a stream?
- How many times was a stream viewed by the same IP address?
- Which streams are more popular than others?
- What was the average length of time a streamed was viewed?
- What was the peak time of day, week or month for stream requests?

If you've done an analysis of web server logs, you'll notice some similarities. The client log formats are based on the standard web server log format. However, the client logs store data that web server logs do not, such as the amount of time a media player played a streaming file.

ALERT It's important to remember that logging will be affected by how a user sets his or her privacy settings on Windows Media Player. Fortunately, most users are happy with the default settings.

Audience Measurement

Log files provide detailed information about the stream. But logs can't tell you anything about the person playing the stream. You could infer preferences. For example, if you see the same IP address requesting the same set of football video highlights week after week, you could say the person likes to watch a lot of football. But this kind of inference is prone to all kinds of errors. How do you know it's the same person every week?

Streaming producers should pair log analysis with standard types of market analysis, such as telephone surveys and focus groups. Compare the results of your marketing studies against your log files. Do the types of files stored in your server logs match the preferences expressed by individuals in your surveys? Do focus groups say they watch movie trailers all the way through, but your logs show people stop the stream after a few seconds? An integrated approach using a variety of tools is likely to provide the most accurate answers.

Stream Quality Measurement

Client logs can also give you some insight into the quality of the user experience and the ability of your network to deliver the streams in a reliable way. The logs store various kinds of networking data, such as the number of packets lost during a streaming session. These logs are different than the logs created by Windows Media Load Simulator, because they're done in a production environment, as opposed to a controlled, protected environment.

Networking gurus and programmers can design software tools that make use of the error reporting in the real-time protocol (RTP), assuming the client is using RTSP to request the stream. These tools are very complex to build and maintain.

Many streaming producers who want to monitor quality over the long-term make use of content monitoring services, such as Keynote or WebTrends. These companies use automated tools that contact your streaming server on a regular basis from several locations and report reliability statistics. You can use these to find bottlenecks in your network, for example.

 ALERT All this gobbledygook about log analysis and focus groups and automated monitoring isn't going to make a whit of difference if you don't click your own streams once in a while. It's stunning how streaming producers forget to click links on their own webpages. And when they do, and something is broken, they act surprised. First rule of quality assurance: *Use your own products every day*!

Conclusion

Microsoft's Windows Media technologies offer more than just a way to deliver a stream of audio and video. You can create a completely unique media experience with tools such as skins and borders. You can fine tune your delivery system with detailed testing, raising the quality of the experience for more users. And you can measure the success of your streaming projects, demonstrating that you have made a wise investment. Streaming media is a promising technology that delivers results today.

APPENDIX

Streaming PowerPoints with Producer

Microsoft PowerPoints are the communications tool of choice for speeches, conference presentations, and boardroom discussions. Until recently, you could only view a PowerPoint presentation in person, either in the meeting or downloaded to your personal computer. Today, a free downloadable tool, Microsoft Producer, lets you stream your PowerPoint presentation complete with audio and/or video narration. The following tutorial takes you through the following steps:

- Using the New Presentation Wizard
- Timing your narration to your slides
- Adding a video to your presentation
- Publishing your final project

The tutorial assumes you have a completed PowerPoint (**.ppt**) file, a recorded audio narration in **.wav** format, and a video in **.avi** format. You also need access to a web server and a Windows Media Server. (Check with your Internet service provider or IT department for details.) You should also have a script with slide changes and other actions written down. As you build your presentation with Producer, refer to the script as your blueprint.

Using the New Presentation Wizard

The following instructions walk you through the importation of slides from an existing Microsoft PowerPoint presentation and a previously recorded audio narration file.

1. Download and install Microsoft Producer 2003 from the Microsoft Windows Media website, *http://www.microsoft.com/windowsmedia/*.
2. Open Microsoft Producer by clicking Start → Programs → Microsoft Producer. The opening user interface is shown in **Figure A-1**.

3. Select "Create a New Presentation Wizard" in the dialog box. If the dialog box does not appear as shown in **Figure A-1**, select File → New Presentation Wizard. Click OK.

Figure A-1
The opening user interface of Microsoft Producer.

4. Click Next in the Wizard Welcome box.
5. In the Presentation Template box, select Default, as shown in **Figure A-2**. Click Next.

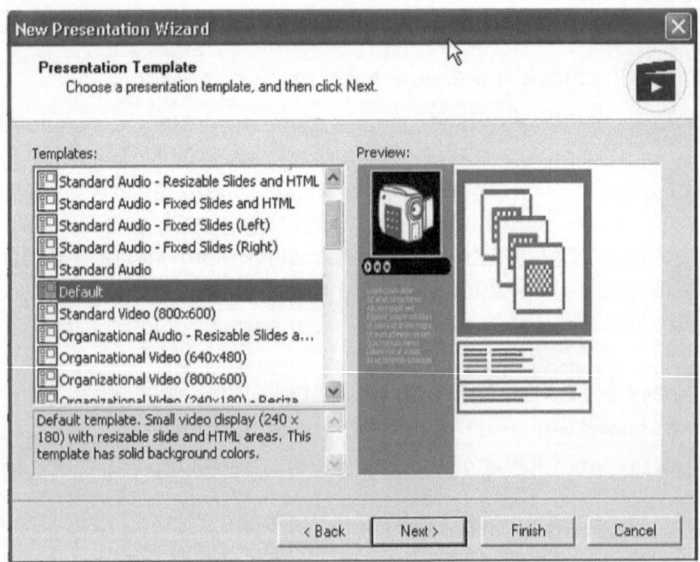

Figure A-2
Select the Default presentation template.

6. In the Choose a Presentation Scheme box, as shown in **Figure A-3**, leave the default fonts and colors as is. Click Next.

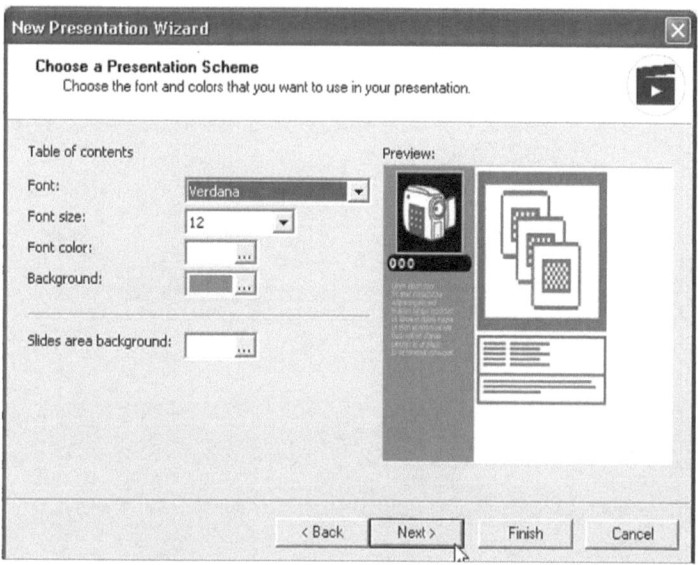

Figure A-3
Leave the default fonts and colors as loaded in the Choose a Presentation Scheme box.

7. In the Presentation Information box, fill out each text box and add an opening page image, if needed, as shown in **Figure A-4**.

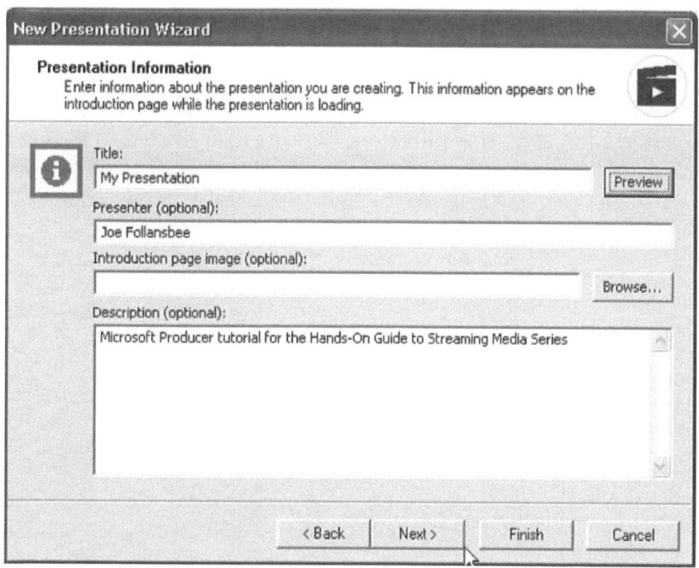

Figure A-4
Enter title, author, and description information.

8. In the Import Slides and Still Images box, click "Browse" to locate your Power-
    Point (**.ppt**) file. Select the file, and click OK. The path will display in the "Files:"
    text box, as shown in **Figure A-5**. Click Next.

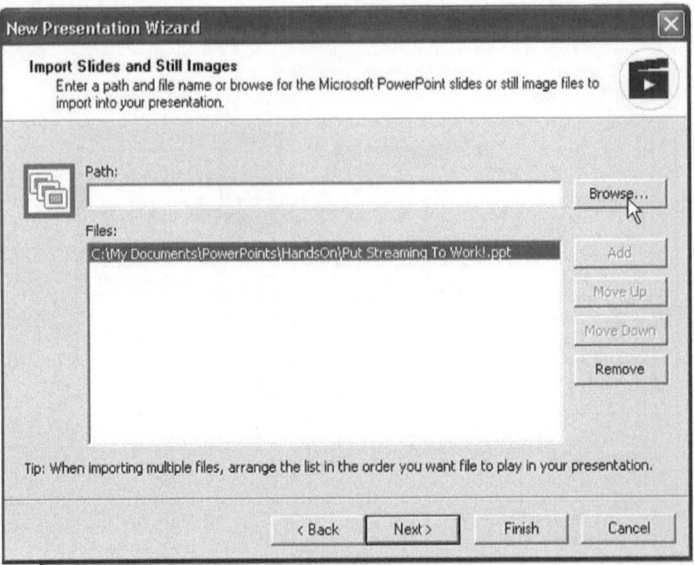

Figure A-5
Import your PowerPoint (**.ppt**) file via the "Browse" button in the Import Slides and Still Images box.

9. In the Import or Capture Audio or Video box, click "Browse" and locate your WAV
    (**.wav**) audio narration file. Select the file, and click OK. The path will display in
    the "Files:" text box, as shown in **Figure A-6**. Click Next.

10. In the Synchronize Presentation Box, select "Yes" to synchronize slides to your
    audio narration after the slides are imported, as shown in **Figure A-7**. Click Next.

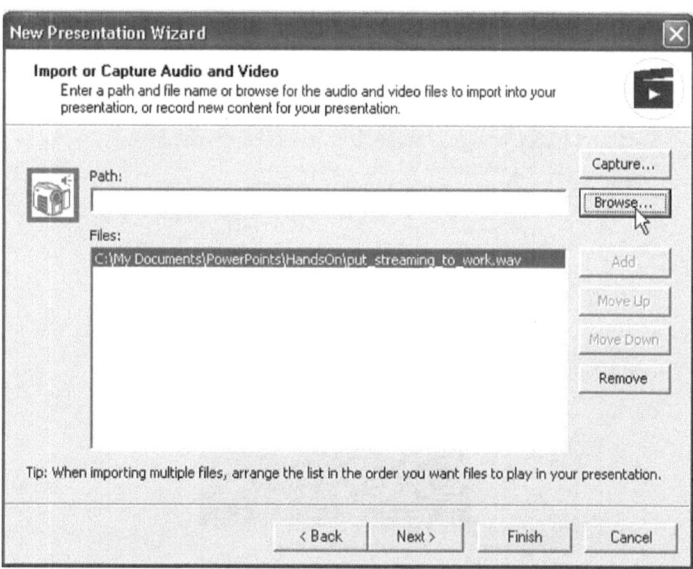

Figure A-6
Import your WAV (**.wav**) audio narration file via the "Browse" button in the Import or Capture Audio or Video box.

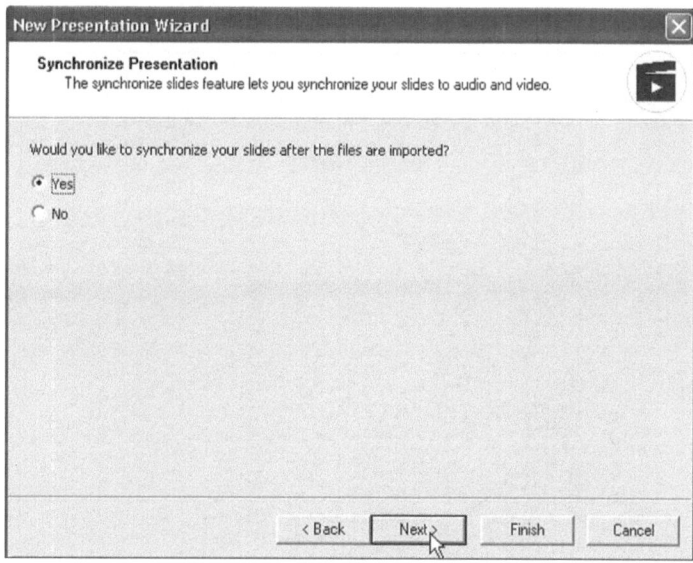

Figure A-7
Select "Yes" to synchronize your audio narration to the slides after the slides are imported.

11. In the Complete Presentation box, click Finish. Producer imports the files, and presents a user interface similar to that shown in Figure **A-8**.

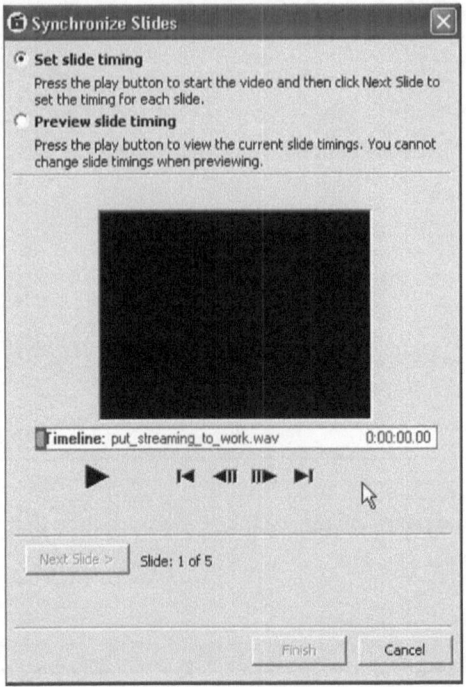

Figure A-8
Microsoft Producer after it has imported slides and an audio narration.

Setting Slide Timing

The next steps demonstrate how to adjust slide timing in Producer.

1. In the Synchronize Slides box, click the "Set slide timing" radio button. Click the Play icon, as shown in **Figure A-9**.

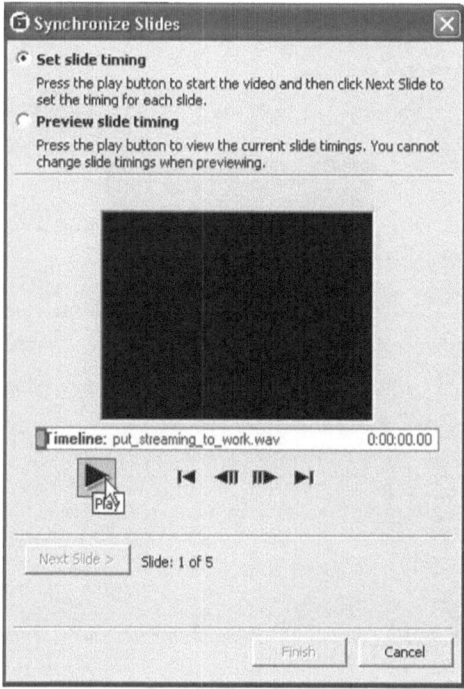

Figure A-9
Click the "Set slide timing" radio button and click the Play icon to start the timing procedure.

2. After clicking Play, the audio narration starts to play. Click the "Next Slide" button, timing your clicks to your narration, as shown in **Figure A-10**. If you make a mistake or want to re-time the slides, click the "Back" icon, which is nearest to the Play button. (You can also fix the timings in later steps.)

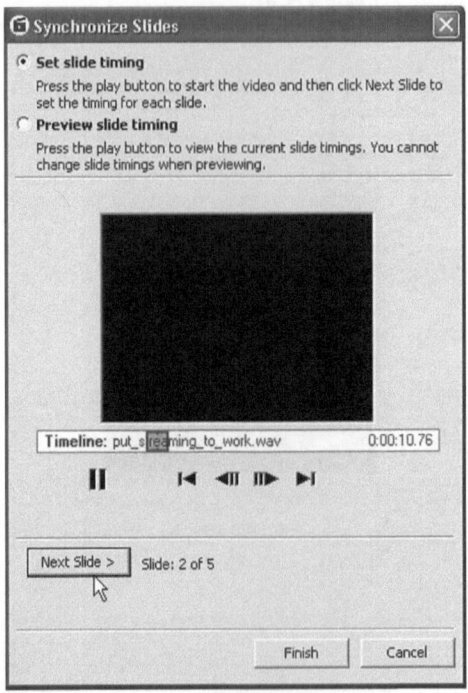

Figure A-10
Click the "Next Slide" button when your script calls for a new slide.

3. When you are satisfied with your timing, click Finish. The "Preview Presentation" tab in Microsoft Producer contains the media and timings, similar to those shown in **Figure A-11**. You may need to click the "Zoom Timeline In" button to see details of your presentation timeline more easily.

4. To view a specific section of the presentation, click the mouse over the bar displaying the minutes, seconds and milliseconds within the timeline. Click Play to play that section.

5. To adjust timings, place the mouse near the timing boundary between two slides. Click and hold. Then move the boundary as needed. See **Figure A-12**.

6. Save your Producer project by clicking File → Save.

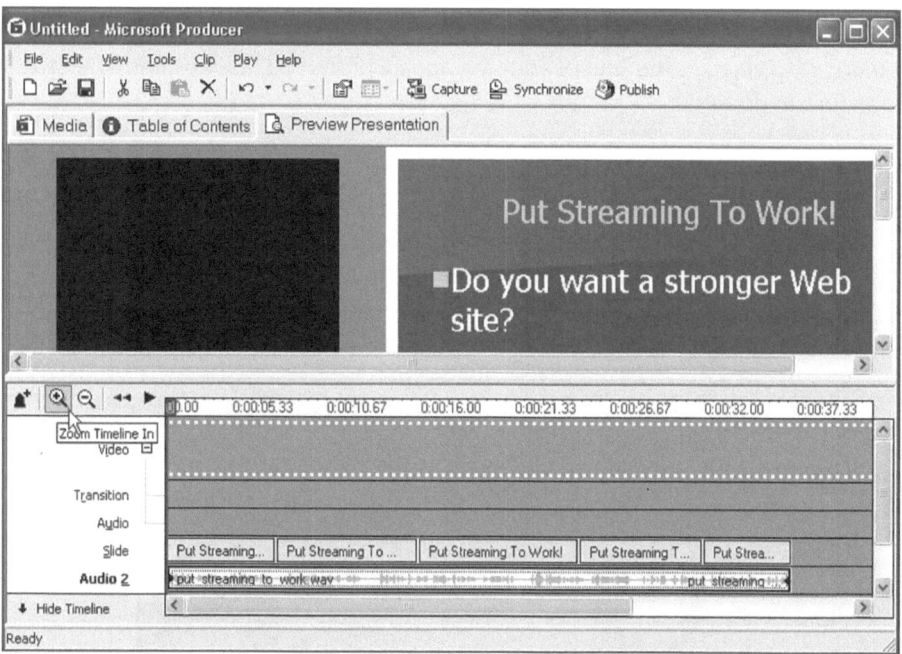

Figure A-11
The Preview Presentation tab displays media and timings.

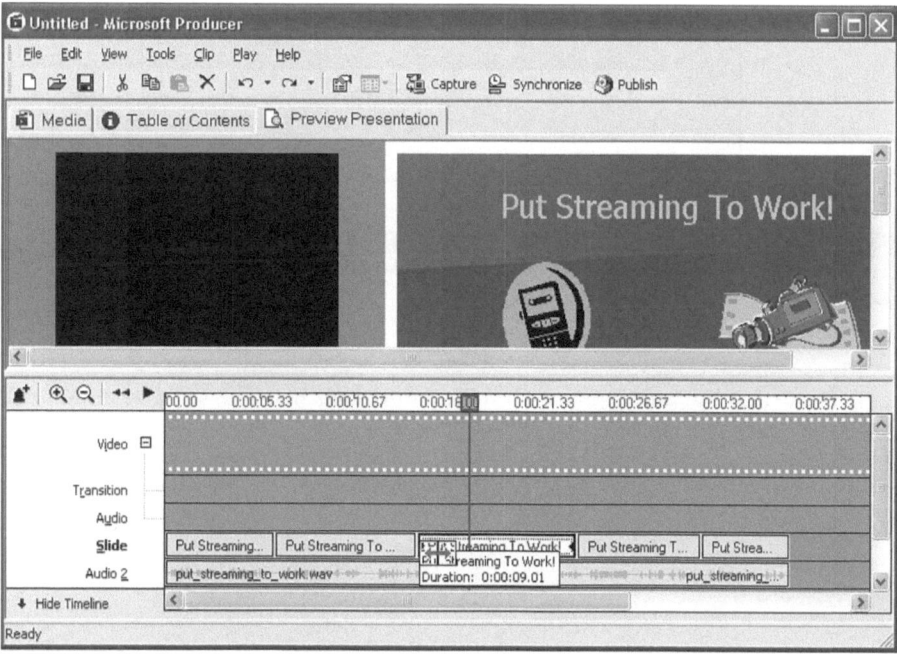

Figure A-12
Click and hold the mouse over a slide boundary to adjust timing.

Add a Video to Your Project

You'd like to add a video to the end of your previously produced PowerPoint. The next section shows how to do this.

1. Open your Microsoft Producer project, and click the "Media" tab.

2. Click File → Import and locate your previously produced AVI file. Select the file and click Open. Producer imports the file into your project, as shown in **Figure A-13**. Preview the video by clicking the Play icon to the right.

3. Drag and drop the video icon to an appropriate place in the timeline pane, as shown in **Figure A-14**.

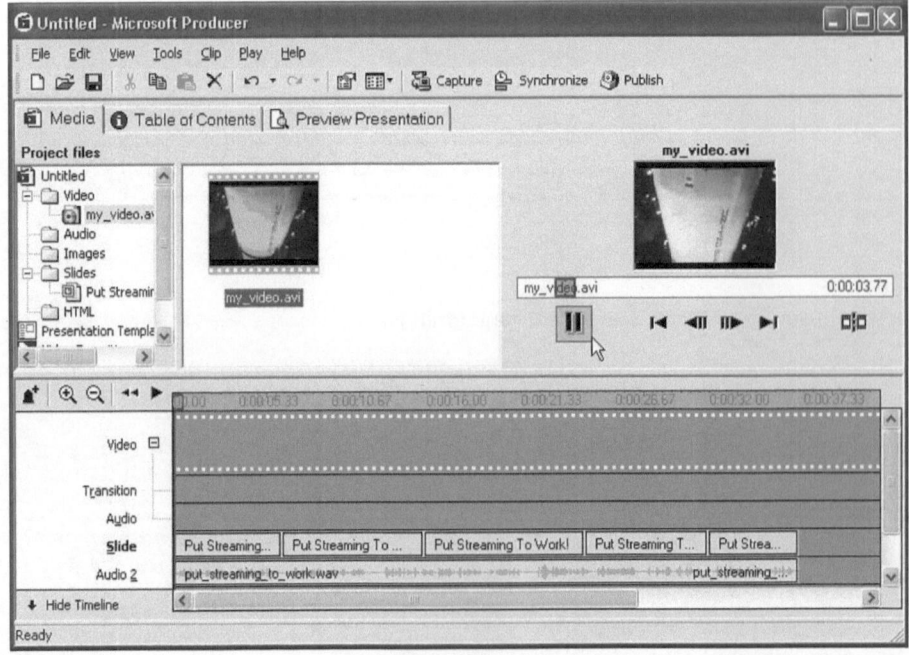

Figure A-13
The Media tab in Producer with an imported video.

4. To preview the presentation with the video, click the "Preview Presentation" tab and click the Play icon.

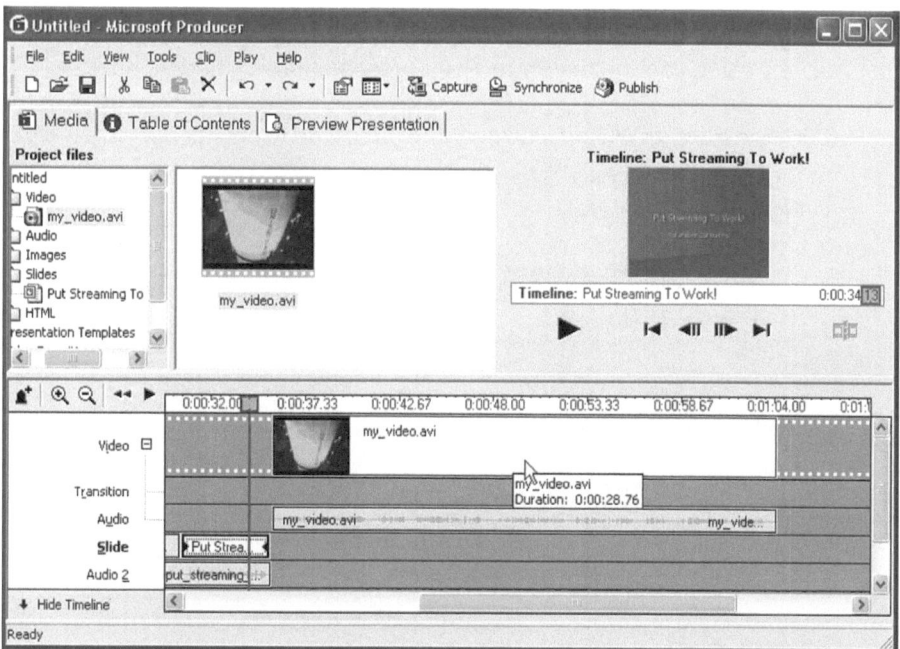

Figure A-14

Drag and drop the video to the desired place in the timeline.

Publishing Your Producer Project

Now that you've created your online PowerPoint presentation, it's time to publish it.

1. Click the Publish Wizard icon near the top of the Producer user interface.

2. In the Select a Playback Site box, click the "Web server" radio button, as shown in **Figure A-15**. Click Next.

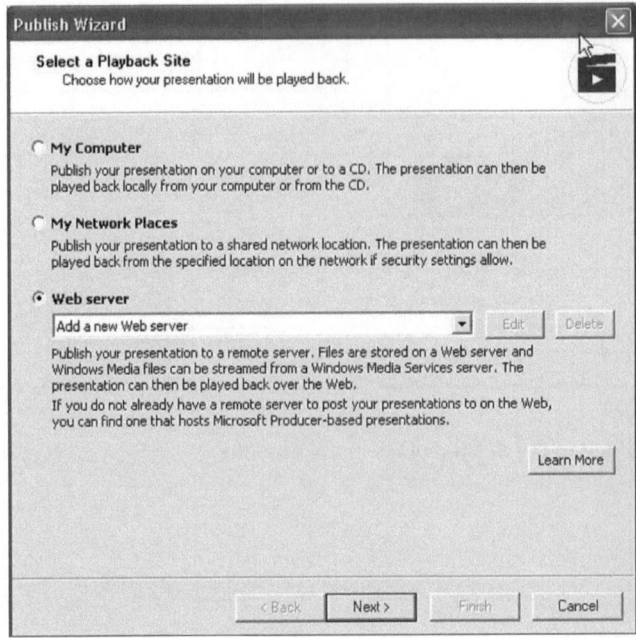

Figure A-15
Select "Web server" in the Select a Playback Site box.

3. In the Internet or Intranet Host Settings box, enter the following items, as shown in **Figure A-16**:

    *   **Friendly host name**: An easy-to-remember name for this host.

    *   **Publish Web files to**: Enter the location of the folder on the web server hosting the files.

    *   **Playback presentation address**: Type the Internet or intranet address for the presentation.

    *   **Publish Windows Media files to**: Network location for the Windows Media files.

    *   **Playback address for Windows Media files**: Type the publishing point of your Windows Media file on the Windows Media server.

4. Click Next.

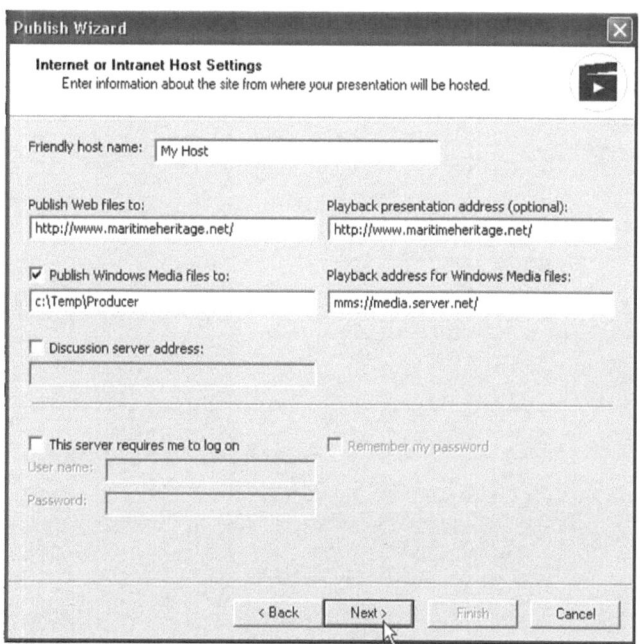

Figure A-16
The Internet or Intranet Hosting Settings box with addressing data.

5. In the Web Publishing Destination box, type in a file name for your Producer project. Also, select the "Save Files:" radio button and select a place on your computer or your network to save the files, as shown in **Figure A-17**. Click Next.

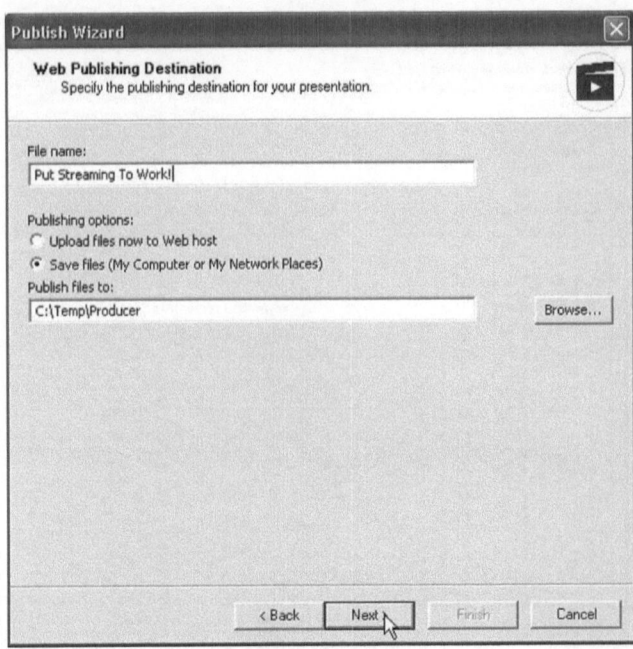

Figure A-17
Save the files to your hard drive or a network drive for testing.

6. The Presentation Information box from the New Presentation Wizard appears. (See "Using the New Presentation Wizard" above.) Modify the information as desired, and click Next.

7. In the Playback Quality box, select an appropriate target audience based on your understanding of the audience's bandwidth capability, as shown in **Figure A-18**. Click Next.

8. In the Publish Presentation box, click Finish, and Producer will create the needed HTML files, image files, and encode your audio and video. When Producer is finished, it asks whether you want to view the finished presentation. Click Close to end the publishing process. **Figure A-19** shows the finished product as displayed in a web browser.

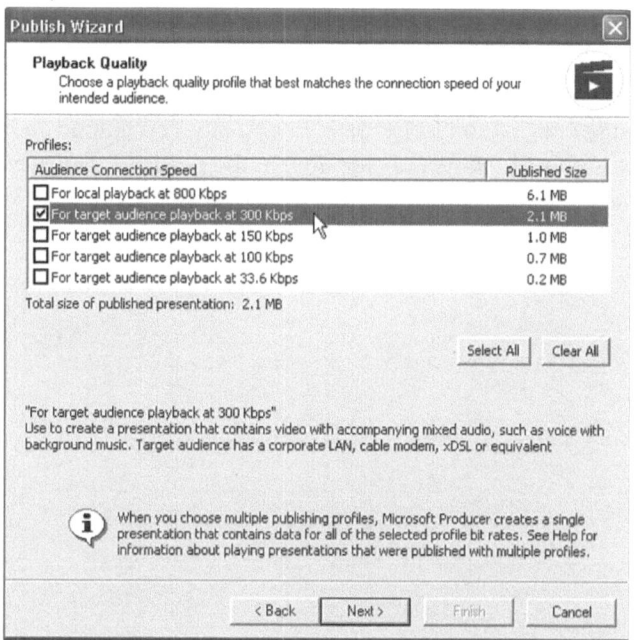

Figure A-18
Select a target audience bandwidth.

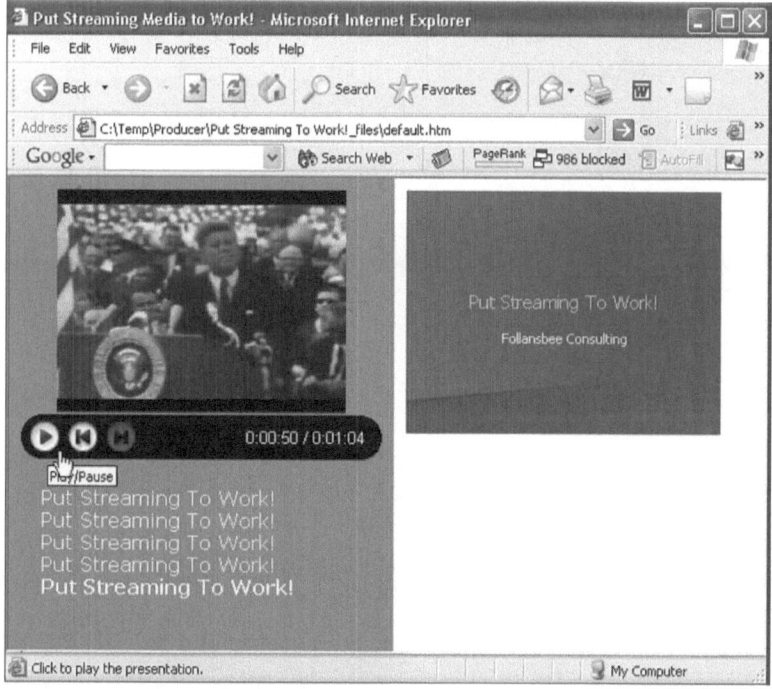

Figure A-19
The finished presentation as published by Microsoft Producer.

Conclusion

The Microsoft Producer files are stored in the folder on the hard drive you designated, allowing you to modify them directly if you see a problem. Or you can load your Microsoft Project file and modify information from there. Eventually, you upload your Windows Media files to the Windows Media Server you designated in the production process, and the HTML, images and other files to the web server. Test your presentation again, and let everyone know about your hard work.

Glossary

3G wireless network: Third-generation wireless networks, available primarily in Asia and Europe. Most American wireless network are considered second generation.

3-point lighting: The standard method of lighting a video subject, using a key light, a fill light, and a back light.

Analog: Describes data flowing in a continuous, often variable manner.

Announcement file: Also called a *metafile*, the announcement file contains the URL for the Windows Media audio or video file to be played via a Windows Media Server.

Archive: A set of on-demand streaming files.

Artifacts: Lines, distortion, snow or other unwanted data in a video image usually introduced by poor quality equipment. Artifacts can appear in audio as odd sounds, dropouts, or distortion.

Aspect ratio: The ratio of width to height of a video frame. Common ratios are 4:3 and 16:9.

ASP: Active server page.

ASX: The Microsoft Windows Media Services metafile file type.

Attenuate: In audio production, turning down the volume level.

Authentication: A process that verifies a user's identity. (See *Authorization*.)

Authorization: A process of granting access to a server or set of files with certain access rights.

AVI: Audio video interleaved. A standard uncompressed or compressed video format for personal computers.

Back light: A light shone behind a subject to bring it out of the background.

Bandwidth: The amount of data that can be transmitted over a network in a given moment.

Bit: A single unit of data.

Bit rate: The flow rate of data (bits) over a computer network.

Boost: In audio production, turning up the volume level.

Border: A customized user interface for Windows Media Player that functions similarly to a skin.

Broadband: Usually refers to DSL and/or cable residential and small business Internet connections, though it may sometimes refer to higher data rates available on bigger connections.

Browser: A software application that displays text, graphics, and some multimedia files downloaded from World Wide Web servers.

Buffer: A portion of RAM reserved for storing streaming data before rendering by a media player.

Bundle: Software is said to be "bundled" if it is included with other software or hardware, often as a giveaway.

Byte: A unit of data comprised of bits.

Cable: 1. An insulated length of wiring connecting two hardware devices. 2. An Internet connection through a cable television operator.

Capture card: See *video capture card*.

Capturing: The process of recording or transferring audio and/or video information from a recording device, such as a digital camera, to a computer hard drive.

CD: Compact disc.

CD-ROM: Compact disc, read-only memory.

Client: Hardware or software primarily used for receiving and rendering information sent by a server.

Client log: A log of client activity created by Windows Media Server.

Client/Server: A network architecture in which one computer (the server) performs a number of dedicated tasks that serve the needs of several other computers or "workstations" (the clients).

Clipping: A type of distortion caused by high audio levels.

Codec: Short for COde/DECode or COmpress/DECcompress. Usually refers to a mathematical formula that removes data from a source audio or video file, leaving a smaller file suitable for streaming over a network. A codec is also used by Windows Media Player to decompress streaming files.

Compression: 1. A signal processing technique whereby the peak volume levels are lowered (attenuated) to reduce distortion. 2. A technique that reduces the amount of storage space needed by a file.

Compressor: A hardware device or software application that compresses audio signals.

Connectivity: A connection to the Internet.

Connector: A hardware device that connects a cable to another cable or other hardware device. They are usually divided into male/female pairs. Common connectors in audio and video production include mini-plug, quarter-inch, RCA, XLR, and BNC.

CBR: Constant bit rate. A constant or steady rate of a fixed amount of data traversing the Internet between a server and a client.

Container tag: An HTML or SMIL tag enclosing other data, often to define its display or action.

Copyright: The right to give someone permission to copy a work.

Covering shot: A brief amount of video that covers a jump cut.

CPU: Central processing unit. The main processor of a computer.

Crop: Removing unwanted portions of a frame, similar to cropping in photography.

Cutaway: An editing technique in which the point of view changes to other person in the scene.

DC (Direct Current) offset: A method for removing inaudible noise introduced into audio when recording equipment isn't grounded properly.

Decompression: The process a media player uses to read and interpret a compressed file.

Deinterlacing: The process of removing video artifacts introduced when one video frame overlaps or interlaces with another.

Dial-up: A method for connecting to the Internet with a modem, usually at 56 kilobytes per second.

Difference frame: Frames in a compressed video file containing image information that changes after a key frame is introduced.

Digital: Describes data divided into discrete binary units, often referred to as 1s and 0s.

DMZ: Demilitarized zone. A peripheral sub-network outside a firewall. Streaming servers are sometimes placed in a DMZ.

Domain: A group of networked computers with a common address.

Downloading: The process of requesting a file and saving it to a hard drive.

DRM: Digital rights management. DRM technologies protect copyrighted content from unauthorized distribution.

DRM profile: A file sent by a DRM license provider containing information for generating encryption keys.

DSL: Digital Subscriber Line. A broadband connection carrying Internet and voice traffic over the same copper telephone line.

DVD: Digital video disc.

Dynamic range: The range of a sound from silence to its loudest point.

Editing: The process of removing unwanted portions of an audio or video file. May include rearrangement of the remaining information.

Electromagnetic radiation: In the context of streaming, visible light.

Embedded: In streaming media, an application is said to be embedded if it performs its task within a browser window.

Encoder: A software application that converts source files into streaming media files.

Encoding: The process of converting a source audio or video file into a smaller file designed for streaming media delivery. (See also *transcoding*.)

Encryption: A method of scrambling data used in digital rights management. (See *DRM* and *protection*.)

EQ: Equalization.

Equalization: A signal processing technique that raises (boosts) or lowers (attenuates) the volume of audio within a certain frequency range.

Ethernet: The dominant method of networking computers on an intranet.

Evergreen: Content that holds its value over time.

File: A file stores information. A streaming file stores compressed audio and video information.

Fill light: A light used to fill shadows on a subject caused by the key light.

Filter: A hardware device or software application that removes unwanted image artifacts or sound from a file.

Firewall: Any of a number of software applications or hardware devices that limit the types of data that pass into or out of a computer network.

Format: A way to organize data on a storage medium, such as CD.

Frame: A single image in a video file, analogous to a single image in motion picture film.

Frame rate: The number of frames shown per second.

Frame size: The pixel dimensions of a frame, sometimes expressed as an aspect ratio, often 4:3.

FTP: File transfer protocol. The network communications protocol used by FTP client software to transfer files from one computer to another, usually for storage.

GB: Gigabyte.

HDTV: High-definition television, sometimes called *HD*.

Head: An electromagnet in an audio or video tape recorder that rearranges metal oxides on the physical tape.

Headroom: 1. The amount of volume available before the sound distorts. 2. A portion of a stream reserved for non-audio or video network packets needed for proper stream performance.

Helper application: A piece of software that assists the browser when it cannot render a file. Most streaming media players are helper applications.

Hertz: A unit of measure for audio frequency.

Hypertext markup language (HTML): The standard language for creating pages rendered in a web browser.

Hypertext transfer protocol (HTTP): The standard communications protocol for delivering most kinds of traffic on the World Wide Web.

HTTP cloaking: A method for sending streams through firewalls.

HTTP streaming: Progressive downloading.

HREF: Hypertext REFerence. The "link" in a webpage.

IDE: Integrated Drive Electronics. A type of hard drive interface.

IEC: International Electro-technical Committee.

IEEE: Institute of Electrical and Electronics Engineers.

IEEE 1394: Also referred to as "FireWire" or iLink. An engineering standard related to high-speed data transfer between electronic devices.

IETF: Internet Engineering Task Force.

iLink: See *IEEE 1394*.

Input: Data that flows into a hardware device or software application.

Interpolation: A method of estimating missing values, such as when a video image is resized. Also called *video smoothing*.

Intranet: A private computer network that functions like the Internet.

Inverse telecine: The process of removing duplicate frames from a video introduced when film content is transferred to video format.

IP: Internet protocol. The standard networking protocol for computers connected to the Internet.

IP Address: The numeric Internet address of a computer.

ISP: Internet service provider. An organization that provides connections to the Internet and other services, such as website hosting.

JPEG: Joint Picture Experts Group. 1. A graphics standards group. 2. A still image compression standard.

Jump cut: A video edit manifested as a sudden change in an image that is not a scene or shot change.

Kbps: Kilobytes per second. An expression of bit rate.

Key frame: A frame in a compressed video that contains information about the entire frame. Its counterpart, the difference frame, contains only information different from the key frame.

Key light: A light used to illuminate the front of a subject.

KHz: Kilohertz.

Knowledgebase: An online archive of experience related to a piece of software.

KVM switch: A switch allowing use of one mouse, keyboard, and monitor for two or more computers.

LAN: Local area network.

Lavalier: A type of microphone used in video production.

LED: Light emitting diode. In audio and video production, LEDs are often used to display audio volume.

Letterbox: Describes the shape of an image with a 16:9 aspect ratio superimposed on frame with a 4:3 aspect ratio.

License provider: A third-party provider of licenses to encrypt audio or video files for digital rights management.

Live: Encoding an audio or video signal as it is created, usually for immediate distribution to an audience.

Live-to-tape: Producing a program as if it were broadcast live, but only recording the program for later broadcast.

Log: A text file that records the activity of a server or application.

Lossless: Refers to codecs that store all input to a file.

Lossy: Refers to codecs that remove data before storing information to a file.

MB: Megabyte.

MBR: Multiple bit rate. The combination of several bit rates into a single encoded file.

Metadata: Data that describes other data.

Metafile: A file that contains metadata. (See *announcement file*.)

Mic: Microphone.

MIME type: MIME (multipurpose internet mail extensions) types are expressed as file extensions, which a software client, usually a web browser, uses to decide how to render an incoming file. When a browser encounters a streaming MIME type, it usually hands off rendering to a streaming media player.

MMS: Microsoft Media Services. A proprietary streaming protocol developed by Microsoft.

Modem: The part of a computer that allows it to connect to the Internet. Modems come in several types, including dial-up, DSL and cable.

Monitor: A hardware device for hearing audio output (speaker) or viewing video output.

MP3: MPEG Audio Layer III. An open standard audio codec approved by the Motion Picture Experts Group.

MPEG: Motion Pictures Experts Group.

MPEG-4: An MPEG open standard usually associated with video compression, though it can be used for other data types, such as still images.

MPG: A file extension for the MPEG format.

Multicast: A means of streaming to a large audience. Clients connect to a stream via a specially configured router, rather than the server delivering the stream. The counterpart to multicast is unicast.

Net weather: A slang term describing the moment-to-moment changeable conditions of the Internet.

Network: Two or more computers connected together for the purpose of communication and resource sharing.

Noise: Unwanted video artifacts or sound in a file.

Noise reduction: A complex algorithm for removing unwanted sound or video artifacts.

Nonlinear editing: Describes the ability to move sections of audio or video around in a software application.

Normal: The standard, hardwired way of routing a signal in a production studio.

Normalization: A signal processing technique whereby an audio signal is turned up as much as possible before distortion occurs.

On-demand: Making a stored streaming media file available to a user whenever the user requests it.

On-the-fly: Refers to the creation of a file at the moment the user requests it.

Open standard: An engineering standard which manufacturers agree to follow to ensure compatibility with each other's devices.

Optimize: The process of improving the quality of data in a captured audio or video file.

OS: Operating system. The software that manages the communication between a software application and computer hardware. Microsoft Windows is an operating system.

Output: Data that flows out of a hardware device or software application.

Outsourcing: The process of contracting a third party to perform some or all services related to streaming media.

Overhead: Data in the stream that controls streaming performance.

Overscan: The area of a video image usually covered by the plastic casing of a TV monitor. Overscan is usually removed before encoding.

Packet: A discrete chunk of data with control and addressing information sent over the Internet.

Patch: Computer code that fixes a problem.

Patch bay: A piece of equipment that allows signals to be routed among several different pieces of equipment.

Patch cord: Used in a patch bay to route signals.

PDA: Personal digital assistant.

Persistence of vision: The principle of optics by which humans perceive still images as moving images when the still images change at high speed.

Pickup: A light gathering device in a video camera.

Picture element: Pixel.

Pixel: The basic unit of composition of the video image on a monitor.

Player: Also media player. Refers to Windows Media Player.

Playlist: In streaming, a list of referenced streamable files in an announcement (**.asx**) or server-side playlist (**.wsx**) file. (See *rollover playlist*.)

Plug-in: A software application that renders audio and video data within a web browser window.

Port: A number in a URL that determines which application on a server handles the data request.

Pre-roll: In streaming, an amount of data placed into the Windows Media Player buffer before playback begins.

Proc amp: Short for processing amplifier. A software application or hardware device that adjusts the quality of a video signal.

Profile: A customized session file meant to be used frequently in similar situations.

Progressive download: A streaming media method using the HTTP protocol.

Progressive scan: The method by which images are drawn on a computer monitor, one line after another.

Proprietary: Refers to the practice of keeping certain methods private to create or protect a competitive advantage.

Protection: A file is said to be protected when it is encrypted via a digital rights management (DRM) system.

Protocol: A set of rules that govern the exchange of data over a computer network.

Proxy: A special type of server that acts as a middleman between a user and the Internet.

Pseudo-streaming: Progressive downloading

Publishing point: A virtual location in Windows Media Server that points to the actual location of streaming media files.

Pull distribution: A method of distributing an encoded stream whereby the server contacts the encoder for the stream.

Push distribution: A method distributing an encoded stream whereby the encoder initiates contact with the server, starting the distribution process.

Rack: A piece of shelf-like equipment for securely stacking electronic equipment.

Rack-mounted: Equipment placed in a rack.

RAM: Random access memory. The part of a computer that stores data temporarily.

Raw: Refers to the format of an audio or video file before encoding for streaming media delivery. Raw formats are usually **.wav** for audio and **.avi** for video.

Redundancy: The practice of building one or more layers of backup systems to a primary system.

Resolution: The number of pixels per square inch on a computer-generated display.

Rights: In digital rights management, the permissions related to playback of a protected file.

Risk management: Planning ahead when producing streaming media helps you lower the risk that unforeseen problems may occur.

Rebuffering: Action by a media player to gather more data in its buffer before continuing playback.

Render: 1. The process of saving certain changes, usually effects, to an audio or video file. 2. The process by which an application displays a video image or plays sound.

Rollover playlist: A playlist containing at least two references to streamable files, the second of which is played if the first file fails for some reason.

RTCP: Real-time control protocol. An open standard protocol that works with RTP packets to check the delivery of other packets.

RTP: Real-time transport protocol. An open standard protocol defining rules for identifying the type of streaming packet, how packets are numbered in sequence, and how they are stamped with the date and time.

RTSP: Real-time streaming protocol. An open standard application level protocol used by Internet clients, i.e., media players, to talk to streaming servers.

Sample: A slice of data taken at a particular time and/or place in a file.

Sample rate: The number of times per second a sample is taken.

SATA: Serial advanced technology attachment. An updated version of the ATA (Advanced Technology Attachment) interface between a hard drive and the computer's motherboard.

SCSI: Small computer system interface, pronounced "scuzzy." A method of connecting peripheral devices to a computer, usually a hard drive.

Script: A set of one or more commands and parameters in a single, executable file that accomplishes a given task.

Server: Computer hardware and software that acts solely as a central storage and distribution device for computer files. In streaming, two types of servers, web servers and media servers, typically work together.

Server room: A climate-controlled, secure room containing most or all the servers for an organization. Also called a *machine room*.

Session file: A file associated with Windows Media Encoder that stores session information. The extension is **.wme**.

Simultaneous streams: The number of streams sent at one time by a server.

Skin: A customize user interface for the Windows Media Player.

Skin definition file: A script telling Windows Media Player how to display a skin and how the skin should behave.

Slide: A frame containing title or other information about a video.

Slide fader: A device in hardware or software for boosting or attenuating audio volume levels.

SMIL: Synchronized multimedia integration language. An open standard markup language designed specifically for combining content types that change over time. Pronounced "smile."

SMPTE: Society of Motion Picture and Television Engineers.

Sound card: Also called audio card. The part of a computer that handles audio data.

Source file: A file before it is compressed into streaming media format. Sometimes called a "raw" file.

Standard: A set of engineering principles often based on patented ideas.

Storage: The permanent or semi-permanent repository of a file on a hard drive, CD, or DVD.

Storyboard: A series of pre-production drawings that describe the shots in a video sequence.

Streamie: A frequent user of streaming media.

Streaming media: The process of sending a time-based computer file, such as audio or video, with a streaming media server in a predictable fashion over the Internet to be rendered in real time by a streaming media client.

Tag: Code in HTML or SMIL that defines data or assigns parameters to data.

Transcode: The process of converting a file encoded in one data format to another. (See *encoding*.)

Transform: The process of modifying the display characteristics of an encoded file, such as enlarging the video image.

TCP: Transmission control protocol. One of the basic Internet communication protocols.

UDP: User datagram protocol. A common Internet protocol used for sending data in a continuous stream.

Uncompressed: Refers to a file where none of the input data is removed before storage.

Unicast: A streaming media method whereby each client is sent a copy of a file. The counterpart is multicast.

URL: Uniform resource locater. The standard method of addressing a file on a computer connected to the Internet.

VBR: Variable bit rate. A method of encoding a file related to hardware device data transfers.

Video card: Hardware in a computer that handles video data displayed on a computer monitor.

Video capture card: Hardware in a computer that takes in video data from an outside source and stores it on a hard drive or other storage device.

Video smoothing: See *interpolation*.

Video switching service: A service that sends and receives a video signal, distributing it as required.

Visible light: The range of electromagnetic radiation visible to the human eye. Also called the *visible spectrum*.

Visualization: A graphical representation of sound that changes as a file is played.

VTR: Video tape recorder.

VU: Volume unit. A expression of audio volume or loudness.

Watermark: A method of identifying the ownership of a file within a digital rights management system.

WAV: A standard method for storing audio information. Pronounced "wave."

Webcast: A live broadcast on the web.

XML: eXtensible Markup Language.

XML compliant: Conforms to XML syntax.

YUY2: A 4:2:2 pixel format.

Resources

The following resources contain information and software related to Windows Media Player 9 and 10 and Windows Media Services. (URLs are subject to change.)

Microsoft and Windows Media resources

- Main site: *http://www.microsoft.com/*
- Windows Media 9 Series: *http://www.microsoft.com/windowsmedia/*
- Windows Media Content Guide: *http://www.windowsmedia.com/*
- Microsoft Developer Network: *http://msdn.microsoft.com/*

Streaming Media and Related Books from Focal Press

- *Get Streaming! Quick Steps to Delivering Audio and Video Online*, by Joe Follansbee
- *The Business of Streaming and Digital Media*, by Dan Rayburn
- *A Practical Guide to Video and Audio Compression*, by Cliff Wootton
- *The Technology of Video and Audio Streaming*, by David Austerberry
- *Single-Camera Video Production*, by Robert Musburger
- *Introduction to Digital Audio*, by John Watkinson

MPEG Resources

- MPEG.org: *http://www.mpeg.org/* – Dozens of links and information about the MPEG standards.
- MP3: *http://www.mpeg.org/MPEG/mp3.html* – For MP3 information, visit MPEG.org's MP3 webpage.
- MPEG-4 Industry Forum (M4IF): *http://www.m4if.org/* – The main website for MPEG-4 supporters.

FTP Clients

- WS_FTP Pro: *http://www.ipswitch.com/downloads/*
- FTP Commander: *http://www.internet-soft.com/ftpcomm.htm*
- Cute FTP: *http://www.cuteftp.com/cuteftp/*

Places to buy audio and video equipment

- Broadcast Supply Worldwide (audio): *http://www.bswusa.com/*
- The Broadcast Store (video): *http://www.bcs.tv/*.
- B & H (audio and video): *http://www.photovideo.com/*.
- Online auction sites, such as eBay or Yahoo! Auctions.
- A local electronics store, such as Radio Shack, Frye's Electronics, or BestBuy, for small items you need immediately.

Periodicals

- Streaming Media: *http://www.streamingmedia.com/*.
- Streaming Media World: *http://www.streamingmediaworld.com/*.

Other Websites

- American Federation of Television and Radio Artists (AFTRA): *http://www.aftra.com/* – Review labor union rules for using actors and other artists in audio and video productions.
- Arbitron/Edison Media Research: *http://www.arbitron.com/* – A rich source of information on streaming and digital media trends.
- National Aeronautics and Space Administration (NASA): *http://www.nasa.gov/* – This is a good place to download public domain AVI files to practice encoding.
- Synchronized Multimedia Integration Language (SMIL): *http://www.w3.org/AudioVideo/* – Check out this page at the W3C standards body for many resources on SMIL.

Index